WHEN THE MARKET MOVES, WILL YOU BE READY?

How to Profit from Major Market Events

Peter Navarro

McGraw-Hill

New York   Chicago   San Francisco   Lisbon
London   Madrid   Mexico City   Milan   New Delhi
San Juan   Seoul   Singapore   Sydney   Toronto

The McGraw-Hill Companies

Library of Congress Cataloging-in-Publication Data

Navarro, Peter.
    When the market moves, will you be ready? : how to profit from major market events / by Peter Navarro.
        p. cm.
    ISBN 0-07-141067-8 (pbk. : alk. paper)
        1. Stocks—United States.   2. Stock exchanges—United States.
    3. Investments—United States   I. Title.

HG4910.N383 2003
332.63'22'0973—dc22   2003016168

        5 6 7 8 9 0   DSH/DSH   0 1 0 9 8 7

ISBN 0-07-141067-8

This publication is designed to provide accurate and authoritative information in regard to the subject matter covered. It is sold with the understanding that neither the author nor the publisher is engaged in rendering legal, accounting, or other professional service. If legal advice or other expert assistance is required, the services of a competent professional person should be sought.

—From a Declaration of Principles jointly adopted by a Committee of the American Bar Association and a Committee of Publisher

McGraw-Hill books are available at special quantity discounts to use as premiums and sales promotions, or for use in corporate training programs. For more information, please write to the Director of Special Sales, Professional Publishing, McGraw-Hill, Two Penn Plaza, New York, NY 10121-2298. Or contact your local bookstore.

This book is printed on recycled, acid-free paper containing a minimum of 50% recycled, de-inked fiber.

To the loving memory of Ruby, my honey. Foresight could have saved her from a fate more cold and cruel than the stock market itself. Let us always remember to look ahead—and never forget the lessons in kindness, gentleness, and peace she taught us.

CONTENTS

ACKNOWLEDGMENTS

David W. Aloyan at Platinum Capital contributed the chapters on Money Management and Technical Analysis. David's grasp of both of these very difficult topics is one of the very best in the business, and I find myself fortunate to have his strong contribution.

Working with the inestimable Bob McCormick of the *KNX Business Hour* on our regular radio feature "The Savvy Investor Minute" helped me clarify and frame much of the material.

I am likewise indebted to John W. O'Donnell and Mike McMahon of the Online Trading Academy. They provided an excellent draft of the chapter on Trade Execution and many useful comments.

Lisa Waataja was meticulous in her preparation of the final manuscript while Laura Coyle from *Active Trader* magazine performed her always-impressive graphic artistry with the figures, charts, and tables.

Pedro Sottile provided insightful comments and a very thorough manuscript review. And Stephen Isaacs offered the steadiest of editorial hands at McGraw-Hill from concept to completion.

Any errors and omissions remain, of course, very much my own.

INTRODUCTION

My name is Peter Navarro, I'm a business professor at the University of California—Irvine, and I'd like to welcome you to the world of the savvy macrowave investor.

This book is a very hands-on companion to my best-selling first investing book, *If It's Raining in Brazil, Buy Starbucks*. In that book, I introduced the revolutionary concept of "macrowave investing"; and since the publication of that book, I have received countless requests from readers to illustrate, in a very hands-on way, just how to apply macrowave investing concepts to the day-to-day management of their individual portfolios.

This, of course, I am happy to do, and that is the purpose of this new book. In *When the Market Moves, Will You Be Ready?* I will walk you step-by-step through the savvy macrowave investor method. As you work through this book—which in many ways *is* a workbook—you will see that each chapter is followed by some review questions you will be asked to answer. I've also provided you with a set of some very interesting exercises that you will be asked to perform. Of course, you can choose *not* to perform these tasks and just keep reading—and that's just fine with me.

However, if I have learned anything in almost 20 years of teaching at one of the top-ranked business schools in the country, it is this: To truly master a set of ideas, you must do much more than simply, and passively, read about them. Instead, you must also *actively* test your reading comprehension and then logically apply that comprehension to very practical applications. That's the purpose of the review questions and investor exercises following each chapter.

As a final note, you certainly do not need to read my first book *If It's Raining in Brazil, Buy Starbucks* to benefit from this one. While I am sure you would enjoy and learn much from *If It's Raining in Brazil, Buy Starbucks*, this new book stands quite sturdily on its own. With that said, let's get to work!

PART ONE

THE BIG PICTURE

The Three Golden Rules of Macrowave Investing

1. Buy strong stocks in strong sectors in an upward-trending market.
2. Short weak stocks in weak sectors in a downward-trending market.
3. Stay *out* of the market and in cash when there is no definable trend.

Chapter 1

SO YOU WANT TO MAKE A MILLION IN THE STOCK MARKET

> Many of today's traders and investors focus all of their energies looking for so-called "great stocks." What they don't understand is this very simple Macrowave principle: You can buy the best stock in the world BUT if it is in the wrong sector when the market is heading down, you are not only going to lose more money than you should; if you are trading on margin, you may lose more than you have.
>
> *If It's Raining in Brazil, Buy Starbucks*

So, how do you make a million dollars in the stock market? Start with two million!

Unfortunately, that joke isn't very funny to the millions of investors who lost trillions of dollars in the last bear market. In fact, in that bear market, which began in March of 2000 and lasted for over three years, 80 percent of individual investors lost over *half* of all their money! This need not happen to you if you follow the basic principles of the savvy macrowave investor.

Macrowave investing is the Big Picture approach to profiting in the stock market that I first introduced several years ago in my book *If It's Raining in Brazil, Buy Starbucks*. To begin to understand this macrowave approach, let me first explain that book name—which is as much a perspective on the stock market as it is an amusing book title.

Brazil is the largest coffee producer in the world. If rain comes to break a drought in Brazil, coffee beans will be cheaper. That means that Starbucks and other coffee retailers will make a few pennies more on every one of those $3 cups of latte they sell us. And when Starbucks' profits rise, so, too, must its stock price.

So, if war breaks out in Iraq, what might you, as an investor, do? You might buy defense stocks like Northrup, which makes the jet fighters needed to bomb enemy targets; or Flir, which produces the night-vision goggles and infrared devices to detect the enemy; or Raytheon, which produces the missiles used to destroy the enemy.

Similarly, if anthrax stalks the U.S. postal system, you might buy SureBeam Technologies, which makes sterilization equipment; or BioReliance and IVAX, which produce anthrax medicines and vaccines.

And if terrorism threatens our airports, stadiums, and nuclear power plants, you might buy InVision Technologies, which makes bomb detection equipment; Viisage Technology, which makes face recognition systems; and Armor, Kroll, or Wackenhut, which provide commercial security guards and perimeter security.

Note, however, that it's not just individual stocks and sectors that move on such macroeconomic "shocks"—as all of the above cited stocks and sectors did in the aftermath of the incredibly tragic and quite literally terrifying events of September 11, 2001. Indeed, a much broader array of macroeconomic events— what I call "macrowaves"—also represent the major fuel that moves the broad stock market indices—from the Dow Jones Industrial Average and Standard & Poor's 500 to the Russell 2000 and, of course, the once highest-flying Nasdaq.

These macrowaves range from the latest government reports about inflation, growth, and unemployment and the earnings news of our largest corporations to major fiscal and monetary policy decisions by the president and the Federal Reserve. And here's both my claim and promise to you:

> *Each of these macrowaves will move the U.S. stock market in very different but nonetheless very systematic and predictable ways. If you come to fully understand these macrowaves, you will become a better investor, no matter what your style of investing.*

Anatomy of a Crash

To fully understand the effects of macrowaves on the stock market, let's analyze all of the various macrowaves that helped pound the Nasdaq market index down from its once lofty heights of 5000 to well below a submissive 2000. This crash was the equivalent of a $5 trillion giant sucking sound out of the pockets of investors, and it happened over the course of many, many months. It was fueled by these major macrowaves, as illustrated in Figure 1-1.

In the months preceding the beginning of the Nasdaq crash of 2000, the over-expansionary U.S. economy was catching what seemed to be a bad case of inflation. Federal Reserve Chairman Alan Greenspan responded by pummeling businesses and consumers with a series of interest rate hikes designed to put on the economic brakes and engineer a so-called soft landing.

Meanwhile, the Justice Department was trying to break up Microsoft. This attempt battered not only the company's stock but the entire tech sector as well as the major players in the tech marketplace, who began to fear the heavy hand of Uncle Sam.

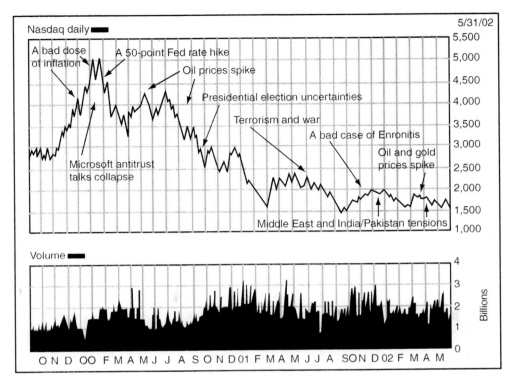

Figure 1-1   Major macrowaves pound the Nasdaq market.

At the same time, oil prices were skyrocketing, adding further contractionary pressures to the Fed rate hikes.

Then, we came into a presidential election season and couldn't even declare a winner for weeks (was it Bush or Gore, Gore or Bush?), and this further roiled the markets.

And just as it looked like the economy and the markets were getting off their knees, we were hit with a vicious and vile terrorist attack and an ensuing war.

Then, as we began to recover from that, lo and behold, the Enron scandal hit, engulfing the markets in accounting uncertainties.

This was followed by near-chaos in Israel, the threat of nuclear war between Pakistan and India, another round of oil price shocks, and soaring gold prices.

Do you get the Big Picture here? *Macrowaves move the markets!* And the most important point is that they do so in both systematic and predictable ways. Of course, the purpose of this book is to help you better understand these ways. To accomplish this goal, we are going to walk step by step through the basic principles and practices of the savvy macrowave investor.

At a bare minimum, I hope to help you protect your investment capital from the kind of ravaging it may have taken in the last bear market. But I also want to arm you with the Big Picture tools you will need to find Big Profits. And once you learn the savvy macrowave investor method, you should be able to prosper in both bull and bear markets.

QUESTIONS

1. If rain comes to break a drought in Brazil, why might the stock price of Starbucks stock go up?

2. List at least five of the major macrowaves that helped bring the Nasdaq Stock Market Index down from over 5000 to well below 2000.

EXERCISES

1. Log on to the Internet and go to the Web site www.bigcharts.com. Use the interactive charting link to create a chart for QQQ: the "tracking stock" for the Nasdaq 100. Specifically, at the "Time Frame" box, use the custom feature to specify the time period from January 1, 2000 to June 30, 2002. Click the "Draw Chart" link after you make the changes. Look at the chart carefully and try to think about all the major macrowaves that drove the market down during this period. After you've done this, compare your chart to Figure 1-1.

2. At www.bigcharts.com, use the same interactive charting link and custom time feature to look at the charts of several companies whose stock price soared after the events of 9/11. Specifically, take a look at the charts of FLIR Systems (FLIR), Viisage Technology (VISG), SureBeam Technologies (SURE), and InVision Technologies (INVN). Use the time period from June 2001 to the present. How many of those stocks managed to hold their initial gains after the events of 9/11?

Not enough money to rapidly rebuild New Orleans or the trade Center in NY

Chapter 2

WHAT'S YOUR
WALL STREET "IQ"?

Author's Note: *This chapter is written primarily for beginning investors. So if you are already an experienced investing hand and simply want to learn about how to master the savvy macrowave investor approach, feel free to just skim this chapter or just skip ahead to Chapter 3.*

Do you think that tomorrow, you could walk into Yankee Stadium and pitch a winning shutout against the meanest men in pinstripes? Of course not!

So why do you think that without the appropriate training and tools and the toughest of mental attitudes, you can plunge right into the stock market and beat the second meanest, and far more ruthless, men in pinstripes—those Wall Street money managers?

David W. Aloyan

In the next chapter, I will present the savvy macrowave investor trading method, and we will begin the exciting task of mastering that method. But before we go there, I need to ask you a prior question—actually 11 questions.

I need to ask you these questions for a very important reason. Together, we need to find out before you walk too far down the stock market's Yellow Brick Road, whether active investing is truly your bag. The fact of the matter is, many people who want to actively manage their own stock portfolios simply are not suited, either mentally, physically, emotionally, or financially, for the task.

I know this because I've met so many of them—unwitting victims who have lost so much money simply because they weren't willing, and in some cases, were quite unable, to maintain the discipline and focus and objectivity necessary to win in what one wag has appropriately called the "loser's game."

So let me perhaps save you a lot of time, and just maybe a lot of money, with my own unique version of the active investor's aptitude test. Our goal here is to measure the Wall Street version of your "IQ"—your "investor quotient." So please take out a pencil and paper if you will—or meander over to your computer—and begin to type or jot down your own personal answers to these at times rather pointed questions:

1. How many hours per week are you willing to devote to actively managing your portfolio?

2. What percentage of your time managing your portfolio do you think you should spend on research and preparation versus actually trading stocks?

3. Do you see the stock market more as a game of roulette or poker? What, in your mind, is the critical difference between these two games?

4. Would you rather win big at the risk of big losses or would you rather consistently win small? Put another way, do you like to swing for the home run fences even if it means you will strike out more? Or are you a "percentage hitter" who is satisfied with a lot of singles and doubles and a high batting average?

5. List your top three investing goals in order of importance.

6. What is the minimum level of capital you are prepared to actively invest?

7. Are you investing with money that you can absolutely, positively afford to lose?

8. If you are in a relationship, how does your spouse or significant other feel about your stock market investing? Would you be comfortable telling him or her that you've sustained a heavy loss? Will it give you pleasure to boast of a big gain? Do you feel you will ever have to hide anything?

9. Is there a comfortable room or office where you can actively manage your portfolio free of distraction?

10. Is your trading platform securely wired to the Internet? Are you computer-literate and quite comfortable surfing the Net?

11. Do you face a high degree of stress in your life? If so, are you ready to handle more? Are you in good health?

Now before we go over your answers and try to calculate your Wall Street IQ, allow me to reveal the underlying structure and intent of these questions.

The first two questions help measure your level of commitment and focus to managing your own portfolio. The next three questions reveal your stock market mindset and investing temperament. Your answers to Questions 6 through 8 will tell us whether you are in a strong enough financial and family position to actively invest in the stock market. Questions 9 and 10 survey the adequacy of your investing environment. Finally, Question 11 highlights the need for a certain level of both mental and physical toughness.

With that as our conceptual overview, let's look at some possible answers to these 11 questions.

1. How many hours per week are you willing to devote to actively managing your portfolio?

   Actively managing your portfolio is hard work—and just as you won't be beating the Yankees any time soon, you won't be beating the *second-meanest* men (and women) in pinstripes on an hour or two of research a week. That's why *if you can't devote at least five to ten hours a week to your portfolio, I humbly suggest that you forget about "playing the market."* Instead, I strongly recommend that you simply stick your money in a very broad index fund and go enjoy your life.

   In this regard, I'm always amazed at how hard people work in their jobs for their next dollar. Yet so many of these very same people are so unwilling to work as hard and as long to protect their portfolio and the dollars they already have.

2. What percentage of your time managing your portfolio do you think you should spend on research and preparation versus actually trading stocks?

   At least three quarters of your time should be devoted to your research and preparation. As we shall see in the next chapter, such preparation includes most obviously your stock picking and stock screening. But it also entails closely following on a daily basis the flow of macroeconomic information as well as carefully crafting your buying and selling strategies.

3. Do you see the stock market more as a game of roulette or poker? What, in your mind, is the critical difference between these two games?

   As you bring your hard-earned money to the investing table, it's absolutely critical that you do so as an intelligent speculator rather than simply a reckless gambler. The reckless gambler inevitably loses because he takes risks when the odds of winning are less than 50-50. Playing roulette or dropping coins into slot machines are both forms of gambling. You bet against the house—and over time, the house *never* loses.

   In contrast, the intelligent speculator only takes a risk when the odds are in his favor. Poker is a form of speculation. If you draw a bad hand, you drop out and forfeit a small ante. But if you draw a strong hand, the odds are in your favor and you play it to the hilt. You will see in this book that if you apply these very same principles of poker strategy to your stock market investing by always "cutting your losses" and "letting your profits run," you will dramatically increase your odds of making money.

4. Would you rather win big at the risk of big losses or would you rather consistently win small?

This question is another way of uncovering any of your possibly "reckless gambler" tendencies. If left uncontrolled, these tendencies will ultimately lead you to ruin. Here's the problem.

The home-run hitter will always expose too much of his or her trading capital on any one bet. This may lead to some spectacular gains, but over time, it likely also will lead to equally heavy losses—and perhaps much worse.

As we shall see in a later chapter, protecting your investing capital is your *most* important responsibility. And while on some very rare occasions, you may want to swing for the fences, most of the time you should be quite content to hit singles and doubles—like Ted Williams, who got his share of home runs with a very smooth swing but who reached the Hall of Fame with the most solid of batting averages.

5. List your top three investing goals in order of importance.

I'm sure that "making money" is somewhere on your list and maybe even at the top—as well it should be. But let me caution you here. If you go into the stock market simply to make the "big bucks," you probably won't. Indeed, *if you only want to make money, do not enjoy the investing process, and find no beauty, elegance, and satisfaction in a well-executed investment strategy, then you will likely run into trouble.*

In this regard, the best investors I know see stock market investing as a complex craft worthy of pride and the pursuit of perfection. Accordingly, one of their top priorities is to "invest well" rather than simply make money. And for many of these same top investors, a second related priority is to be both challenged and entertained by what, in reality, is one of the most interesting and complexly subtle pursuits this side of Grand Master Chess.

6. What is the minimum level of capital you are prepared to actively invest?

I am of two minds on this question. On the one hand, and for you absolute beginners reading this book, the less capital you start with, the less you can lose. And it is the rare beginner who doesn't initially lose in the stock market—something the Wall Street pros caustically refer to as "tuition to the market."

On the other hand, unless you start with a large enough sum of money, whatever profits you may be lucky or skilled enough to generate will be whittled down or completely dissipated by your commission costs. The problem here is that with most brokerage services, it costs the same to buy 50 shares of a stock as it does to buy 5000. But the more shares you deal in, the more you can spread your commission costs over your profits.

To see this, suppose you buy 50 shares of the fictional company Transactions Costs at $20 and sell it at $22 for a gain of $100. After you deduct round-trip commission costs of, say, $20, you're left with a net profit of only $80—and commissions have eaten up a full 20 percent of your gains. In contrast, if you buy 1000 shares at $20 and sell at $22, your commission costs are a miniscule 1 percent of your profits.

The point here? Taking into account the burden of commission costs (and the need for diversity in your portfolio), you should start with a trading account of at least $25,000 and preferably $50,000.

If you don't have that kind of money, please *don't* go out and borrow it or mortgage your house. Instead, as I shall explain in a later chapter, you should consider simply simulating your stock market investing for a while using the STOCKTRAK software I discuss in the last chapter of this book.

7. Are you investing with money that you can absolutely, positively afford to lose?

If you have ever missed a 2-foot putt to lose a key match or forgotten what you were going to say at your first big (and perhaps stammering) speech, you have experienced the effect that pressure can have on both your motor skills and coherent thought. The problem here is that if you are using money in the stock market that you can't possibly afford to lose, you will likely wind up making bad decisions because of that added pressure.

8. If you are in a relationship, how does your spouse or significant other feel about your stock market investing?

If your spouse or significant other is afraid you will lose all of the family's money in the market, the chances increase that you will do precisely that. This is because of the "P" word again, namely, pressure.

If you are not comfortable reporting a heavy loss to your partner, that, too, reflects a level of mistrust or lack of confidence that will cloud your judgment. And if you act proud as a rooster every time you make a "big score" and must declare your victory to your partner, you are simply setting yourself up for a "pride cometh before the fall" embarrassing, and likely huge, loss.

May I gently suggest, then, that you don't need any of this noise or static in your marriage or relationship. What will help most is very open communication between you and yours about what you are attempting to do in the stock market on behalf of your family.

9. Is there a comfortable place where you can actively manage your portfolio free of distraction?

Don't worry. I'm not going to go off on a big meditation rant here. I simply want to make the point that successful investing requires a calm and peaceful trading environment free of distractions.

Put simply, you need to focus. And you can't do that if your investing space is in the middle of the living room with a blaring TV and screaming children. Nor will it be appropriate to try to fit—or sneak—in your stock trading between the tasks you are supposed to be doing at your job.

So find a quiet space. Keep it clean and neat. And if you need further explanation of why this is important, pick up a copy of one of my favorite books, *Zen and the Art of Motorcycle Maintenance*, which is the best-selling discourse on the importance of focus and clarity in one's life.

10. Are you computer-literate and quite comfortable surfing the Net? Is your trading platform securely wired to the Internet?

I'm sure it is just as possible to make money investing in the stock market without the help of a computer or the Internet as it is to live without modern plumbing. But why would you want to do that?

With a computer, you can trade online at substantially lower commission costs. With most online brokers, you can also receive up-to-the-minute market data that will help you get the best prices.

With an Internet connection, you can receive news much faster. You can also gain access to what have now become the preferred sources for most stock research. And you can even get the electronic edition of *Investor's Business Daily*—an indispensable trading tool—a full 12 hours sooner than the print edition.

As for a secure Internet connection, forget about the old-fashioned telephone line modem. You will need either a cable or DSL broadband connection to play in the same league as those Wall Street traders in pinstripes.

Last but hardly least, you will need a fast computer with plenty of random access memory (RAM) and hard drive space; and, if you really want to do this right, get at least two computer monitors for your computer so you can conveniently see all the market action and charts that you will need.

11. Do you face a high degree of stress in your life? If so, are you ready to handle more? And are you in good health?

    If you are already in a high-stress occupation, please be aware that active investing will not provide you any relief from that stress. Indeed, for most people, it will almost certainly add another major layer of stress. This will be particularly true at the beginning of your investing career.

    This is because as a novice investor, you will almost assuredly lose money because of little mistakes, perhaps toss away some big chunks of dough because of big mistakes, and maybe even at times you will do everything right but it will still go so very wrong.

    That's called the Wall Street "learning curve," and it will often seem more like an emotional roller coaster than the Yellow Brick Road to wealth. You need to be ready for that rocky ride, and you also need to be in excellent physical health to absorb the stress. Heart conditions and the faint of heart need not apply.

Now, a drumroll please as we calculate your Wall Street investor's quotient based on your answers to the above 11 questions. So go ahead now and compare your answers to those in the text above, and give yourself one point for every "right" answer.

Ideally, if active investing is going to be for you, you will score at least a 7 or higher out of 11. But if you don't and your score is more like 5 or below, let me humbly suggest that you follow the advice set forth in the answer to Question 1, which is to simply put your investment capital in a broad index fund and go enjoy your life.

QUESTIONS

1. At a minimum, how many hours a week should you devote to actively manage your portfolio?

2. Should you view the stock market more as a game of roulette or poker? And what is the difference between gambling and speculation?

3. Besides making money, list two other important investing goals.

4. What is the minimum level of capital you need to be an efficient active investor?

5. Why is it important only to invest money that you can afford to lose?

EXERCISES

1. If you are already an active investor, sit down with a pad of paper or at your computer and review your investment activities over the last two or three weeks. Try to recall how many hours total you spent on your portfolio. Then, determine how many of those hours were spent doing research versus actually trading stocks.

2. If you are in a relationship, take some time with your spouse or significant other to discuss his or her attitudes toward your stock market investing or your plans to begin actively investing.

3. If you are still using an old-fashioned telephone modem to connect to the Internet, call up both your local cable company and your phone company that may provide a DSL connection. Go ahead and price these services and determine what it would take to upgrade your computer to a high-speed broadband connection.

4. Take a trip to your local computer store and get the lowdown on putting dual monitors on a computer. If you have a computer, find out how much it would cost for the hardware and software to add a second monitor. Or, if you don't want to travel for the information, log on to the Internet and visit www.google.com. Type in *dual monitor systems* in the search window, and see what you come up with.

Chapter 3

THE FOUR STAGES OF MACROWAVE INVESTING

Author's Note: *This chapter is a very important one because it will lay out for you the entire structure of the book that follows. While it may take you a little extra time to read through it, after you do so, you should have an excellent overview of the entire savvy macrowave investor method.*

To become savvy macrowave investors, we must begin, of course, at the beginning. This means we must first learn the Three Golden Rules of Macrowave Investing. Even more importantly, we must also come to understand the important implications of these rules for the four stages of the macrowave investing approach.

The Three Golden Rules of Macrowave Investing

1. Buy strong stocks in strong sectors in an upward-trending market.
2. Short weak stocks in weak sectors in a downward-trending market.
3. Stay *out* of the market and in cash when there is no definable trend.

The implications of these three rules for the skills we must develop as investors should be clear: First, we must be able to determine the present and likely future direction of the broad *market* trend. Second, we must be able to determine individual sector trends. And third, we must be able to identify both strong and weak stocks once we have determined the market and sector trends.

Of these three tasks, many investors are very good at identifying strong and weak stocks, some investors are pretty good at assessing the broad market trends, but very few investors have cultivated a sophisticated sector approach to the markets. A big part of my job in this book will be to address these possible gaps in your investing armor. Now here is the fourth important implication of our Three

Golden Rules of Macrowave Investing: Once we have determined the broad market and individual sector trends *and* we have picked our strong and weak stocks, we must learn to strategically enter—and exit—the market with discipline.

In particular, we shall learn that *no* successful entry strategy can come without a well-defined *exit* strategy. We shall also learn that intelligently crafting solid entry and exit strategies will depend on a strict adherence to both sound risk management and solid money management rules as well as a mastery of trade execution rules to efficiently buy and sell your stocks.

The Four Stages of Macrowave Investing

Figure 3-1, which establishes the structure for the remainder of this book, summarizes the four and highly interrelated stages of macrowave investing.

In *Stage One*, the savvy macrowave investor uses "macrowave logic" to process the flow of information from the "four dynamic factors" that move the markets. As I will show you, macrowave logic is simply a big-picture method of systematically thinking about how the stock market works.

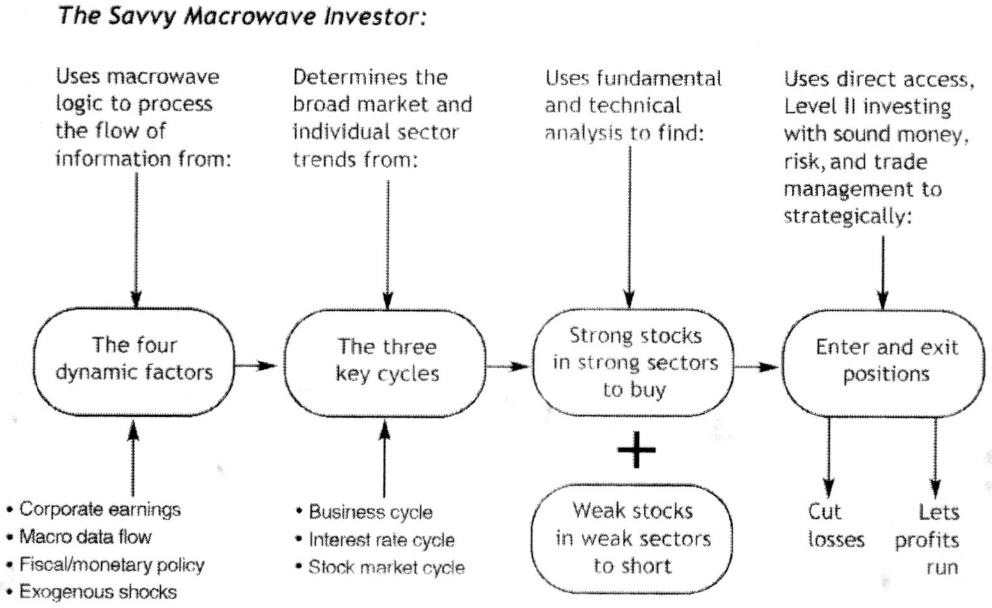

The Savvy Macrowave Investor:

Uses macrowave logic to process the flow of information from:	Determines the broad market and individual sector trends from:	Uses fundamental and technical analysis to find:	Uses direct access, Level II investing with sound money, risk, and trade management to strategically:
The four dynamic factors	The three key cycles	Strong stocks in strong sectors to buy	Enter and exit positions
		+	
		Weak stocks in weak sectors to short	Cut losses Lets profits run
• Corporate earnings • Macro data flow • Fiscal/monetary policy • Exogenous shocks	• Business cycle • Interest rate cycle • Stock market cycle		

Figure 3-1   The four stages of macrowave investing.

As we shall discuss in detail, the following are the four dynamic factors:

1. Corporate earnings news
2. The flow of macroeconomic data on issues like inflation and unemployment
3. The conduct of fiscal and monetary policies by the government
4. So-called exogenous shocks, from war and terrorism to, yes, rain in Brazil.

In *Stage Two*, the savvy macrowave investor uses a mastery of the "three key cycles" to determine the broad market trend and the individual sector trends. The following are the three key cycles:

1. The business cycle
2. The stock market cycle
3. The interest rate cycle

In *Stage Three*, the savvy macrowave investor uses *both* fundamental analysis and technical analysis to select strong stocks in strong sectors to buy and weak stocks in weak sectors to short. Technical analysts focus purely on the price action of a stock. In contrast, fundamental analysts believe that a stock's price simply reflects key characteristics ranging from a company's growth prospects and earnings per share to its debt loads and quality of management. We shall see that every stock must go through both a fundamental and technical "screen."

Finally, in *Stage Four*, the savvy macrowave investor uses solid risk management, money management, and trade management tools together with direct access, Level II investing to enter and exit positions so as to cut losses and let profits run.

We shall work together in the remainder of this book to systematically and sequentially work our way through these four stages. To prepare for this task and as a means of providing you with a broad overview of where we will be going, I will briefly summarize each of the major elements of Figure 3-1 in the remainder of *this* chapter and indicate in which chapter or chapters each of these elements will be discussed.

Stage One: The Four Dynamic Factors

Stage One: The savvy macrowave investor uses macrowave logic to process the flow of information from the four dynamic factors that move the markets

Signals from the Corporate Earnings News

All publicly traded companies release extensive quarterly and annual earnings reports and issue periodic announcements about future earnings prospects. This may seem like a *micro*economic factor because it's about individual companies, but such corporate earnings news can signal the health of a sector and the broader economy.

For example, if the semiconductor equipment manufacturer giant Applied Materials (AMAT) fails to meet its earnings estimates or issues a downward revision of its forecast, it won't just be AMAT that suffers. The effects will ripple upstream to semiconductor manufacturers like Intel and Texas Instruments and forward to consumer electronics companies like Nokia.

The key points for this dynamic factor, which are discussed in Chapter 4, are: You must first be intimately aware of the earnings calendar—and not get caught by any earnings surprises. You must also learn the difference between what's called the "consensus estimates" versus the so-called whisper numbers.

Messages of the Macroeconomic Calendar

Both government agencies and private institutions release regular reports on all phases of the economy—from production and capacity utilization to inflation, recession, and productivity. Following the flow of macroeconomic data is the very bread and butter of the savvy macrowave investor. Our task in Chapter 5 will be to come to better understand just some of these points:

The macroeconomic calendar provides the major fuel that moves the stock market. More subtly, some reports are more important than others. Most importantly, certain reports are more important at different stages of the business cycle than others.

For example, in inflationary times, the Consumer Price Index (CPI) reigns supreme. But, in a recession, all eyes are on the Institute of Supply Management or "purchasing managers'" index. Perhaps most inscrutably, the macroeconomic news isn't always what it seems, for "good news" can indeed be "bad news."

Don't Fight the Fed—or Fiscal Policy

We will see that monetary policy, which controls the supply of money and credit, is the most crucial policy for investors to watch. Every trader on Wall Street knows that you can't—and shouldn't—"fight the Fed." Indeed, as we shall see in Chapter 6, the Federal Reserve can do you far more harm as an investor than any 10 wily market makers can.

In addition, fiscal policy uses decreased government spending and increased taxes to contract an overheated economy—and increased government spending or tax cuts to stimulate a recessionary economy. Such stimulative policies can pull an economy more quickly out of recession—and lift the stock market. But the savvy macrowave investor also knows that such policies can also spark a virulent inflation and kill a bull market.

The Market Shocks from "Exogenous Shocks"

War and terrorism, global warming and drought, an AIDS epidemic or outbreak of Ebola, oil price hikes, and, yes, rain in Brazil. These are all examples of what economists call "exogenous shocks." The key point for the savvy macrowave investor is this: While many of these shocks occur unpredictably, the impacts of the shocks on the broad market trend and sector trends as well as individual stocks are *quite* predictable and systematic—and thus potentially a very lucrative source of investment opportunities. We will explore these opportunities in Chapter 7 within the context of a very powerful investment strategy called the "macroplay."

Stage Two: Three Key Cycles That Shape Market and Sector Trends

> **Stage Two**: The savvy macrowave investor uses a mastery of the business cycle, the stock market cycle, and the interest rate cycle to determine the broad market trend and individual sector trends.

In this second stage of macrowave investing, our central premises are these:

1. The so-called twin cycles—the stock market cycle and business cycle—move in tandem.
2. The stock market cycle is a leading indicator of movements in the business cycle.
3. The pattern of sector rotation within the stock market cycle is a key to identifying strong and weak sectors.

The Crucial Business and Stock Market Cycles

In Figure 3-2, note first how the business cycle moves from peak to trough to peak. It charts the roller-coaster ride of the economy from expansion to recession to expansion.

Next, please note how the stock market moves through six clear stages. In the early bull, middle bull, and late bull stages, both the market trend and the prices of most stocks are moving *upward*. Then, when we get to the early bear, middle

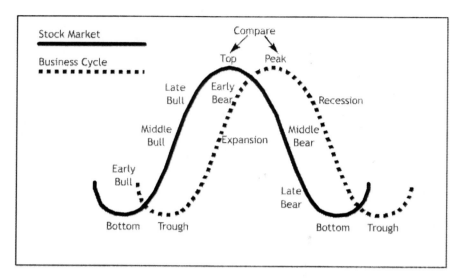

Figure 3-2   The stock market cycle leads the business cycle.

bear, and late bear phases, the market trend is clearly *down*—along with the prices of most stocks.

Finally, and most importantly, we can see very clearly that the stock market line hits its top well *before* the business cycle hits its peak. This means that the stock market starts declining *before* the recession actually hits. That's why the stock market is seen as a "leading indicator" of the business cycle—a critical point we shall explore in much more detail as we examine the twin cycles, and sector trends within these cycles, in Chapters 8 and 9.

The Powerful Patterns of Sector Rotation

The real power of using the stock market as a crystal ball lies not just in its ability to forecast recessions and recovery. No, the *real* power of following the stock market cycle lies in the underlying pattern of what's called "sector rotation" that occurs in the typical cycle. These patterns of sector rotation will be examined in Chapter 9, and they represent the keys to the Macrowave Kingdom. This is because they allow you to better discern the various sector trends—an essential element of the macrowave investing approach.

Figure 3-3 illustrates the typical patterns of sector rotation. You can see, for example, that the transportation and technology sectors typically outperform other sectors in terms of stock price increases in the early bull phase while health

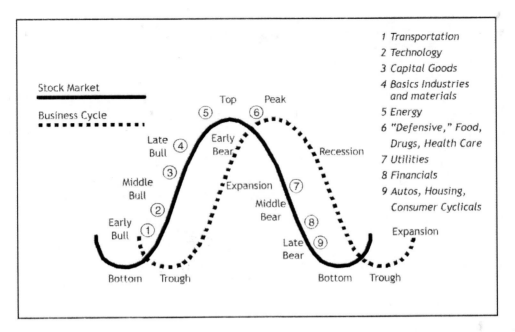

Figure 3-3   The stock market's powerful patterns of sector rotation.

care and "consumer staples" like food and drugs have their day in the late bear sun. Note also how the energy sector peaks in the late bull phase of the stock market while "consumer cyclicals" like autos and housing lead the recovery. In fact, much of the work we will do in this book will be dedicated toward better sensitizing you to these patterns of sector rotation.

The reason is as simple as it is powerful: By understanding the patterns of sector rotation, you will be better able to identify strong and weak sectors. This is perhaps the most crucial element of savvy macrowave investing. Remember: You can buy the strongest stock in the world, but if it is in a weak sector, you lose—big time!

Market Secrets of the Interest Rate Cycle

Let's turn now to the interest rate cycle and a related tool known as the "yield curve." They are examined in more detail in Chapters 10 and 11.

The interest rate cycle charts the progression of Federal Reserve policy from a series of rate hikes to dampen inflationary pressures during an expansion to a series of rate decreases to stimulate an economy out of a recession. Like the stock market cycle, the interest rate cycle is likewise a leading indicator of movements in the business cycle as well as a key driver of interest—sensitive activities of the firm—from the management of short-term debt to the financing of longer-term capital expansion.

More specifically, the savvy macrowave investor uses the ever-changing shapes of the yield curve to forecast changes in the business cycle. This yield curve, which is illustrated in Figure 3-4, defines the relationship between short- and long-term bonds.

Note that Line A is the "normal" shape. This normal yield curve is moderately sloped upward with the spread between the short and long ends of the curve a few hundred basis points. This type of curve generally reflects an ongoing and stable economic expansion without significant concern for inflationary pressures. It also typically signals an upward-trending and bullish stock market.

Line B is a steeper version of Line A. As we shall learn, we often observe such a steep yield curve at the *start* of an economic expansion—just after a recession ends. Such a steep yield curve often augurs a major change in the market trend and the onset of a new bull market. Accordingly, it broadcasts a very important "buy signal" for the market.

Perhaps even more important is the "sell signal" offered up by the inverted yield curve in Line C. In fact, the inverted yield curve is one of the most reliable— and dangerous!—signs of both a coming recession and new bear market.

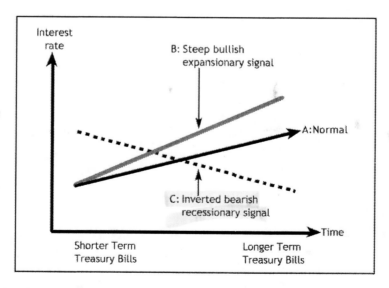

Figure 3-4 The yield curve's powerful market signals.

Stage Three: Picking Strong and Weak Stocks and Sectors

> **Stage Three**: The savvy macrowave investor uses both fundamental analysis and technical analysis to select strong stocks in strong sectors to buy and weak stocks in weak sectors to short.

As we shall discuss in Chapter 12, there are a myriad of ways to find potential stock picks. These range from combing the newspapers and Internet for hot new ideas to applying easy-to-use but highly sophisticated computer programs to perform your stock searches. Wherever you find your stocks, you can fruitfully apply both a fundamental and technical "screen."

The Phony Battle between Technical versus Fundamental Analysis

Technical analysis focuses purely on the price action of a stock—and it cares not whether the stock is for computer chips or potato chips. As a macrowave investor, you don't necessarily have to understand the full complexities of technical analysis. You just need to develop a working knowledge of technical analysis tools like "moving averages" and "on balance volume" and learn how to apply technical screens. This will be the goal of Chapter 14.

In contrast, the fundamental analyst believes that a stock's price simply reflects its underlying fundamentals, and key fundamental characteristics range from a company's growth prospects, market capitalization, and earnings per share to its sales-to-profit ratio, leverage, institutional ownership, float, and even its labor management relationships. Note, however, that (as we shall see in Chapter 13), the fundamentalist who fails to adopt a macrowave perspective invariably falls into two kinds of traps:

1. Investing in a fundamentally strong company but doing so in a bad overall *market*.
2. Investing in a great company in a bad market *sector*.

Both traps can be avoided, however, by combining your fundamental screens with solid technical analysis.

In fact, technical and fundamental analysts fight like cats and dogs, with fundamental analysts accusing the technicians of "chartist witchcraft" while technicians often rightfully ridicule fundamental analysts for picking stocks with great fundamentals that drop like a stone.

So who's right? Both camps are! As I shall continually remind you throughout this book, any stock you buy should be strong both technically and

fundamentally—and any stock you might want to short should be both technically and fundamentally weak.

Stage Four: Using Solid Money, Risk, and Trade Management Tools to Buy, Sell, and Short Stocks

---

Stage Four: The savvy macrowave investor uses solid risk management, money management, and trade management tools together with direct access, Level II investing to strategically enter and exit positions so as to cut losses and let profits run.

Managing Your Risk and Your Money

Protecting your investment capital and managing your risk are the two most important keys to successful, long-term investing. There are some great stock pickers who still go bust simply because they don't know how to manage their money or risk. That's why we shall review the basic rules of strict risk and money management in Chapters 15 and 16.

As a preview, and with my tongue only partly in cheek, I can tell you that the first three money management rules of successful investing are as follows: Cut your losses, cut your losses, and—you guessed it—cut your losses! But you must also learn to "let your profits run."

As for risk management, a portfolio consisting of Merck (a drug stock), Yahoo! (an Internet stock), Schwab (a financial sector stock), and Halliburton (an energy sector stock) clearly diversifies sector risk. However, a portfolio featuring AT&T, Sprint, and Nextel—all of which operate in the same industry sector—does not diversify risk. *In essence, you are not holding three positions but merely one.* The point is this: We have to learn to diversify risk.

Managing Your Trades

The key to any successful trade is your initial entry into the market. In order to craft efficient and intelligent entry strategies, you must know the critical differ-ence between market and limit orders and when to use each kind. Before you actu-ally ever get into a stock, you must also decide both how and when you are going to get out. That is, you must have an "exit strategy" to go along with your "entry strategy." This requires a mastery of valuable tools like the "stop loss," the "trail-ing stop," and the "buy stop" order. Such trade management techniques will be the topic of Chapter 17.

Managing Your Trade Executions

In Chapter 18, we will explore the exciting and intricate world of direct access, Level II investing platforms. The Level II feature of the modern investing platform takes you far beyond the bid price and the ask price of a stock to the entire underlying market for a stock—from the market participants and share sizes to a streaming ticker of market clearing prices. The resultant "market transparency" will help you greatly improve the timing of your trade executions.

Besides providing lightning fast trade executions, the direct access feature of the platform will also help you more efficiently implement your risk, money, and trade management rules. The tools you will have quite literally at your fingertips to do so go far beyond the simple "buy stops" and "sell stops" that are available from the Level I discount broker crowd and extend to much more sophisticated "programmed ordering."

Preparing for the Investing Week and Stock Simulations

In Chapter 19, I will put it all together by showing how to thoroughly prepare for each investing week. Finally, in Chapter 20 I will emphasize the importance of first "simulating" your stock trading before you actually put your money down. You will see that that's great advice not just for the novice but for any investors who may have run into a tough losing streak or who want to try out some new investing strategies.

With that as our overview of the savvy macrowave investor method, let's move now to Part Two and learn about the four dynamic factors.

QUESTIONS

1. What are the Three Golden Rules of Macrowave Investing?
2. Name the four stages of macrowave investing.
3. Name the four dynamic factors.
4. Name three key cycles.
5. Why does a better understanding of the patterns of sector rotation help you become a better investor?
6. Upon what does technical analysis focus?
7. Name at least one of the traps that the fundamental analyst tends to fall into.
8. What are the first three rules of money management?
9. Before you actually ever buy a stock, you must also decide both how and when to do what?

EXERCISES

1. Please sit down with a pen and paper and, without referring to the figure in the book, try to illustrate the four stages of macrowave investing. Include as many details as possible. Go back and check your work with Figure 3-1 in the book.

2. With that same pad of paper, draw and label the twin cycles. Can you see from your figure why the stock market cycle is viewed as a leading indicator of the business cycle?

3. To become more familiar with the earnings calendar, visit the Web site http://yahoo.finance.com and click on the link "Site Map." In the "Calendars" section under the column "Tools & Community," find the link "Earnings Calls." Click on the link and take a look at some of the companies that might be announcing earnings in the current week and in some of the weeks that follow.

4. To become more familiar with the macroeconomic calendar, visit http://economy.com/dismal. I will use this Web site in many of the exercises that follow in this book so I strongly urge you to sign up for the free trial subscription. Once you do so, please then go to the front home page. Where it says "View All Indicators," hit the Go button and see what's on tap for the month.

5. Visit www.federalreserve.gov and take a spin around the site. Read about what's going on at the "Monetary Policy" link and also check out "About the Fed."

6. Visit www.nber.org. This is the Web site for the National Bureau of Economic Research. It is the "official" agency that determines when our economy is in a recession. Check out the "Business Cycle Dates" under the Data Link.

7. To see what the current yield curve looks like, visit www.bloomberg.com and click on the "Markets" link at the top of the page. Then go down to the "Rates and Bonds" category and click on the "U.S. Treasuries" link.

PART TWO

THE FOUR DYNAMIC FACTORS

Stage One: The savvy macrowave investor uses macrowave logic to process the flow of information from the four dynamic factors that move the markets: corporate earnings news, the macroeconomic data flow, fiscal and monetary policy, and exogenous shocks.

Chapter 4

FOLLOW THE
EARNINGS CALENDAR!

The earnings season has disappointed Wall Street once again. Many investors had hoped that the latest batch of quarterly earnings would indicate a profits recovery, and so reflect the spate of rosy economic data that came out in the first quarter. Those hopes have faded.

Financial Times

Over the longer run, a company's stock price represents no more—and no less—than investors' expectations about the company's future stream of earnings. If those earnings expectations change, so, too, must a stock price.

Of course, the most direct way that investor expectations can change is from earnings news from the company itself. That's why the savvy macrowave investor carefully follows our first dynamic factor: the "earnings calendar." He or she does so not just for a company he or she may invest in. He or she also carefully follows other key stocks in that company sector as well as more general "bellweather" companies whose earnings news can help shape the broader market trend.

In fact, there is a very well-defined earnings season on Wall Street. It is an interval that spans the weeks following the end of each quarter when most companies release their earnings news. In parsing this earnings news, the savvy macrowave investor wants to answer three major questions:

1. Are the company earnings for the quarter likely to meet, beat, or fall short of the consensus estimate?

2. More subtly, is the company likely to meet, beat, or fall short of its earnings "whisper number" for the quarter?

3. Is the company likely to prospectively change its "earnings guidance" for the next quarter or next several quarters?

As we work our way through these questions, these will be this chapter's key macrowave points.

Author's Note: *Each of the remaining chapters will feature a summary of the key macrowave points. You should find this feature very helpful both for preparing to assimilate the chapter information as well as for going back and reviewing the information.*

Key Macrowave Points

1. The clear danger during earnings season is that you will be caught on the wrong side of a "gap opening." To mitigate this risk, the savvy macrowave investor always follows the earnings calendar.

2. The market typically moves before earnings are announced so you need to "buy on the rumor" but "sell on the news."

3. The so-called whisper numbers can be more important than the "consensus" earnings estimates.

4. The savvy macrowave investor watches not just the earnings news for his own stocks but also for other key companies in the sectors in which those stocks reside. This helps determine sector trends.

5. The savvy macrowave investor looks at the largest companies like GE and GM as bellweathers for the broader market trend.

Key Point #1: Fall into the Gap?

Williams-Sonoma gapped up out of a long base Wednesday on huge trade . . . . The home furnishings retailer raised its earnings outlook to 17-19 cents a share for the first quarter vs. prior views of 3-4 cents.

Investor's Business Daily

As a rule, individual companies release their earnings news *after* the close of the market or right before the next day's market open. The clear danger for investors is that upon release of the news, the stock price of a company will "gap down." With a gap down open, the stock's opening price of the day will be significantly lower than the previous day's close.

If you are holding a long position in a gap down opening on bad news, you can lose a lot of money. Symmetrically, if you are holding a short position in a "gap up" opening on unexpected good news (as with Williams-Sonoma in the news excerpt above) you can lose big as well.

Indeed, in the worst gap down scenario, the stock opens at a price not only far below the previous day's close but also far below your "stop loss," which is the predetermined stock price at which you had decided to sell the stock if it became a loser.

To mitigate this risk, the savvy macrowave investor always follows the earnings calendar.

Key Point #2: Buy on the Rumor, Sell on the News

> Take a quick look at how Coca-Cola shares are trading right now. They're trading down. You'd never expect that, based on what Coca-Cola said today.
>
> *CNBC Business Center*

In this example, what Coca-Cola "said" was that their earnings were great! So why did the stock fall?

For starters, you have to understand that Wall Street doesn't wait for the actual earnings news to change its assessment of a stock's price. Quite the contrary!

In the days preceding the release of a company's earnings news, a company's stock may experience higher volume and a rising price amid speculation of a positive "earnings surprise." This is "buy on the rumor" activity. And, in fact, in our Coca-Cola example, Coke's stock price actually had a very nice run-up prior to the announcement of the actual news—amid rumors that the news would be very good.

Now what can be so disconcerting—and costly—to the novice investor is that once the actual earnings news hits, a stock's price can fall quite significantly, even on such good news. This is the result of what's called "sell on the news" behavior among Wall Street's professionals, and if you think it through, this behavior is perfectly rational.

Indeed, by selling just before or as the news hits, the pros are eliminating the risk that the actual news might actually not meet the rosy expectations that have driven the stock's price up. So they get out with a nice profit and then let the amateur money perhaps take the beating.

But this is not the only reason why a stock's price can fall after a positive earnings surprise. The stock price of a company may still gap down if the company's top executives change their guidance about the profitability of future quarters, where guidance is simply the company's best estimates of its future profitability. Put another way, a company like Coca-Cola may report great earnings for the last quarter but warn that the next quarter will be a bit rocky. In such case, the stock most assuredly will take a hit.

Finally, and most subtly, a stock price may gap down on the news even if the reported earnings beat the "consensus estimate" of stock market analysts but fail to beat the so-called whisper number. This distinction between the consensus estimate and the whisper number is important, so let's take a short digressionary detour here to explain it.

Key Point #3: Consensus Estimates versus Whisper Numbers

We'll see it in the case where a whisper number is very optimistic, let's say 3 or 4 cents over the consensus number. A company will come in and beat that consensus number, but miss the whisper number. The analysts will get excited about that, yet the stock will fall, in the days after the earnings announcement, sometimes 20 percent, 30 percent. Those are big moves.

David Haffenreffer, CNNfn

The consensus estimate is compiled and published by the financial data powerhouse First Call (www.firstcall.com). This company relies exclusively on the judgment of professional stock market analysts, and this can create a very big problem.

In a strategy that Microsoft has now made famous, the management of many companies tries to "game" the consensus estimate system. The game is one of *deception*. It is to try to keep analyst estimates below the company's internal targets by feeding analysts misleading information.

Of course, the reward for management winning this game is that when the *actual* earnings number comes out and beats the consensus estimate, the company's stock price goes through the roof.

Because of this gaming behavior, so-called whisper numbers have emerged as an alternative way of assessing a company's profitability. They can be found on the Internet at sites like www.WhisperNumber.com, which is a paid subscriber site, and www.Earningswhispers.com, which at the time of this writing was free.

Now here's an important distinction: Whereas the consensus estimates are provided by Wall Street's insider stock market analysts, the whisper numbers are compiled using a much broader sample of opinion. And here's where it gets tricky for the individual investor: It is now quite possible for a company to beat its consensus estimates. However, if the whisper number calls for even higher earnings and the company fails to meet or beat that whisper number, the stock can swoon.

Key Point #4: Sector Watch

> Comverse Technology, an Israel-based maker of telecom software, and Avaya, a communications network provider which spun off of Lucent, also rattled the sector after both companies lowered their earnings guidance because of tough conditions in the telecom industry.
>
> *Financial Times*

The savvy macrowave investor not only checks the earnings calendar for a company he or she is evaluating. He or she also checks that calendar for other key companies in the sector and *related* sectors. This will be particularly important if the stock under consideration is a relatively smaller player in the sector.

In such a case, it is important to watch the sector leaders because any good or bad news offered by these companies is seen by Wall Street as a bellweather for the broader sector *and* perhaps the cluster of sectors the company does business in or with.

To understand this point, suppose you are evaluating a small cap stock like MKS Instruments (MKSI). This company manufactures sophisticated sensing equipment for semiconductor manufacturers. The equipment is used to improve the quality of chip production.

Of course, it's important to follow the earnings news of MKSI itself if you are thinking about buying or shorting the stock. But it can be equally, or even more important, to keep an eye on big chip players like Applied Materials, which is the market leader in capital equipment for semiconductors, and Intel, which is the world's largest chip maker. Any sign of weakness in these companies would likely ripple negatively through to MKSI while any sign of unexpected strength might provide a nice little macrowave boost of support for MKSI.

Key Point #5: Earnings and the Broad Market Trend

> The Nasdaq composite index, thick with technology stocks, soared 7.8 percent, its biggest gain in more than a year and the eighth biggest ever. The Dow Jones Industrial Average posted its best performance since September. And why? Because Cisco beat its modest earnings-growth target.
>
> *The New York Times*

Besides viewing the earnings news at the company and sector levels, the savvy macrowave investor also looks at the economy's largest companies like GE, GM, and Procter & Gamble as *bellweathers for the broader market trend*. As a famous president once put it, what's good for General Motors is good for the United States—or, as a president might say today, what's good for Microsoft is great for the United States.

More broadly, the savvy macrowave investor sees the whole earnings *season* as a huge mosaic. Collectively, each earnings announcement represents a dot in this mosaic. When these dots are properly connected with a Big Picture perspective, this mosaic paints a portrait of an economy and stock market either in an expansionary and bullish mode or recessionary and bearish mode, as the quotation leading off this chapter from the *Financial Times* alluded to.

Of course, the value of painting such a portrait from following the earnings news is that it helps the savvy macrowave investor better assess the direction of the broad market trend. Put simply, if the earnings season has been a very successful one for the majority of companies, this signals a healthy next several months in the stock market. In contrast, a dismal earnings season is very bearish for the market trend while mixed news foreshadows several more months of a market that is likely to simply trade sideways rather than trend up or down.

QUESTIONS

1. Over the longer run, what does a company's stock price depend on?

2. In processing the earnings news, the savvy macrowave investor wants the answers to what three major questions?

3. When do companies typically release their earnings news?

4. If a company releases bad earnings news, what is likely to happen to the stock price when the market opens the next day?

5. Provide at least two reasons why the stock price of a company may *gap down* after very good earnings news.

6. Why do consensus estimates tend to be unreliable?

7. Who provides the consensus estimates?

8. Why does the savvy macrowave investor also check the earnings calendar for other stocks in the sector in which he or she may be investing?

9. Why is it useful for the savvy macrowave investor to look at the earnings reports of the economy's largest companies?

10. Most broadly, what does a healthy earnings season signal and, conversely, what does a dismal earnings season signal?

EXERCISES

1. This exercise will show you how to research a company's earnings calendar, consensus estimates, and whisper numbers. Compile a list of the stocks in your portfolio and be sure to have their stock symbols ready. Then go to www.earningswhispers.com. Take a few minutes to peruse the site and look at some of the latest earnings news reports. After you do so, find the "Get Whisper" box and look up the latest whisper numbers for your stocks and compare them to the "Analysts' Estimate." Determine how you can actually put in your own estimate of earnings for a stock or two. [If you don't have any stocks at this time, use Cisco (CSCO), General Electric (GE), and Applied Materials (AMAT).]

2. Go to www.firstcall.com and click on the "About Us" link and go to the "Overview." This is not a Web site that you will be able to use much as an investor. But it's useful to be aware of it because First Call is such a big clearinghouse for all of the Wall Street analyst information. But beware! As we shall discuss later in the book, most of the Wall Street analysts are not worth listening to—and their track records prove it.

3. This exercise will begin to tune you into sector awareness. Go to www.bigcharts.com and click on the "Industries" link. Pick one of the "Dow Jones U.S. Sectors" like "Technology" or "Healthcare" and click on it. Note all the different sectors under the category. For example, "Technology" houses sectors like "Software" and "Computers." Pick one of these sectors and look at the Best and Worst Performing Stocks. Then go down to the bottom of the page and click on "Show All Stocks in This Industry." Peruse the list for familiar names and look at some of the charts.

4. Visit the Savvy Macrowave Investor Web site at www.peternavarro.com. Click on the "Macrowave University" link. To understand how short-term traders react to gap openings, read the article "The Dilemma of the Gap Down Opening" from www.tradertalk.com.

Chapter 5

FOLLOW THE MACROECONOMIC CALENDAR!

The Macrowave Calendar provides the daily dance of data that is the single most important source of fuel that moves the stock market.

Ron Vara

On an almost daily basis, both government agencies and private institutions release regular reports on the major macrowaves that move the markets, from inflation, recession, and productivity to budget deficits and trade deficits. Learning how to anticipate the possible effects of this macrowave calendar on the stock market is one of the most important tasks of the savvy macrowave investor—what is called "macro scenario building."

Key Macrowave Points

1. The macrowave calendar provides the major fuel that moves the stock market, but all economic indicators are *not* created equal. Different clusters of indicators are more important at different stages of the business cycle.

2. Use macro scenario building around the macrowave news to better gauge the market and sector trends and thereby exploit profitable opportunities.

3. Mr. Market hates inflation because inflation raises the probability that the Federal Reserve will raise interest rates. Higher interest rates choke off both business investment and consumption and can lead to recession.

4. Mr. Market hates recession because recession means lower production and sales and ultimately lower prices for the products firms sell. As earnings fall so, too, must stock prices.

5. Mr. Market hates falling productivity because lower productivity is inflationary and lowers growth over time.

6. Mr. Market (mostly) hates trade deficits because trade deficits can weaken the dollar and raise interest rates. But some trade deficits can be very bullish.

Key Point #1: The Market's Major Fuel

It will be both a light and heavy week on the macroeconomic calendar front. The light part is that very few reports are coming out. The heavy part is that we will see at least three key reports that have the power to significantly move the market.

The Savvy Macrowave Investor Newsletter

The macrowave calendar provides the major fuel that moves the stock market, but all economic indicators are *not* created equal. This is clearly evident in the four-star rating system in Table 5-1, which illustrates a typical monthly chronology of the macro data flow.

For example, the Consumer Price Index (CPI), the Producer Price Index (PPI), and the jobs report all rate three or four stars for their strong ability to move the markets. In contrast, the latest news from one-star reports like those for construction spending and consumer credit rarely move the markets in any appreciable degree.*

At the same time, it's important to understand that different *clusters* of economic indicators take on more importance at different stages of the business cycle. For example, when the economy is in recession, there typically is far less focus on key inflationary indicators like the CPI and PPI. Instead, Wall Street follows key recessionary indicators like the jobs report, housing starts, and auto sales.

Key Point #2: Use Macro Scenario Building

On Thursday, it's the Retail Sales and Producer Price Index reports. Neither is likely to offer any good news. Risk on the PPI is to the upside—sending a ripple of fear of Fed rate hikes through the markets. A budding

---

*The reasons why some indicators are more important than others are discussed at length in Part Three of *If It's Raining in Brazil, Buy Starbucks*.

Table 5-1   The Monthly Macrowave Calendar (Quarterly reports in italics)

Indicator	Rating	Source	Time of Release
Construction spending	*	Department of Commerce	First business day.
Institute of supply management index	****	National Association of Purchasing Managers	First business day.
Personal income and consumption	**	Department of Commerce	First business day.
Auto and truck sales	**	Department of Commerce	Third business day.
The Jobs Report	****	Department of Labor	First Friday.
Index of leading indicators	*	Conference Board	First week.
Consumer credit	*	Federal Reserve	Fifth business day.
Productivity and costs	****	Department of Labor	Around the 7th of the second month of the quarter for the prior quarter.
Retail sales	****	Department of Commerce	Between the 11th and 14th.
Producer price index	***	Department of Labor	Around the 11th.
Industrial production and capacity utilization	***	Federal Reserve	Around the 15th.
Business inventories	*	Department of Commerce	Around the 15th.
Consumer price index	****	Department of Labor	Between the 15th and 21st.
Housing starts	***	Department of Commerce	Between the 16th and 20th.
International trade	***	Department of Commerce	Around the 20th.
Consumer confidence	***	Conference Board University of Michigan Survey Research Center	Last Tuesday of month. Second and last weekend.
The treasury budget	**	U.S. Treasury	Third week.
Durable goods orders	**	Department of Commerce	Third or fourth week.
Factory orders	*	Department of Commerce	About a week after the durable goods report.
Employment cost index	***	Department of Labor	Near end of month of the quarter for prior quarter.
Existing home sales	**	National Association of Realtors	Around the 25th.
New home sales	**	Department of Commerce	Around the last business day.
Gross domestic product	***	Department of Commerce	Quarterly. Third or fourth week of the month.

softness in the auto sector is likely to leak a little air out of the retail balloon—so it will be interesting to watch whether the retail holder RTH goes into the red that day and maybe takes GM and Ford with it.

The Savvy Macrowave Investor Newsletter

Every Saturday morning, I open my fresh new copy of the weekly *Barron's Magazine* and go to the "Review and Preview" section to study the macroeconomic calendar for the coming market week. This calendar not only provides me with a list of the key reports. It also provides estimates of what the experts think the key numbers in each report will be.

After reading *Barron's*, I typically talk with my hedge fund partner David Aloyan, and we will speculate on the likely effects that the key macroeconomic reports will have on the stock market in the coming week. We call these sessions "macro scenario building."

At a minimum, we macro scenario build for defensive purposes. We don't want to be caught in any big positions on the wrong side of the economic news. For example, if the CPI comes out unexpectedly hot, we don't want to be caught in any long positions because the market will likely tank. By the same token, unexpected good news on the retail sales or jobs report front can, under certain conditions, give the market a nice upward boost; and of course, we don't want to be caught short selling.

The broader goal of our macro scenario building is to proactively use the macroeconomic news to better gauge the market and sector trends and thereby exploit opportunities that may arise when the actual news that is reported deviates significantly from the consensus estimates of the Wall Street experts. In this regard, it is critical to understand that, as with the earnings news dynamic factor we discussed in Chapter 4, the biggest effects on the stock market from the macroeconomic calendar will come when the actual macroeconomic news *deviates significantly* from the consensus estimates of the experts.

Perhaps the best way to illustrate the important role of expectations and our broader macro scenario building process is to start with this small excerpt from the *Savvy Macrowave Investor Newsletter* that David and I publish on a weekly basis:

> *Major reports of the week include: The ISM Index, a superb measure of the supply side of the economy, and Auto Sales, an important demand-side signal—both on Monday. Be ready for a nice upside surprise on the ISM Index to get the market moving upwards—at least if last week's robust Chicago PMI is the past to this prologue. Be wary of any unexpected drop off in auto sales that would indicate a crack in the consumer demand façade.*

At least in this particular case, we were dead on in our analysis. The ISM number came in well above the consensus expectations and gave the broad market a boost. At the same time, auto sales were unexpectedly weak and the major U.S. automakers took a haircut. In both cases, we were able to use this information to our profitable advantage.

Now at this point, you probably want to ask why our own expectations about the coming reports were different from the Wall Street consensus. The answer to this question is, however, that in some sense it's really the *wrong* question to ask. In this regard, it wasn't that we necessarily believed that the consensus estimate would be wrong. Rather, we formed a more subtle expectation of the *likely direction* of any possible deviation from the consensus.

For the ISM Index, we saw little risk that the index would come in below the consensus estimate and therefore little risk of a downside surprise and negative effect on the market. On the other hand, data from other reports in the previous week suggested that the supply side of the economy was building strength, which increased the odds of a nice upside surprise. *In other words, the odds in our view were better than 50-50 that the actual number would meet or beat the estimate so our bias was to the long side for the broad market.* That made a long position in a market index fund like QQQ or SPY or a strong semiconductor stock very attractive.

In contrast, in looking at auto sales, we saw a sector that had had a very nice upward run for many, many weeks. We didn't see much risk of auto sales being higher than the consensus even as we saw a much greater chance of a downside move as the sector (based on our technical analysis) seemed to be losing considerable momentum. That gave us a bearish bias for this particular sector and a short selling signal for companies like GM or Ford.

The broader point, of course, is that we used our awareness of the macroeconomics calendar to move the odds in our favor. That, by definition, is the very essence of practicing the art of intelligent speculation, as we discussed in Chapter 2, rather than submitting to the fool's game of reckless gambling. And that's why in this book, I will be encouraging you to engage in the same kind of macro scenario building that David Aloyan and I regularly practice.

Key Point #3: Mr. Market Hates Inflation

> U.S. stock markets ended a volatile week with record single-day plunges in the Dow Jones Industrial Average and the NASDAQ Composite Index . . . . The free fall was ignited by the early-morning release of a monthly Labor Department report on inflation. . . . The inflation report raised fears that the Federal Reserve . . . would raise interest rates higher than an expected quarter-point increase at its upcoming session in May.
>
> *Global News Wire*

Mr. Market hates inflation because inflation raises the probability that the Federal Reserve will raise interest rates. Higher interest rates choke off both business investment and consumption and can lead to recession, which in turn can lead to a reversal of an upward market trend and new bear market.

The problem, however, with tracking inflationary pressures is that there are two main kinds—"demand-pull" and "cost-push"—that can have very different effects on the market.

Demand-pull inflation comes with economic booms and "too much money chasing too few goods." It is very bullish. It is also readily curable using contractionary fiscal or monetary policies (as discussed in the next chapter).

Not so with *cost-push inflation*, which is the result of "supply shocks" such as oil price hikes or drought-induced food price spikes. This is a much more bearish inflation because supply shocks can create simultaneous inflation and recession—the dreaded "stagflation."

Consider a jump in the price of a barrel of oil. This price shock significantly raises the costs of energy-intensive businesses, discourages production, and is thereby recessionary. But the higher prices also act like an inflationary "tax" on consumers who have to pay more for their fuel oil and gasoline—and therefore have less money for other consumption.

Now here's the punch line: While the Fed is likely to very swiftly raise interest rates in the presence of demand-pull inflation, the Fed is likely to be much more cautious in the presence of cost-push inflation. In fact, the presence of cost-push inflation can actually *reduce* the probability that the Fed will raise interest rates because the Fed recognizes the contractionary nature of supply-side shocks.

For the savvy macrowave investor, this observation has a very real and practical significance. While the stock market, and particularly inflation-sensitive sectors like banking, finance, and housing, are likely to react very negatively to an unexpected jump in demand-pull inflation, the market may well shrug off bad news on the cost-push front—*if* it thinks the supply shocks are transitory. That's why the savvy macrowave investor reviews the news about inflation indicators like the CPI and PPI very carefully to distinguish between demand-pull and cost-push pressures.

Key Point #4: Mr. Market Hates Recession

All 16 companies in the U.S. Philadelphia Semiconductor Index gained yesterday, helping push the Index up 1.9 percent, after a report on U.S. housing starts that was better than economists forecasted boosted confidence about an economic recovery. A rebound in growth would boost demand for semiconductors, which are used in everything from cars, to mobile phones and Christmas greeting cards.

Bloomberg News

Mr. Market hates recession because recession means lower production and sales and ultimately lower prices for the products firms sell. As earnings fall so, too, must stock prices. That's why the savvy macrowave investor carefully follows at least four key recessionary indicators: the ISM Index, auto sales, housing starts and building permits, and the jobs report. A key point here is that each of these indicators offers a subtly different message.

For example, the ISM Index provides a very powerful and highly accurate yardstick of the manufacturing or "supply side" of the economy. It is based on a survey of purchasing managers in more than 300 companies representing over 20 industries in all 50 states. Any reading over 50 indicates the economy is in an expansionary mode. More importantly, any *change* in this index can signal a possible turn in the business cycle from recession to expansion or vice versa.

In contrast, both auto sales and housing starts and building permits are regarded as key "leading indicators." That's because the auto and housing sectors are typically the first to surge when the economy is recovering from a recession—*and* the first to falter when a recession is on the way.

The reason is simply that when consumers begin to worry about recession, they postpone or cancel decisions to buy big-ticket items like autos or homes. But when the economy is coming out of its recessionary trough, interest rates typically have bottomed and the unleashing of pent-up demand for these big-ticket items typically leads the recovery—and confirms the start of a new bull market.

Note, then, that these kinds of reports not only help the savvy macrowave investor gauge the broad market trend. They can also help on a sector level as well.

For example, if auto sales are booming, other sectors in the "auto cluster"—from tires and glass to aluminum and steel—will likely get a boost. In contrast, if housing starts and building permits are way down, the stock prices of the companies that make the carpet, dryers, dishwashers, furniture, and other accoutrements that will fill new homes will likely suffer with the home builders. And as the quote leading off this chapter illustrates, even sectors like semiconductors will respond to changes in this data at key turning points in the business cycle.

Key Point #5: Mr. Market Hates Productivity Decreases

> U.S. stocks rose as surging productivity and falling jobless claims boosted confidence corporate profit growth will rebound faster than expected.
>
> *Bloomberg News*

Productivity measures the growth in real output per worker, and it is the single greatest determinant of earnings and, by extension, both stock prices and the broader market trend. One reason is that faster productivity growth means the U.S. economy can grow at 4 percent to 5 percent rather than 2 percent to 3 percent *without* fear of inflation.

While a few percentage points may not seem like much, the economy can double in less than 20 years rather than in more than 30 years. For the corporations providing the clicks and bricks and mortar to fuel that faster growth, this means higher earnings and stock prices.

Over the long term, productivity is driven by the rate of capital investment, better education, improved management, and more rapid technological change. But in scenario building around the productivity report, the savvy macrowave investor is keenly aware that *productivity is also strongly affected by short-run movements in the business cycle*. This is a crucial observation, because the Federal Reserve and the stock market react much differently to changes in productivity, *depending on where the economy is in the business cycle*.

For example, when the economy begins to slide into a recession, productivity tends to fall because businesses cut back on production at a faster pace than they lay off workers. Such a fall in productivity is "normal" and unlikely to provoke much of a response from either the Federal Reserve or the stock market.

In contrast, when the economy is in a strong expansion, labor markets will begin to get tight and the cost of energy and raw materials will increase. At this point, the Fed will interpret any sign of falling productivity as highly inflationary and move to begin raising interest rates. This can send the stock market into a swoon, reverse the broad market trend, and hit key interest-rate-sensitive sectors hard.

Key Point #6: Mr. Market (Mostly) Hates Trade Deficits

> U.S. bonds posted their worst loss in two weeks after the government said imports and exports surged to records in March, fueling concern the Federal Reserve will raise interest rates soon to ward off inflation. Stocks fell.
>
> *Bloomberg News*

Mr. Market (mostly) hates trade deficits because they can weaken the dollar and are inflationary. But macro scenario building around the monthly trade data is one of the most complex tasks of the savvy macrowave investor. It is so because a trade deficit is not always what it seems to be.

The problem is that a trade deficit can arise *for more than one reason*. For example, a deficit due to rising exports can be very bullish while a deficit due to rising imports can signal inflationary troubles ahead. To better understand this phenomenon, let's look at two different scenarios.

First, let's assume that both the European and Asian economies are growing but that the U.S. economy is growing at an even faster rate and sucking in imports. In this case, the stock market is unlikely to react negatively to a trade deficit because it has resulted from robust economic growth.

In contrast, consider the case where U.S. exports are falling because the Japanese economy is on its knees and Europe is stagnant. In this case, a rising trade deficit will be very bearish, particularly for export-dependent sectors like aerospace, agriculture, autos, industrial equipment, and telecommunications to lead the decline.

Tracking the Macroeconomic Calendar

As I said earlier, I start every Saturday morning with my copy of *Barron's*. Alternatively, *Investor's Business Daily* offers its own calendar and provides excellent coverage of the release of the data and their effects on the markets.

Still and all, *the truly platinum standard* for the macroeconomic calendar news may be found on the Internet at www.dismalscience.com. This Web site provides the most comprehensive news and analysis available. The downside of this otherwise superb site is that it has evolved from a totally free and open site to a paid subscriber model. In this case however, you still get a lot more than you pay for, and I strongly recommend subscribing.

QUESTIONS

1. The process of speculating on the likely effects that the key macroeconomic reports will have on the stock market is called "macro scenario building." What are the goals of such speculation?

2. When we say that all macroeconomic indicators are not created equal, what exactly do we mean?

3. Why does the stock market hate inflation?

4. Is the Federal Reserve more likely to raise interest rates in the presence of demand-pull inflation or cost-push inflation?

5. Why does the stock market hate recessions?

6. Why are both auto sales and housing starts regarded as key leading indicators?

7. Why does the stock market love increases in productivity growth?

8. What happens to productivity when the economy begins to slide into recession? Is this likely to worry the Federal Reserve?

9. Why does the stock market hate budget deficits?

10. Why does the stock market (mostly) hate trade deficits?

11. If the trade deficit increases because the U.S. economy is growing faster than the European and Asian economies, is this bullish or bearish?

EXERCISES

1. This exercise will test your macroeconomic calendar reading comprehension. So sit down with a pad and pencil or at your computer keyboard and note from memory as many of the different economic indicators as you can remember from Table 5-1. In a second column, try to rate each of the various indicators that you can remember by one to four stars based on their importance in moving the stock market. After you finish this exercise, go back and compare your table to the table in the book. Be sure and try to fix in your mind at least those indicators that are rated three or four stars.

2. On Saturday of this next weekend, please go to your local newsstand and buy a copy of *Barron's*, if you don't already subscribe. In the Preview Section, check out the coming week's macroeconomic calendar and note the "consensus estimates" for each of the previewed indicators. Then, cross-check the indicators with Table 5-1 to see which economic reports are likely to most move the markets based on the four-star system. (Note: *Barron's* is also available online at www.barrons.com, but you must pay to gain full access to the site.)

3. After you have finished Exercise 2, visit the Dismal Scientist Web site at www.dismalscience.com. This would be a good time to try a free trial subscription. Use this free subscription to read in more detail about each of the economic reports that have been previewed in *Barron's*. Do this by going to the box "View All Indicators" and hitting "Go" to see the indicators by month. Find the current week's indicator lineup, compare it to the *Barron's* lineup, and begin to systematically read through some of the reports.

4. Visit my Web site, The Savvy Macrowave Investor, at www.peter navarro.com and read the current weekly newsletter featured on the main page. Read with particular interest the section that analyzes the likely effect of the current week's economic reports on the stock market.

5. This exercise draws on the fine work you did completing Exercises 2, 3, and 4. Specifically, I'm going to ask you to watch on a daily basis both how the macroeconomic calendar unfolds that week and how the stock market reacts—or does not react—to the breaking news. In this regard, you can read about the new data releases every day at the Dismal Scientist site. You can also note how the stock market reacts each day to the data releases by visiting a Web site like http://money.cnn.com or http://smartmoney.com. The day's feature story should have some analysis of how the economic reports of the day moved (or did not move) the markets.

Chapter 6

UNCLE SAM AND
THE STOCK MARKET

> Put Fed Chairman Alan Greenspan and the Incredible Hulk in the stock
> market ring and I'll put my money on Greenspan every time.
>
> *Ron Vara*

The third dynamic factor that moves the stock market involves the government's application of discretionary monetary and fiscal policies to fight inflation and recession.

The Federal Reserve sets monetary policy, and monetary policy is the most crucial policy for the savvy macrowave investor to watch. Since the 1970s, *the Fed has used monetary policy to intentionally cause at least one major recession and bear market. The Fed also inadvertently helped trigger several other bear markets*, including the quite painful bear market that began in 2000 and has lasted several years.

On the other hand, the Fed has miraculously ridden to the market's rescue in numerous other crises, most notably the 1987 "Black Monday" stock market crash, the 1997–1998 Asian financial meltdown, and, less successfully, the terrorist attack of September 11, 2001. For these and other reasons, virtually every Wall Street pro follows the adage "Don't fight the Fed" and carefully follows monetary policy. But the savvy macrowave investor also knows that you can't fight fiscal policy either.

Fiscal policy uses increased government spending or tax cuts to stimulate a recessionary economy and decreased government spending or tax hikes to rein in an overheated, inflationary economy. And just as monetary policy has had some spectacular successes and failures, so, too, has fiscal policy.

Indeed, well-executed fiscal policies helped trigger at least four of the most robust bull markets in history—from a spectacular recovery from the great depression to the incredible longevity of the Clinton bull market. On the other hand, the dismal *misuse* of fiscal policy in the 1970s helped result in the worst bear market since the Great Depression. So let's roll our sleeves up in this chapter and master the art of both fiscal and monetary policy. Both of these policies will have a tremendous ongoing influence over both the broad market trend and individual sector trends.

Key Macrowave Points

1. Monetary policy expands the money supply and lowers interest rates to stimulate a recessionary economy, or shrinks the money supply and hikes rates to contract an overheated and inflationary economy.

2. The Fed lowers or raises rates in a cycle over a period of many months in small increments rather than in isolated steps and thereby exerts enormous influence over the broad market and individual sector trends.

3. An interest rate hike will ripple through the economy and stock market in a complex pattern that will hurt some sectors far more than others but will always turn the broad market trend down.

4. Fed policy is much more successful at fighting inflation than recession because "you can't push on a string."

5. The key to understanding how fiscal policy affects the stock market lies in understanding the two basic methods used to finance budget deficits. "Selling bonds" can "crowd out" private investment while "printing money" can cause inflation. Both are bearish.

6. Fiscal policy is a much blunter instrument than monetary policy. It works more slowly and is much more difficult to reverse. Still, fiscal policy is generally viewed as more effective in fighting recessions while monetary policy is seen as more effective fighting inflation.

7. A tax cut to stimulate the economy is a blunter and more uncertain tool than increased government spending.

Key Point #1: The Tools of Monetary Policy

Last year, the Fed sponged the liquidity back up, and the Nasdaq crashed.

Don Bauder, San Diego Union Tribune

Monetary policy expands the money supply and lowers interest rates to stimulate a recessionary economy, or shrinks the money supply and hikes rates to contract an overheated and inflationary economy. This involves raising and lowering what are called the discount rate and the target federal funds rate.

The *discount rate* is the interest rate that the Fed charges banks when they borrow money from the Fed while the *federal funds rate* is the rate banks charge one another for making loans. Lowering these rates makes it cheaper for banks to borrow money, and when they borrow more money, the money supply expands. In contrast, raising these rates makes it more expensive for banks to borrow from the Fed, which contracts the money supply.

In terms of keeping an eye on monetary policy, what you need to know is that the Federal Open Market Committee (FOMC) meets regularly to discuss its interest rate policy and announce any changes. As with other important aspects of the macroeconomic calendar, you can get plenty of advance notice of when these meetings are simply by regularly looking at the weekly calendar in *Barron's* or *Investor's Business Daily*. But also note that you can go directly to the Federal Reserve's Web site—www.federalreserve.gov—for both its FOMC calendar as well as the notes and transcripts of its meetings.

While I'm not suggesting that you regularly check out the Fed's Web site for FOMC updates, I do highly recommend that you do so at least once. This is because the FOMC meetings are a very crucial part of the macroeconomic calendar that the savvy macrowave investor closely follows. You simply don't want to be caught on the wrong side of a Fed surprise!

Key Point #2: The Fed Moves in Cycles, Not Isolated Steps

> We're looking for a 25 basis point rise by the central bank. We think the Reserve Bank will try and get ahead of the inflation curve. They will only need to tap on the brakes a couple more times. We'll see the peak in the interest rate cycle in the middle of the year.
>
> *Bloomberg News*

As this news clip implies, once the Fed begins to lower or raise interest rates, it usually does so in a clearly defined cycle over a period of many months. These rate changes typically come in very small increments—usually 25, and no more than 50 basis points, which is a quarter to half an interest rate percentage point.

Understanding that these rate changes are part of a cycle rather than isolated events is important because the interest rate cycle, which we will examine in more detail in Chapter 10, has a huge impact on the broader market trend. Put simply, it is very difficult for the market trend to continue moving upward once an increasing interest rate cycle takes hold.

Key Point #3: Monetary Policy Ripples through the Stock Market

> History has taught us that markets tend to rise after rate cuts. However, some sectors respond better and more quickly to interest rate cuts than others. The first sectors to react are generally those with direct exposure to interest rates such as financial firms and banks.
>
> *The Jerusalem Post*

It's not just the broad market trend that is affected by the Fed's interest rate cycle. At the front lines, the first casualties of a Fed rate hike are interest rate–sensitive *sectors* such as autos, banking, brokerage, financial services, home finance, and construction. In contrast, a Fed rate hike will have much less of a negative impact on so-called defensive sectors such as food, tobacco, and drugs.

Accordingly, an awareness of the Federal Reserve's "orchestration" of the interest rate cycle will help you considerably in your task of constantly assessing and reassessing both broad market and individual sector trends.

To see this, let's do a little macro scenario building around an interest rate change by the Federal Reserve. By doing so we can come to better understand how to anticipate, and profit from, the sector movements and broad market movements that are triggered by a change in Fed rates. Suppose, then, that the Fed starts to raise interest rates in reaction to a perceived increase in inflation.

For starters, this can lead to higher mortgage rates, a fall in new home sales and, eventually, a decline in new home construction. Slower new home construction reduces consumer spending on appliances such as washers and dryers, dishwashers, and refrigerators. Carpet manufacturers and other home improvement businesses likewise take big hits.

Similarly, fewer people buy automobiles, as car financing becomes more expensive and job prospects become uncertain. This decreased buying has a ripple effect on sectors that make tires, windshield glass, car stereo systems, and the like. As layoffs begin to mount, other sectors—from gaming, leisure, and retail to various technology subsectors—are affected by the collateral drop in consumer spending.

That's not the end of the story, however. In an international economy, higher interest rates may raise the foreign exchange rate of the dollar (that is, make the dollar more expensive versus other currencies). This rate increase, in turn, depresses exports because they are now more expensive. That's why stocks in export industries such as agriculture, pharmaceuticals, and steel are likely to react more sharply to Fed policy.

Eventually, the total effect of a fall in consumption, investment, and net exports is that the gross domestic product and the rate of inflation both get pushed down, thereby achieving the desired policy goal. Of course, during this time the broad market trend is likely to be decidedly down while some sectors will be falling much faster than others. Got the Big Picture?

Key Point #4: You Can't Push on a String

Interest rates have plummeted. Unemployment has not. Governments wonder why. The answer—which for some reason has eluded them—is that you can't push on a string.

Toronto Star

Prudent monetary policy is not a sufficient condition for a stable, non-inflationary financial climate. Fiscal policy must also play a role.

Fed Chairman Alan Greenspan

When the Federal Reserve raises interest rates, this development will most assuredly contract the economy and fight inflation. But does this policy work in reverse?

In particular, does *lowering* interest rates have an equally successful effect at stimulating the economy out of recession? The perhaps surprising answer is "not always," and the reason is captured by the old adage: "You can pull on a string, but you can't push on a string."

Specifically, in a recession, the Fed may cut interest rates to try to stimulate the economy back to full employment. However, there is no guarantee that either consumers or businesses will respond to the interest rate reductions.

Consumer fears about a deepening recession may motivate a more cautious approach to buying new cars, homes, or consumer durables such as refrigerators or washing machines—even if interest rates drop lower. At the same time, businesses looking at idle production capacity and inventories piling up in their warehouses might not want to increase their investment even if interest rates were falling.

This is a case of being unable to "push on a string." In such circumstances, the government will likely have to turn to expansionary fiscal policy (spending and cutting taxes) to stimulate the economy out of its recessionary funk—a graphic case in point being the massive infusion of government expenditures into the economy in the aftermath of the terrorist attack. The fact that the Fed can't "push on a string" offers us an excellent segue to our next set of key points as we discuss Uncle Sam's other major policy option to fight recession, namely, fiscal policy.

Key Point #5: The Two Problems with Financing Fiscal Policy

We are left with a budget that embraces the tried and failed fiscal policies that led our nation into deficit, debt and economic despair. It is anchored by a tax cut that is irresponsible in its size and unfair in its structure.

Senator Tom Daschle

The key to understanding how fiscal policy affects the stock market lies in understanding the two basic methods used to finance budget deficits. The two main options are selling bonds or printing money. Selling bonds can crowd out private investment while printing money can cause inflation. Both are bearish for the stock market but in subtly different ways.

Let's look at the first option, selling bonds. Here, the U.S. Treasury sells bonds to the private financial markets to finance a deficit. The big danger is that the sale of these government bonds will raise interest rates and thereby crowd out private investment. The result will be a lower level of private investment, and the higher interest rates might reduce consumption.

Note the irony here. The purpose of fiscal policy is to stimulate consumption and investment during a recession, not discourage it. But in a worst-case scenario, crowding out can completely offset the fiscal policy stimulus, leaving us simply with higher interest rates.

Bad as this might sound, the second way the government can finance fiscal policy is absolutely devastating to the stock and bond markets. This is to print money, which happens when the Fed purchases U.S. Treasury bonds *before* they hit the open market.

In this case, the Fed is said to be "accommodating" the government's fiscal policy because it is buying the bonds rather than letting them compete with corporate bonds on the open market. This method of financing the budget deficit is equivalent to "printing money" because the Fed simply pays for the Treasury bonds with a check that increases bank reserves. Banks, in turn, can lend more money out based on these increased reserves so the effect is to increase the money supply.

One short-run benefit of the option of printing money is to *lower* interest rates—the directly opposite result of bond financing. However, over time, the printing of money is highly inflationary and also weakens the currency, eventually driving interest rates up. So you can see why when the Fed starts printing money to finance a budget deficit, investors get very nervous.

Key Point #6: Fiscal Policy's Blunt and Irreversible Tool

> An activist fiscal policy, however well designed, is a blunt instrument that is exceedingly difficult to reverse.
>
> *Henry Kaufman, The Washington Post*

While monetary policy can work relatively quickly and is easily reversible, just the opposite is true of fiscal policy. Here, the sad truth that the stock market has learned time after time is that by the time a fiscal stimulus finally takes hold, it often is no longer needed. Instead, all the fiscal stimulus does is to create very unwanted inflationary pressures down the road.

The classic case in point involves the famous Kennedy tax cut of 1964. This tax cut was passed in honor of the slain president and initially was a success. But as the Vietnam War began to heat up, it became very clear that the economy would soon suffer from a far-too-powerful fiscal stimulus, one that would trigger a virulent inflation in the late 1960s and later, an even more virulent stagflation in the 1970s.

The broader point here is that fiscal policy can be a very dangerous tool to use to "fix" the economy. Still and all, look for fiscal policy fixes when the economy is in a significant recession because of monetary policy's can't-push-on-a-string problem. But look for monetary policy to fix inflation when the economy is at or near full employment.

That said, let's now go one layer deeper and ask the question that arises every time the use of fiscal policy to fight recession is debated: Should the government use a tax cut or increase government spending as the stimulus?

Key Point #7: The Problem(s) with Tax Cuts

> A year ago, even as the recession was starting, the federal government projected surpluses far into the future. Today there are deficits to contend with once again. The administration attributes them to the slump. But neutral calculations by the Congressional Budget Office demonstrate clearly that the lavish Bush tax cut is responsible for most of the disappearance of the surplus.
>
> *The New York Times*

Just as fiscal policy is a blunter tool than monetary policy, a tax cut to stimulate the economy is a much blunter and more uncertain tool than increased govern-

Politics make fiscal policy often counterproductive
f all physical assets or limited at a point in time of at money
56 *Need for increase   Monopoly game*   THE FOUR DYNAMIC FACTORS

ment spending. To understand this key point, let's do some more macro scenario building.

Suppose the economy goes into a significant recession, and monetary policy fails to provide sufficient stimulus for recovery so the government turns to fiscal policy. On the one hand, the president favors a tax cut to stimulate the economy. On the other hand, Congress is pushing for an increase in government spending. So who's right?

To get to the bottom of this, let's examine what turned out to be the unfortunate failure of the Bush tax cut of 2001. The tax cut failed as a stimulus because many recipients failed to actually spend the money. Instead, they simply put their check in the bank or used the money to pay off credit cards.

In this sense, tax cuts suffer from the same kind of can't-push-on-a-string problem as monetary policy. In particular, you can give a person a tax cut but cannot force her or him to spend it.

To end this chapter, I will leave you to ponder Table 6-1, which provides a short summary of the pros and cons of monetary versus fiscal policy. If you understand these pros and cons, you will be able to readily understand how changes in fiscal and monetary policy can move the markets.

Table 6-1   Monetary versus Fiscal Policy

	Monetary policy	Fiscal policy
Most appropriate for:	Fighting inflation or trying to cure a minor recession	When the economy is in a deep recession or depression
Upside	The best "fine-tuning" instrument; works relatively quickly; easily reversible	Provides a very powerful stimulus to a recessionary economy; can choose either tax cuts or spending increases
Downside	"Can't push on a string" so may be ineffective in periods of significant or severe recession; hits some sectors like autos and housing much harder than others; potential negative effects in international currency markets; A much blunter tool	Any stimulus takes much longer to work its way through the economy; much greater danger of "missing the target" and being inflationary; harder to reverse; increased government spending may crowd out private sector investment and harm productivity; tax cuts may be ineffective in times of increased uncertainty

QUESTIONS

1. What is the difference between fiscal and monetary policy when it comes to fighting recession?

2. Why is it important to understand that interest rate changes are part of a cycle by the Federal Reserve rather than isolated events?

3. What are some of the sectors likely to be hurt by a Fed rate hike?

4. How might an interest rate hike by the Federal Reserve affect the housing sector and the various sectors that depend on home construction?

5. Is the Federal Reserve more likely to be successful fighting inflation or recession? Why?

6. What are the two main ways to finance a budget deficit created by expansionary fiscal policy? What are the problems associated with each of the two methods?

7. Is it better for the government to use a tax cut or increased government spending to stimulate a recessionary economy?

EXERCISES

1. Visit the Web site of the Federal Reserve at www.federalreserve.gov. Click on the "Monetary Policy" link and then go to the "Federal Open Market Committee" link. Read more about the structure and function of the FOMC and check the FOMC meetings calendar.

2. At www.federalreserve.gov, go again to the Monetary Policy link and then click on the link for "Open Market Operations." Review the history of the Fed's rate changes, as demonstrated by the changes in the "Intended federal funds rate."

3. Spend some additional time perusing some of the other links at www.federalreserve.gov. Read some of the chairman's speeches, for example, under the "Testimony and Speeches" link in "News and Events."

4. Let's try to see how rate changes by the Federal Reserve can affect the stock market. For illustrative purposes, let's focus on the May 16, 2000 rate hike of 50 basis points. This was the last in a series of six total hikes. It is now generally believed to have been an overreaction by the Fed that helped trigger the bear market of 2000. To see the impact of this rate hike on the markets, let's go to my favorite Internet Web site to draw stock charts, www.bigcharts.com. Enter the symbol "$comp" in the "Enter Symbol or

Keyword" box, where $comp is the symbol for the broad Nasdaq market. Click on the red "Interactive Charting" box. Then, go down to the "Time" box and choose the "Custom" option. In the "Custom Time Frame" boxes put in the dates from "5/4/2000" to "5/30/2000." Click the "Draw Chart" box. Looking at this chart, you can see how the market was trying to rally in the early part of May. However, once the Fed raised rates by 50 basis points, the market went into a tailspin.

5. Left-of-center Democrats and right-of-center Republicans have a very different view of fiscal policy. For example, Democrats generally favor increased government spending to stimulate the economy while Republicans favor tax cuts. For a flavor of this debate and to learn more about fiscal policy, check out the following Web sites: For a left-of-center Democratic perspective, visit the Progressive Policy Institute at www.ppi online.org. Go to the "Economic and Fiscal Policy" link. For the right-of-center perspective, try the Cato Institute at www.cato.org. Go to "Research Areas" and click on "Budget and Taxes." Skim some of the articles to get a flavor of the fiscal policy debate.

Chapter 7

EXOGENOUS SHOCKS AND THE STRATEGY OF THE MACROPLAY

"Exogenous shock," the term that economists use for events from outside the economy but that affect economic activity, has a grim redundancy when applied to the Sept. 11, 2001, attacks on the N.Y. World Trade Center and Pentagon. The term literally means "a blow from outside the system"—like a fuel-laden jetliner crashing into a skyscraper.

Edward Lotterman

We turn in this chapter to "exogenous shocks"—the fourth dynamic factor that moves the stock market. Such shocks run the gamut from oil price spikes, war, terrorism, and natural disasters like earthquakes and drought to more human-made phenomena like accounting scandals and the advent of "disruptive technologies" like the Internet or wireless cell phones.

Key Macrowave Points

1. Exogenous shocks are random and unpredictable but the effects are not. The savvy macrowave investor uses a powerful investment strategy called the "macroplay" to profitably exploit these effects.

2. Oil price spikes are contractionary for the economy and bearish for the stock market but some sectors like oil services and gold may thrive.

3. War has historically been bullish for the stock market in the short run but can be very bearish in the longer term.

4. The terrorist threat is fundamentally restructuring the economy in a way that is creating clear sectoral winners and losers in the stock market.

5. The stock market impacts of events like accounting scandals can spread first from a company to a sector and eventually to the broader market.

6. "Disruptive technologies" ranging from the Internet and DVD recording to cures for cancer and aging are likely to be the single most important sources of large movements in stock prices in the twenty-first century.

Key Point #1: The Art of the Macroplay

The great dampener on American shares has been Enronitis; the fear that profits have been highlighted or losses airbrushed away by creative accounting and that nasty shocks are liable to hit any day. In two weeks' time even the mighty General Electric has promised to issue a more open and much more detailed annual report.

The Times (London)

Exogenous shocks may be quite random and unpredictable; however, the effects on the economy and the stock market are decidedly not. Such shocks can significantly affect companies and sectors and ultimately influence the broader market trend. To understand these effects, you must be a "chess player," looking many moves ahead. Such a Big Picture perspective is, in fact, the essence of a very powerful investing strategy that I often use to analyze the effects of exogenous shocks on the stock market—a strategy I call the "macroplay."

Every macroplay begins with some kind of shock or news event. The macroplay then travels along an often-winding trail of facts and assumptions. Finally, it winds up at its destination—a stock, a group of stocks, or a sector poised for a sharp movement up or down.

Consider, for example, the infamous Enron scandal of some years ago. This was a highly unpredictable event that caught almost everyone by surprise. This scandal involved a highly sophisticated "pump-and-dump" scheme in which company executives used a variety of accounting tricks to inflate profits as a way of artificially boosting the company stock. Enron executives also used highly sophisticated "gaming" techniques to illegally drive up electricity prices and likewise boost profits. With the stock thus "pumped" on two fronts by inflated or illegal profits, executives proceeded to "dump" millions of shares on the market at premium prices to enrich themselves.

At first blush, it appeared that the Enron scandal was about only one company. But using macroplay logic, the savvy macrowave investor quickly came to two very clear conclusions.

First, given the nature of the accounting tricks used by Enron and the scrutiny that was brought to bear on its illegal electricity trading, it was highly likely that other companies in the sector like Dynegy, Reliant, and Mirant may have likewise engaged in similar chicanery. Thus, it was equally likely that the stocks of these companies would also fall precipitously like Enron's stock—making them excellent short-selling opportunities.

Second, given the scope and magnitude of the Enron collapse and the likelihood that other companies in other industries might have practiced similar kinds of dubious accounting, it was only a matter of time before "Enronitis" spread to the broader market—and indeed, it quickly morphed into a broader crisis in corporate confidence that infected the likes of Global Crossing, Tyco, WorldCom, IBM, and even the mighty GE.

From this crisis, the savvy macrowave investor could foresee strong downward pressure that suggested an excellent shorting opportunity on the broader market. In this way, the Enron scandal provided a very rich and textured macroplay in which the most nimble of investors could capitalize on huge movements of 10 and 20 points in some stocks and large percentage moves in the market.

To further hone our macroplay skills and come to better understand the role of exogenous shocks in moving the market, let's look now at how some of the most common shocks typically ripple through, or severely rock, the stock market.

Key Point #2: Contractionary Oil Price Spikes

In the late 1960s, oil prices began to rise faster in response to the U.S. involvement in the Vietnam War. In the 1970s, oil prices shot up as a result of the 1973 Arab oil embargo in retaliation for U.S. aid to Israel. I wonder whether investors today remember how the stock markets reacted to the backdrop of rising oil prices. The Dow peaked at 1,000 in 1968 and investors had to wait until 1982 for the Dow to break above 1,000 and resume an up-trend. This flat period also contained one of the great bear markets of the 20th century.

The Toronto Star

Since the mother of all oil price spikes hit during the 1973–1974 Arab oil embargo, the world economy has periodically experienced sharp runups in the price of a barrel of oil. The very bearish problem with such spikes is that they act as a contractionary "tax" on the economy.

To the extent that consumers wind up paying more for gasoline at the pump, they spend less at the malls and the movie theaters and car dealers. Moreover, unlike an actual *domestic* tax, oil price shock revenues are not recycled by our government for the building of roads or bridges or defense. Instead, these oil revenues simply flee the country and wind up in the pockets of foreigners, making this shock a nasty tax indeed.

But that's not all. As oil prices rise, so, too, does the cost of producing goods and services, particularly for energy-intensive companies, from the airline, rail, and trucking sectors to the companies that make products like aluminum and steel and even plastic bags. This increase in costs also looks like a tax to businesses even as these businesses try to pass these costs on in the form of inflationary higher prices.

For all these reasons, oil price spikes can be highly contractionary and bearish for the broad market trend. That said, it is equally clear that at least a few sectors benefit from the shock. Most obviously, the companies that drill for oil and natural gas as well as the companies that look for the oil or make the drills will get a boost from higher oil prices. More subtly, so, too, will alternative fuel producers that market solar cells for businesses and homes and companies that make fuel cells for use in automobiles.

Key Point #3: War Premiums and Penalties

> The Vietnam War may have important lessons for the generals in the Persian Gulf war, but it also has a valuable lesson for politicians: Refusing to face up to the cost of fighting can cause serious economic trouble for years.
>
> *The Bergen Record*

War has historically been bullish for the stock market in general and defense stocks in particular, at least in the short run. However, a government's shift in budget priorities from "butter" to "guns" can lead to larger budget deficits, higher inflation, higher interest rates, and lower productivity and be decidedly bearish in the longer term. To see this, let's look at the effects of three major wars.

World War II came on the heels of the Great Depression, and it was the single greatest catalyst for economic development in American history. It transformed the United States from a minor player on the world stage with a moderate production base to a global superpower and represents the perfect model of a "good war," both morally and economically. For not only did it defeat a heinous set of enemies, it also was a great boost for the stock market and economy.

But what about Vietnam? Increased defense spending triggered a booming economy and stock market in the 1960s but the stimulus turned out to be too much. We got a very bad case of demand-pull inflation that set the stage for economic collapse in the stagnant years of the 1970s.

As for the Gulf War with Iraq in 1991, it was great for defense stocks like Raytheon and Northrop in the short run. But it, too, came at a very heavy price. The basic problem is that unlike previous wars, the Gulf War was accompanied by oil price shocks that helped push the economy into a recession. Moreover, the war came when the United States was already struggling with huge budget deficits.

The broader point here is that contrary to the conventional wisdom that war is always good for the economy, it can pose very big problems. For starters, wars must be financed by running budget deficits, raising taxes, or shifting expenditures from the "butter" of education, health care, and infrastructure to "guns." All three financing methods are quite bearish.

Budget deficits are inflationary. Raising taxes is contractionary. Most perplexing from a longer-run perspective, productivity is likely to suffer from the shift from butter to guns. This is because increasing productivity relies, to a major extent, on the education, infrastructure, and other public goods that government provides.

Key Point #4: The Terrorism Tax

> We're going to have to spend more for our security: security of airplanes, security of buildings, security of facilities, Internet security, financial security. This "terrorist tax" is going to have a long-term weight on the economy. The market will have to take that into consideration as well.
>
> *Robert Hormats, Goldman Sachs*

The nation's ongoing war on terrorism offers the savvy macrowave investor an absolute macroplay clinic on how an exogenous shock can lead to major structural changes in an economy—and thereby create large classes of winning and losing stocks and sectors.

Just consider what happened in the wake of September 11, 2001—America's second day that will live in infamy. When the stock market reopened on September 17, all three major indices fell by double digits, with a loss in total market capitalization and shareholder wealth of almost $2 trillion.

What was most interesting about these sharp declines, however, is how the different sectors fared. For obvious starters, airline and hotel and gaming stocks all took very heavy hits on expectations of reduced travel demand while insurance stocks fell sharply because of anticipated huge payouts to cover the damages. No macroplay mystery there. On the other side of the ledger, defense stocks all rose on expectations of increased defense expenditures. No mystery there either.

But if we probe deeper into the markets, we see some very interesting additional macroplays, with some stocks rising by 50 percent and 100 percent or more.

For example, one macroplay involves the cluster of firms that operate in the high technology area of security. These include InVision Technologies, which makes three-dimensional baggage scanners; Magal Security Systems, which specializes in airport perimeter defense; and Viisage Technology, which is a leader in face recognition systems. The stocks of all of these companies took off like rocket ships in the weeks following 9/11 and there was plenty of time to make money on the moves. Just look at Figure 7-1, which shows the incredible move of InVision Technologies. It was transformed from a flat-lining "penny stock" trading below five bucks to one that climbed a macroplay mountain all the way up toward $50.

A second cluster involves some firms that provide traditional armed security. These include companies like Armor, Kroll, and Wackenhut. Clearly, in the wake of the terrorist attack, there would be increased demand for the services of these firms, and this was reflected in large price movements in the several-week period following the market's reopening.

Still a third cluster of firms provide a very important airline travel alternative, namely, video and Web conferencing. In the wake of 9/11, both WebEx and Act Teleconferencing returned absolutely monster gains, and this is about as pure a macroplay as you can imagine.

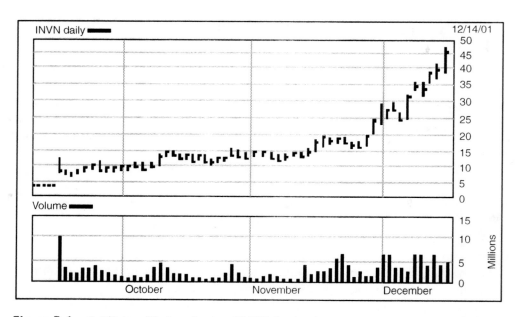

Figure 7-1   InVision Technologies (INVN) climbs a macroplay mountain.

More broadly, these short-run price movements in key sectors have been followed by longer-run movements that confirm an ongoing shift in the fortunes and fate of terrorist-sensitive sectors. Moreover, after a strong rebound from the lows reached in September 2001, the broader stock market fell once again to retest those lows. There were concerns about a variety of macrowaves, ranging from a weak dollar and a profitless recovery to the very much ongoing terrorist threat. At the heart of understanding this threat from an investor's viewpoint is understanding both the sectoral shifts and the negative pressure on the broader market trend that terrorist shocks can have.

Key Point #5: The Market Stain of Scandals

I certainly hope that Martha Stewart is cleared of illegally trading ImClone stock and that the "ridiculousness," as she terms it, does not negatively affect her perfect-homemaking empire. But even if worse comes to worst, . . . I'm sure she'll be able to do as much for Cellblock H of federal prison as she did for the house wares aisle of Kmart.

Martha's fellow prisoners may or may not be interested in Martha's seminar on edible pansies, but they're sure to give her their full attention when she describes for them the proper way to sharpen a knife.

David Grimes, Sarasota Herald-Tribune

In our earlier explanation of the investment strategy of the macroplay, we used the Enron scandal to illustrate how an isolated event can spill over to other companies in a sector and eventually to the broader market trend. There are numerous other such examples of such macroplay ripples and waves.

For example, when the scandal over alleged insider trading hit the biotech firm of ImClone, the scandal spread first to a more traditional drug company, Bristol-Myers Squibb. This is because Bristol-Myers was partnering with ImClone on the development of the drug called Erbitux that failed to pass the required FDA tests. But the scandal soon spilled over into the entire biotech and pharmaceutical sectors.

Perhaps most interestingly from a macroplay perspective, the ImClone affair absolutely torched the stock of Martha Stewart's company, even though the retail consumer products sold by this company were as far removed from the biotech industry as one can get. The reason? As soon as Stewart became linked to the insider trading scandal, the loss in her perceived reputation spilled over to tarnishing her company's "brand name." Such a loss in brand name could only spell trouble for the Stewart line, and Mr. Market quickly figured that out, as Figure 7-2 graphically illustrates. Note, however, that the fall in Stewart's stock didn't

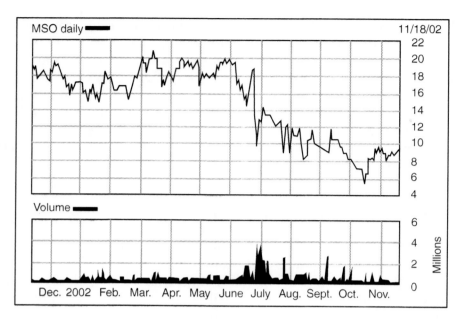

Figure 7-2   Martha Stewart Living (MSO) falls off the edge of scandal.

come overnight but rather over a period of a month or more, which would have left you plenty of time to short-sell the stock.

Key Point #6: The Role of Disruptive Technologies

> Technological innovations like the steam locomotive or the personal computer are yet another category of exogenous shock.
>
> *The Bismarck Tribune*

The auto killed the horse and buggy, the computer killed the typewriter, and digital technologies have killed audiotapes and VCRs. In fact, "disruptive technologies" ranging from the Internet and DVD recording to cures for cancer and aging are likely to be the single most important sources of large movements in stock prices in the twenty-first century. That's why I always recommend to those practitioners of the savvy macrowave investing method to keep abreast of new technological developments.

Consider, for example, what the combination of the Internet, compressed audio file technology like MP-3, and CD-ROM recording devices have done to the music industry. This is an industry in which it is almost impossible now to protect the product from illegal copying and distributing. As a result, the stock prices of many of the top entertainment companies have suffered.

In this regard, the industry reached a quite undesired milestone back in the year 2001 when more blank CDs were sold than music CDs. Not surprisingly, in that same year revenues and profits for the music industry declined significantly. On the other hand, the stock prices of the purveyors of these disruptive technologies—companies like Roxio, Sonic, and Pinnacle Systems, which market the hardware and software to capture music files—all benefited handily from the trend.

As for how to keep abreast of such technological developments, I can recommend at least several sources of information. In the print media, both the magazines *Red Herring* and M.I.T.'s *Technology Review* provide powerful glimpses into the technological future. On the Internet, the paid subscriber site www.red chip.com is an important source of information about the kind of "small capitalization companies" that are on the cutting edge of technological change. And Tobin Smith and his paid subscriber Web site, www.changewave.com, do a good job identifying new companies with disruptive technologies—that Smith calls "ChangeWaves."

We've now completed the first stage of macrowave investing through our analysis of the four dynamic factors—the fuel that moves the markets. Let's turn now to Stage Two where we will learn how a mastery of the business cycle, the stock market cycle, and the interest rate cycle—the three key cycles—will help us better gauge both the broad market and individual sector trends.

QUESTIONS

1. Define, and provide several examples of, exogenous shocks.
2. Why are oil price spikes very bearish for the stock market?
3. Is war bullish or bearish for the stock market?
4. What is the nature of the "terrorist tax"?
5. What is likely to be the single most important source of large movements in stock prices in the twenty-first century?

EXERCISES

1. This exercise will demonstrate how Enron's accounting troubles spread to the stock prices of other companies in its sector—with enough of a lag for you to have taken profitable advantage of on the short-selling side. So go

to www.bigcharts.com. Type in the symbol for Enron in the "Enter Symbol or Keyword" box (at the time of this writing, the symbol was ENRNQ) and click on the "Interactive Charting" box. Go down to "Time Frame," specify "Custom," then type in the dates 6/01/2001 to 1/01/2002. Finally, under the "Compare To" box, put in the symbol DYN for Dynegy—another very major player in the energy sector with a business model very similar to Enron. Hit the "Draw Chart" box. Note how Enron's stock price began to fall after the first of the year in 2001. It took several months, but Dynegy stock price eventually followed suit.

2. Stay at www.bigcharts.com and use the "compare" function to draw charts for WebEx (WEBX) and Act Teleconferencing (ACTT). Use a time interval beginning three months before the September 11 attacks and going right up to present day. Note how the stock prices of both companies soared right after 9/11. Which one now appears to be outperforming the other in the race to replace conventional air travel with cyber alternatives?

3. Visit the New York Mercantile Exchange at www.nymex.com. It is at this exchange where literally billions of dollars worth of futures contracts for oil, precious metals, and other commodities are traded. At the markets link, go to "Energy" and then "Light, Sweet Crude Oil." Click on it and learn a little bit about the world's largest oil futures market. Click on "Historical Data" and use the charting function to look at a graph of the price of oil over the last several months.

4. Visit your local bookstore and peruse a copy of *Red Herring* magazine or M.I.T.'s *Technology Review* for the latest in disruptive technologies. If you are a dyed-in-the-wool Internet surfer, visit alternative sites like www.changewave.com, www.redchip.com, and the cyber edition of *Red Herring* at www.redherring.com.

5. For more information about the macroplay investing strategy, visit my special Internet link at www.peternavarro.com/macroplay and view the free Internet presentation "The Art of the Macroplay."

PART THREE

THE THREE KEY CYCLES

Stage Two: The savvy macrowave investor uses a mastery of the business cycle, the stock market cycle, and the interest rate cycle to determine the broad market trend and individual sector trends.

Chapter 8

TRACKING THE MARKET AND SECTOR TRENDS

The market trend is your friend.

The statement just quoted is one of the oldest clichés in the Wall Street playbook, and the wisdom underlying it never really grows old or wrong. You simply don't want to be caught buying or holding stocks when the market trend is heading down or shorting stocks when the market trend is moving up or turning up. Still and all, this powerful cliché tells only half of the story. For the savvy macrowave investor, the amended cliché should read more like this:

Both the market and sector trends are your very best friends.

In fact, this amended cliché provides the cornerstone of the Three Golden Rules of Macrowave Investing. I'm sure that you recall these rules from Chapter 3. They are as follows:

- Buy strong stocks in strong sectors in an upward-trending market.
- Short weak stocks in weak sectors in a downward-trending market.
- Stay out of the market and in cash when there is no discernible trend.

Now here's the Big Picture point: The key to anticipating changes in both the broad market trend and individual sector trends lies in understanding the intimate relationships between the three key cycles: the business cycle, the stock market cycle, and the interest rate cycle.

In the next several chapters, we will systematically work our way through the three key cycles. More specifically, I will show you how to use an increased awareness of the movements in these cycles to better gauge both the market and sector trends as well as key market turning points.

Before we do that, however, I want to use this chapter to illustrate why it is so very important—and can be so highly profitable—to invest with both the market and sector trends. In this chapter, I also want to arm you with a very powerful, practical, and easy-to-use tool to detect trend changes. This tool is known as the

"3-point-break method," and it should prove very useful to you in timing your investment decisions.

Key Macrowave Points

1. The stock market either trends up, down, or sideways. To invest against the trend is to recklessly gamble. To invest with the trend is to intelligently speculate. Stay in cash when there is no clear trend.

2. Every market sector—from chemicals, paper, and steel to hardware, software, and semiconductors—likewise is trending up, down, or going sideways at any given point in time. Sectors do not move in "lockstep" with the broad market but rather trend according to the broad market's underlying patterns of "sector rotation."

3. Use broad market exchange-traded funds like QQQ for the Nasdaq, DIA for the Dow, and SPY for the S&P 500 to follow the broad market trends. Use sector-specific exchange-traded funds like SMH for semiconductors and BBH for biotechnology to follow the sector trends.

4. It's easy in hindsight to identify market and sector trends. The skill in real time is to better anticipate trends as they unfold. That's where a deeper understanding of the three key cycles—and a mastery of the 3-point-break method—comes into play.

5. Use the 3-point-break method as a very practical tool to identify the market and individual sector trends.

Key Point #1: The Market Trends Up, Down, or Moves Sideways

A market not busy being born is busy dying.

Ron Vara

Over any given time interval, the market trend is either quite busy moving up or equally busy moving down. Moreover, at certain times as the market ponders its direction, it may also "trade 'sideways' in a range."

Figure 8-1 illustrates this point for the Nasdaq market over a one-year period. Specifically, the chart tracks the trend of QQQ, where QQQ is an exchange-traded fund (ETF) based on the Nasdaq 100 Index. (More about ETFs below.)

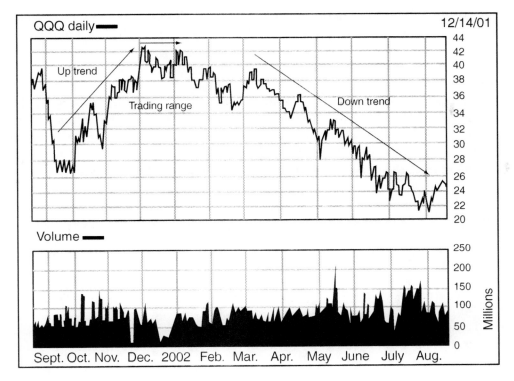

Figure 8-1   Tracking the market trend.

In the figure, we can observe a very interesting "three-act play." For several months, the market is trending up. In Act Two, the market begins to trade "sideways" in a trading range for several more months. Finally, in the third act, we see the market trending down for a number of months.

Now, it should be clear from this figure why the trend is your friend and why you should *never* trade against the trend. Indeed, when the market is in an up trend, you do *not* want to be shorting stocks. During such up trends, 8 out of 10 stocks generally are moving up *with the trend*. That means from a simple statistical probability point of view, you've only got a 20 percent chance of being right about your short position. That's a very bad gamble—*not* an intelligent speculation.

Of course, when the market is in a clear down trend, the same rules and laws of probability apply—but they do so in reverse! In such a down trend, going long is the sucker's gamble while going short is the intelligent speculation.

Finally, note in the figure the interval in which the market is trading in a range. According to the Third Golden Rule of Macrowave Investing, this is a time when it is very dangerous to do anything other than either sit in cash or engage in much shorter-term day trading or "swing trading" (whereby you only hold on to stocks for a few days at most).

In fact, sitting in cash in such conditions is one of the hardest things for the undisciplined investor to do. However, I strongly urge you to cultivate such a discipline. As you can see from the charts—and as I shall illustrate in an example below using the 3-point-break method—once the trend does declare itself, investing *with* the trend comes as close to a license to printing money as you can get.

Key Point #2: Individual Sectors Move Up, Down, or Move Sideways

> If you're really looking to try to outperform the market, investing in even the best stocks in under-performing sectors isn't the way to do it.
>
> *CNBC's Bob Pisani*

Just as the broad market is always trending up, down, or sideways at any point in time, so, too, does every market sector exhibit such movements. This is true for every market sector, from "Old Economy" industries like chemicals, paper, and steel to the "New Economy" sectors of hardware, software, and semiconductors. This point is illustrated in Figure 8-2 for semiconductors using the exchange-traded fund SMH over the same period as we examined QQQ in Figure 8-1.

Now here's an interesting point: Even though we see in Figure 8-2 that the semiconductor sector is going through the same phases that we observed the broad market went through, it does not necessarily follow that every individual sector moves up and down in lockstep with the broad market. Quite the contrary!

As we shall learn in the next chapter, there are very clear patterns of "sector rotation" within the broader stock market cycle that will determine the timing of the movements of any given sector relative to the broad market. The important point to understand for now, however, is that the same rules of probability and intelligent speculating apply when you are investing in a given sector as they do when you are investing in the overall market. *To wit, the odds will always be against you if you insist upon buying stocks in sectors that are trending down or shorting stocks in sectors that are trending up.*

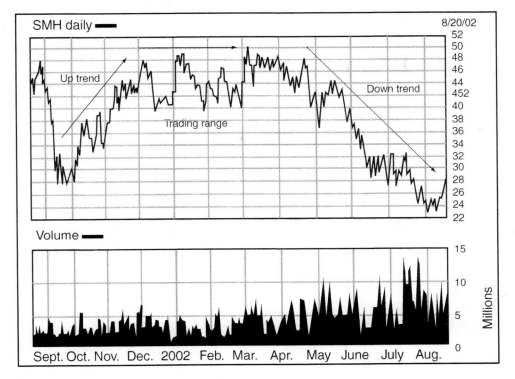

Figure 8-2 Tracking a sector trend.

Key Point #3: Use Exchange-Traded Funds to Track Market and Sector Trends

One of the most heavily traded items on Wall Street, ranking right up there with Cisco and Intel shares, is an obscure instrument nicknamed Cubes. Cubes—shorthand for their trading symbol, QQQ—is an instrument made up of the 100 biggest companies on the Nasdaq Stock Market . . . Cubes merge two of the biggest recent investing trends: aggressive technology speculation and investing in mutual funds that mirror a broad market index.

Washington Post

In Figures 8-1 and 8-2, we charted the movements of the Nasdaq market and the semiconductor sector by charting the price movements of QQQ and SMH. As I indicated earlier, both QQQ and SMH are part of a broader family of exchange-traded funds, or ETFs.

It is certainly worth a short digression now on ETFs because the advent of such investing vehicles back in the 1990s has turned out to be one of the most important innovations in the stock market for several reasons.

For one, ETFs trade exactly like stocks. That means that if you want to hold the broad market or a particular sector, you don't have to do what investors had to do in the old pre-ETF days, that is, put your money in a mutual fund tied to the broad market or a sector. The ETF alternative is a great leap forward because mutual funds typically have much higher fee and expense ratios.

Second, and unlike mutual funds, *you can both buy and short sell ETFs.* Moreover, unlike the stocks for individual companies, the ETFs are not subject to the so-called up-tick rule. This is a big advantage!

In particular, if you are going to engage in short selling, the up-tick rule is very important to understand. It dates back to the days of the Great Depression and the stock market crash of 1929, and it was instituted by the Securities and Exchange Commission to promote stability in the markets. It basically says that *you can't short a stock that is falling in price.* The clear intent of this rule is to prevent short selling from driving a stock into a death spiral.

Note, however, that you can short sell ETFs without worrying about the up-tick rule. Essentially, it allows you to be much more nimble and get your short sale in at better prices.

Table 8-1 provides a list of some of the major ETFs. For tracking the broad market trends, this list includes the aforementioned cubes, or QQQ, for the Nasdaq; "spiders," or SPY, for the Standard & Poor's 500 Index; and the "diamonds," or DIA, for the Dow Jones 30 blue-chip stocks.

The list also includes a small sampling of the many sector-specific ETFs available on the market. These range from our now-familiar SMH for semiconductors and BBH for biotechnology to IAH for Internet Architecture, SWH for software, and so on.

It is in the spirit of this book that I am trying to teach you how to "fish for a lifetime" rather than "give you a fish for the day." Accordingly, I will ask you in the exercises at the end of this chapter to visit several Web sites to investigate further the world of ETFs. I will also ask you to learn about the important difference between two kinds of ETFs: "HOLDRS" and "iShares." (In Table 8-1, SMH, SWH, and TTH are, for example, all HOLDRS but IYR, IYE, and IYD are iShares.)

As a final comment on ETFs, let me note that on my own online Direct Access Investing screen, I always reserve a special box for a select group of ETFs. I watch them daily; frequently review their weekly, monthly, and yearly price charts; and also apply the same kind of technical analysis tools to these ETFs as I do to stocks.

Table 8-1   A Sampling of Market and Sector Exchange-Traded Funds (ETFs)

	Exchange-traded funds (ETFs)
Nasdaq 100 Index	QQQ
S&P 500	SPY
Dow Jones Industrial Average	DIA
Biotech	BBH
Chemicals	IYD
Energy	IYE
Financial	IYF
Health care	IYH
Internet	HHH
Internet architecture	IAH
Internet B2B	BHH
Internet infrastructure	IIH
Pharmaceuticals	PPH
Real estate	IYR
Semiconductors	SMH
Software	SWH
Telecommunications	TTH
Telecom — broadband	BDH
Utilities	UTH

(Technical analysis is a tool that we will discuss in much more detail in Chapter 14.) The short and long of it—pun intended—is that ETFs represent a very valuable tool to track both the market and sector trends and help you adhere to the Three Golden Rules of Macrowave Investing.

Key Point #4: It's Easy in Hindsight to Spot Market and Sector Trends

Studies this year by the European Central Bank and the International Monetary Fund . . . suggest share prices do have a generally good track record as a leading indicator. They also show that the relationship between the Business Cycle and share prices is symbiotrophic: Business Cycles drive share prices and share prices help drive Business Cycles, particularly in the US.

The Weekend Australian

Symbiotrophic? My, those Aussies love to use big words. The previous quotation nonetheless helps make the point that there is a complex interrelationship between the business cycle and the stock market cycle. By better understanding this relationship—explored in detail in the next chapter—you will gain a very powerful strategic edge over other investors. That's because you will be much better able to anticipate both movements and changes in market and sector trends.

The perhaps painfully obvious problem we are trying to solve is to clearly identify market and sector trends *before they happen*. Of course, it is very easy in hindsight to identify these trends. Just look again at the charts in Figures 8-1 and 8-2. The lines are quite easy to draw once you've seen the whole picture.

The fact is, however, that it is much more difficult to track and clearly see these trends in real time—minute by minute, day by day, and week by week—as you are trading or investing. That's because on any given day or in any given week, the market and its sectors do not move in straight lines. Instead, in an up trend, it's more like "two steps forward and one step back," while in a down trend, it's two steps back and one step forward. In such a world of volatile fits and starts, it is particularly easy for the myopic investor to hold on to his or her stocks far too long as the market trends downward.

It is precisely this "trend myopia" that led over half of all individual investors to lose more than half of all their stock market wealth when the market *quite clearly* began trending down from its dizzying peak in March of 2000. In this regard, the 3-point-break method described in the next key point should prove to be a very useful tool for you to spot major trend changes as well as to better cultivate an ongoing "trend awareness."

Key Point #5: Use the 3-Point-Break Method to Spot Changes in Trends

If you were swimming in a river, would you rather swim with the current or against it?

Manila Standard

The 3-point-break method is a very simple but useful shorthand tool to quickly identify trends and trend reversals in real time. By identifying such reversals, this tool can also be very helpful in generating both buy and sell signals for your entry and exit strategies.

Here's the basic idea behind the 3-point-break method: In an up trend, a stock's price forms new highs as it climbs Wall Street's "Wall of Worry." By systematically relating these new highs to the previous highs and closing prices, you can better pinpoint the time when the trend is broken.

The best way to understand how the 3-point-break method works is to simply illustrate it, as I have done for you in Table 8-2. This table uses *weekly* (not daily) closing prices for QQQ over a time period very similar to that for which we charted the various trends for QQQ in Figure 8-1.

Note that in columns 1 and 6, we have the dates of QQQ's closing price, and in columns 2 and 7, the QQQ closing price itself. Columns 3 and 8 chart the progression of the "higher highs" and "lower lows" defined by the 3-point-break while columns 4 and 9 note the relevant 3-point-break comparison of this progression *typically used to identify a break in trend*. Finally, in columns 5 and 10, we note when the various trends are broken.

Follow along now as we work our way through the table. As we do so, let's see how good it is at generating both "buy and sell" and "short and cover" signals.

Table 8-2   The 3-Point-Break Method

1	2	3	4	5	6	7	8	9	10
Date	QQQ price	Three point break	Compare	Trend changes	Date	QQQ price	Three point break	Compare	Trend changes
9/21	$28.19	0			3/8	$38.67	0		Down trend broken
9/28	$28.98	1		Begin up trend	3/15	$37.23	-1		Begin new down trend
10/5	$31.76	2			3/22	$36.68	-2		
10/12	$34.55	3		Confirm up trend	3/29	$36.06	-3		Confirm down trend
10/19	$33.55				4/5	$34.37	-4	-4 to -1	
10/26	$36.01	4	4 to 1		4/12	$33.52	-5	-5 to -2	
11/2	$35.60				4/19	$34.46			
11/9	$37.73	5	5 to 2		4/26	$31.04	-6	-6 to -3	
11/16	$39.37	6	6 to 3		5/3	$29.74	-7	-7 to -4	
11/23	$39.28				5/10	$29.56	-8	-8 to -5	
11/30	$39.65	7	7 to 4		5/17	$32.93			
12/7	$41.73	8	8 to 5		5/24	$31.24			
12/14	$40.11				5/31	$30.04			
12/21	$39.48				6/7	$28.30	-9	-9 to -6	
12/28	$40.33				6/14	$27.62	-10	-10 to -7	
1/4	$41.67				6/21	$25.82	-11	-11 to -8	
1/11	$40.85				6/28	$26.10			
1/18	$38.59				7/5	$26.34			
1/25	$38.83				7/12	$24.80	-12	-12 to -9	
2/1	$38.14				7/19	$23.99	-13	-13 to -10	
2/8	$36.17	0	Three point break	Up trend broken	7/26	$22.67	-14	-14 to -11	
2/15	$35.78	-1		Begin down trend	8/2	$22.25	-15	-15 to 12	
2/22	$33.65	-2			8/9	$23.33			
3/1	$35.74				8/16	$24.70			
					8/23	$25.15		Three point break	Down trend broken

The Up Trend

We begin on September 21 (9/21) with QQQ at a price of $28.19, and we mark 0 in column 3 to set our starting point. At this point, if the price closes lower than $28.19 in the following week, we will have the possible beginning of a down trend. Alternatively, as it actually happens in the table, if the price closes higher than our starting point, we will have the beginning of a possible up trend.

We see, then, that the price does indeed close higher so we put a number 1 in column 3 to denote the first higher high of $28.98. Then, the following week, we reach a second higher high of $31.76 and note this with a number 2 in column 3. Finally, in the third week of October 12 (10/12), we reach a third higher high of $34.55 and are well on the way to a nice up trend. Note that at this point with three higher highs, *the up trend is solidly confirmed*. At this point, according to the 3-point-break method, QQQ would have to close below the starting point of $28.19 *three* higher highs away to break the up trend!

Now please note the next move carefully. When the third higher high is topped on October 26 (10/26) with a fourth higher high, we put in the number 4 in column 4. Here, however, we also note in column 4 that we will be comparing the fourth higher high not to our starting point of $28.19 but to our first higher high of $28.98. On the basis of this comparison, QQQ would have to close only below $28.98 to indicate the break in the up trend instead of our starting point of $28.19. *Because we continually advance the threshold for breaking the trend so that it always remains three higher highs away, we call this the 3-point-break method.*

For example, when on November 9 (11/9) we reach a fifth higher high of $37.73, we will compare that to the second higher high of $31.76, and that becomes the new benchmark for any break in the trend. And so it goes.

You can see from the table that we continue in a nice upward trend and finally reach our eighth and final higher high of $41.73 on December 7 (12/7). You can also see that we *never again* reach that high in the table. In fact, we see that the up trend established by that eighth higher high is finally broken on the week of February 8 (2/8) when QQQ closes below $37.73. Put another way, for a full *two months*, the market has traded sideways in a trading range, unable to further advance the upward trend.

The Trading Range Morphs into a Down Trend

What is really interesting next in Table 8-2 is how, beginning on February 8 (2/8) when the up trend is broken, the trend begins to oscillate for a number of weeks. On February 15 (2/15), it starts to move down with a price of $35.78 but by March 8 (3/8), the short downward trend is broken with a price of $38.67.

You can see from the table, however, that this is but a very temporary reprieve. The very next week of March 15 (3/15), the market begins a very strong downward trend that will move forcefully over the next five months, reaching a full *15* lower lows.

Note in the table that this down trend is confirmed with a third lower low of $36.06 on March 29 (3/29). Note also that by the tenth lower low of $27.62, *QQQ falls below our original starting point of 9/21*! And not until August 23 (8/23) is the down trend finally broken, when the closing price of $25.15 is higher than the twelfth lower low—our 3-point-break threshold.

Buy and Hold versus Investing with the Trend

It should be clear from Table 8-2 how valuable this 3-point-break method can be in generating profitable buy and short signals. If, as a position trader, you had bought 1000 shares of QQQ on September 21 (9/21) at $28.19 and sold those shares at $36.17 once the up trend was broken, *you would have realized a $7980 profit.*

Likewise, suppose you were conservative and had shorted 1000 shares of QQQ on March 29 (3/29), after the confirmation of the down trend at a price of $36.06. That point was after the down trend had reached at least its third lower low. If you then sold those shares, or "covered your short," on August 23 (8/23) at a price of $25.15, you would have realized another $10,910 profit. Your total profit would have been $18,890!

In contrast, as a buy-and-hold investor, if you had bought QQQ on September 21 (9/21) for $28.19, as of August 23 (8/23) of the following year, you would be showing a *loss* of $3040.

The broader point is this: Invest with the trend and profit, and use the 3-point-break method as a simple tool to guide you.

QUESTIONS

1. What are the Three Golden Rules of Macrowave Investing?

2. At any one time, the stock market trend will be in one of three possible states. What are they?

3. Why is trading against the trend a bad gamble rather than an intelligent speculation?

4. What is the hardest thing for the undisciplined investor to do when there is no clear trend?

5. Does a market or a sector trend move in a straight line?

6. Name two advantages of exchange-traded funds over mutual funds.

7. Name the exchange-traded funds for the Nasdaq market, the Standard & Poor's 500 Index, and the Dow Jones Industrial Average.

8. Name the exchange-traded funds for the semiconductor and biotechnology sectors.

9. The 3-point-break method is a very useful shorthand tool to identify what? How can this knowledge help you in your trading and investing strategies?

EXERCISES

1. Go to www.bigcharts.com, enter "QQQ" in the "Enter Symbol or Keyword" box, and click on the "Interactive Charting" link. Check that the time frame is for "1 year" with a frequency of a "Daily" chart. Click on "Draw Chart." Study the resultant chart carefully. See if you can spot any trends over the period. Look for both up and down trends as well as any trading ranges.

2. Go through the same exercise for SPY and DIA as in Exercise 1 at www.bigcharts.com. Explore different time periods to study the various trends.

3. Go to www.ishares.com and spend some time learning more about just what an iShare is. Find the list of all of the different kinds of iShares that are offered on the market—for example, IYH for health care and IYE for energy. Note that besides sector iShares, there are others like "International."

4. Find the iShare for one of your favorite industry sectors at www.ishares.com and then go back to www.bigcharts.com and appraise the trends for its one-year chart.

5. Go to www.holdrs.com and read up on this particular kind of ETF. As you read about HOLDRS, try and figure out the key difference between a HOLDR and an iShare. You will see that one reflects a very broad index while the other is based on a smaller number of companies. Which one is which? Think about which one would be a little less risky.

6. At www.holdrs.com, find the list of all the HOLDRS. For a specific HOLDR such as RTH or SWH, look at all of the individual companies that make up the HOLDR.

7. Go to www.wallstreetcity.com and enter the symbol of your favorite stock in the "Enter Symbol or Name" box. Click on the "Historical Quotes"

link. At this link, change the "Type" of data you want from "Daily" to "Weekly." Then choose a start date and an end date that reflects the last six months of trading in this stock. Click on the "Get Quotes" box. Print out the page and then use the 3-point-break method to analyze the various trends and buy, short, and sell signals over the period. Note that the use of weekly data is more useful for "position traders," who hold stocks for weeks and months, than for "swing traders," who hold positions for just a few days or weeks. Assess whether the 3-point-break method that uses weekly data may be helpful to you if you are a position trader.

8. At www.wallstreetcity.com, repeat the above exercise but change the type of data back to "Daily." Also, look at the data over only a two-month period rather than a six-month period. Examine the trends and any buy, sell, and short signals that may be generated. Do so for a number of stocks. Assess whether this method may be helpful if you are a swing trader.

Chapter 9

THE BUSINESS CYCLE AND THE STOCK MARKET CYCLE

Ride the Stock Market Cycle—or be run over.

Ron Vara

Stocks are considered a barometer on the health of the economy, not to mention a leading indicator of the business cycle, rising and falling in advance of economic activity.

Bloomberg News

Movements in stock prices and the broader stock market cycle reflect nothing more than changing shareholders' expectations about the future stream of corporate earnings. Movements in the business cycle, in turn, are critical in shaping these corporate earnings expectations for a very simple reason: Corporations just make a heck of a lot more profit when the economy is strongly expanding than they do when the economy is in recession.

For example, if stock market investors expect a strong economy, they will bid up stock prices on the expectation of improved earnings, and we will have an upward-trending bull market. On the other hand, once investors begin to see even the glimpse of a recession on the horizon, no more than a nanosecond will go by before stock prices begin to bearishly suffer on the expectation of lowered earnings. For these reasons, the stock market cycle is viewed as a "leading indicator" of the business cycle—a powerful crystal ball that predicts future economic conditions.

In this chapter, we are going to look much more closely at the relationship between the business cycle and the related stock market cycle. Understanding these twin cycles is at the core of better anticipating movements in stock market trends—a critical task of the savvy macrowave investor. Equally important, we will also examine the patterns of sector rotation within the stock market cycle, because understanding these sector rotations is a key to identifying both strong and weak sectors over time.

Key Macrowave Points

1. The business cycle moves from peak to trough to peak, from expansion to recession to expansion. It varies in both amplitude and duration, with expansions generally longer than contractions.

2. The stock market cycle moves from bottom to top, from early, middle, and late bull phases to early, middle, and late bear phases. The stock market cycle moves in tandem with the business cycle but always ahead of it and therefore is a valuable leading indicator of future economic conditions.

3. The stock market cycle's ability to predict movements in the business cycle is the result of a complex adjustment process involving the four dynamic factors. Understanding these movements and this adjustment process are critical tasks of the savvy macrowave investor and essential to tracking the broad market trend. Remember, we never want to invest against the trend.

4. Different sectors of the stock market outperform other sectors at different intervals of the stock market cycle, meaning that prices rise faster in some sectors than in others. By using these patterns of sector rotation to choose your stocks and sectors, your portfolio will outperform both buy-and-hold investors and "market timers."

Key Point #1: The Business Cycle's Ups and Downs

The standard, postwar business cycle begins with an expansion, when demand picks up after the previous recession. Before long, this modest growth evolves into an outright boom, in which the economy begins expanding faster than its long-term growth rate and very near its overall capacity to produce goods and services. Next is what economists refer to as the "crunch" period, during which time the onset of inflation—as consumers demand more goods and services than can be produced—provokes the Fed to raise interest rates. These higher interest rates cause consumers to scale back big-ticket purchases and, usually not long after, businesses cut back production to compensate. This stamps out inflation, but triggers a recession, as layoffs and bankruptcies ensue. The final phase, "reliquefication," describes the financial restructuring that occurs when businesses and consumers pay off the debts they accumulated during the boom period, and businesses liquidate the inventories that had piled up along the way. Some time after that happens, the assumption goes, consumers (and then businesses) start spending, and the cycle begins all over again.

New Republic

My kind thanks here to the *New Republic* for doing some very heavy lifting with this quotation. I use this quote, long though it may be, because it perfectly captures all of the important elements of the business cycle.

Figure 9-1 illustrates a typical business cycle as it moves from peak to trough to peak, from expansion to recession to expansion. Note the very sharp peak that we sometimes get with a boom. This kind of overexpansion is sure to provoke the Federal Reserve to sharply—and very bearishly—raise interest rates to contract and cool down the overheating economy.

As for both the duration and amplitude of the business cycle, this can vary significantly. An expansion can last as little as six months or as long as five years or more. In general, however, we can say that expansions are generally longer and more gradual than contractions.

Now note in the figure also how the economy grows over time along a "growth trend" line, despite the cyclical volatility. This growth trend is crucial because it

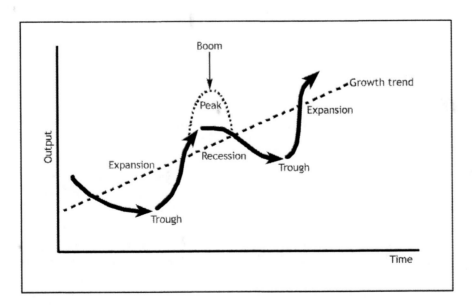

Figure 9-1   The business cycle.

tells us how fast our economy will grow over the longer term. Will it be a mere 2 percent as it was in the stagnant 1970s or a robust 4 to 5 percent a year like it was in the roaring 1990s? This is a crucial question because *the difference between these two scenarios can spell the difference between a prolonged secular bear market in which stock prices stagnate and a sustained bull market in which the market trends ever higher.*

Given the overriding importance of the business cycle in driving stock prices and the broader market trend, the obvious question for the savvy macrowave investor must be this: How can one predict movements of the business cycle and therefore better forecast the market trend? The answer lies in cultivating a much more sophisticated understanding of the related stock market cycle and its underlying patterns of "sector rotation."

Key Point #2: The Stock Market's Crystal Ball

> The chances of a double-dip recession in the United States are now "compelling," given signs of deflation and the recasting of US GDP figures to show the economy spent longer in recession than earlier believed . . . the forces that have held up the US economy thus far—homebuilding and consumer spending—could weaken, because they are accompanied by a high buildup of debt, mounting layoffs and an intensifying negative wealth effect in the wake of stock market declines.
>
> *The Business Times, Singapore*

The stock market cycle and its relationship to the business cycle are illustrated in Figure 9-2. Note first how the stock market cycle moves through six clear stages.

In the early bull, middle bull, and late bull stages, both the market trend and the prices of most stocks are moving upward. Then, when we get to the early bear, middle bear, and late bear phases, the market trend is clearly down, along with the prices of most stocks.

Now look very carefully again at the figure to understand one of the most important relationships in stock market investing. Specifically, compare the "top" of the stock market cycle to the "peak" of the business cycle. Do you see clearly that the stock market cycle reaches its top *before* the business cycle reaches its peak? Do you also see that the stock market cycle reaches a corresponding bottom *before* the business cycle reaches its trough? What this means is that *the stock market is an excellent predictor, or "leading indicator," of movements in the business cycle.*

This is a very powerful insight for investors because it means that the stock market trend can begin to fall before a recession hits and it can begin to rise in anticipation of an economic recovery. Unfortunately, far too many investors don't

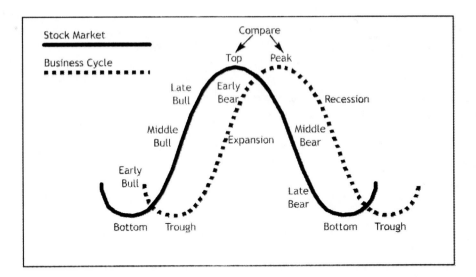

Figure 9-2 The stock market cycle leading the business cycle.

understand this simple relationship. The practical result is that they hold on to their stocks too long in a declining market and are not nimble enough to enter the stock market as it begins turning back upward. The reason is that they focus too narrowly on the business cycle and do not understand how that cycle lags stock prices.

Key Point #3: The Stock Market and Four Dynamic Factors

The overall wealth effect is currently undoubtedly negative, even though the severe losses sustained on the equity market over the past two years have been balanced in part by rising housing prices. At the end of June, private households' net worth was $1.4 trillion lower than a year earlier. This negative wealth effect is likely to dampen households' propensity to consume for the foreseeable future.

Quest Economics Database

There is nothing really mysterious about the ability of the stock market to predict movements in the business cycle. Yet the stock market cycle's movements do reflect a rather complex adjustment process, one driven by the four dynamic factors that we have discussed in previous chapters. In fact, this ongoing adjustment process always begins with fresh news from one of the four dynamic factors.

In a typical instance, the latest report on the Consumer Price Index might reveal an unexpected increase in the core rate of inflation. Investors will react to this inflationary news by raising their expectations that the Federal Reserve will increase interest rates to contract the economy and dampen the inflationary pressures. These recessionary fears, in turn, will lower expectations about the future stream of earnings for corporations. And quite soon the stock market will make a downward and bearish move in anticipation of a possible downturn in the business cycle.

Alternatively, the economy may experience an exogenous shock like an oil price spike. This fourth dynamic factor triggers recessionary fears because of its contractionary effects—and the stock market swoons.

Understanding how the stock market cycle moves in response to the four dynamic factors is a critical task of the savvy macrowave investor. This task is at the very heart of tracking the broad market trend. Remember, we *never* want to invest against the trend.

That said, the even greater power of using the stock market as a crystal ball lies not just in its ability to forecast recessions and recovery but rather in the market's underlying patterns of "sector rotation." These patterns of sector rotation represent the keys to the Macrowave Kingdom, precisely because they allow you to better discern *sector* trends—an essential element of the Three Golden Rules of Macrowave Investing.

Key Point #4: The Profitable Patterns of Sector Rotation

> If you are in the right sector at the right time, you can make a lot of money very fast.
>
> *Peter Lynch*

Figure 9-3 illustrates the typical patterns of sector rotation over the course of the stock market cycle and business cycle. Put simply, at different points of the twin cycles, the stock prices of the companies in some sectors will rise faster than the stock prices of companies in other sectors. As a result, these sectors *outperform* both the general market and other sectors during their own period in the sector rotation sun.

For example, in the figure, you can see that the transportation and technology sectors typically shine in the stock market's early bull phase. In contrast, health care and consumer staples like food and drugs are classic "defensive" sectors and

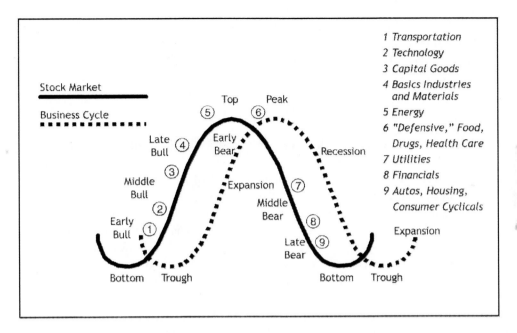

Figure 9-3   The stock market's powerful patterns of sector rotation.

have their day in the late bear sun. Note also how the energy sector peaks in the late bull phase of the stock market while autos and housing lead the recovery.

But here's an important cautionary note: Like fingerprints, no two business cycles are alike, and the stock market *does not always follow these typical patterns* of sector rotation. For example, in the 2001–2003 recession, the housing sector remained remarkably strong over a much greater time interval than was typical. The reasons were many and varied but boiled down to historically high liquidity and low interest rates and a strong move into housing from the stock market's battered investors.

The broader point is this: Don't simply memorize these patterns and expect to grow rich in their predictability. Instead, *seek to understand the underlying logic of these patterns* and why sectors move the way they do. By so doing, you will be able to apply such macrowave logic to future and ever-changing conditions. To help you hone this skill, let's take a macrowave logic walk through the patterns of sector rotation in Figure 9-3.

Let's start at the top of the stock market cycle with the transition from the late bull to the early bear. At this point, the business cycle is in a late expansionary stage and suffering increasing inflationary pressures. The Federal Reserve has likely raised interest rates several times to dampen these pressures.

Despite these rate hikes, unemployment remains low while retail sales and consumer confidence remain high even as consumer credit becomes perilously overextended. Fueling inflationary pressures, however, both factory production and capacity utilization rates are banging up against inflationary constraints and energy prices are spiking.

In this early bear phase, Wall Street's "smart money" starts to defensively rotate funds into the health care sector and consumer staples or "noncyclical" sectors like cosmetics and food and pharmaceuticals. They know from bitter experience that the Federal Reserve will likely raise interest rates one too many times and thereby push the economy off the recessionary cliff.

The hard landing does, indeed, begin to happen as the economy soon crests and begins its recessionary slide. Falling production, sinking consumer confidence, a rising unemployment rate, a shrinking workweek, and increasingly idle factory capacity are just some of the recessionary signs that show up in the second dynamic factor: the macroeconomic reports.

Eventually, the Fed will realize what the Wall Street pros had already figured out. The Fed raised interest rates too high and too fast and killed the economy. At this point, the Fed will reverse course and begin to lower interest rates.

But these rate cuts won't work very quickly because, as we noted in Chapter 6, you can't "push on a string." Indeed, with excess inventories and sales slowing, most business executives will not partake yet of the Fed's new "easy money" and purchase the capital investment that would otherwise stimulate the economy. Nor are wary consumers—now fearful of winding up on the unemployment line—likely to go on any new spending spree for big-ticket items like autos and housing, even if interest rates are falling.

So the recessionary spiral continues downward to find some inevitable, and one hopes not too deep, bottom. During this time, the stock market moves toward its middle and late bear phases as the smart money begins to rotate first into utilities and then into both consumer cyclicals like autos and housing and financial stocks.

Utilities become attractive because they are very capital intensive, and therefore their earnings improve with lower interest rates. In this late bear phase, energy costs are also declining sharply because of weak worldwide demand, and this factor helps the bottom line as well.

Meanwhile, autos and housing have typically reached the bottom of their valuations under ever-weakening demand. But as interest rates head toward a bottom, both of these sectors perk up as consumers rush in with pent-up demand. This helps key financial sectors like banking and home finance just as ever-lower interest rates are helping other sectors like brokerage and financial services. With autos, housing, and financials leading the way, the broader economy soon begins to move back up.

The next expansionary shoe to drop will be a surge in surface transportation sectors like the railroads and trucking in the Old Economy and semiconductors in the New Economy. Still, there will be no need as yet for businesses to invest in new plant and equipment. Indeed, it won't be until the middle bull phase that spending on capital goods will increase. At this point in the business cycle's expansion, equipment will begin to wear out even as increased demand speaks to the need for expanding capacity. In response, the Wall Street pros begin to rotate first into all those sectors that will benefit from the boom in capital goods, from agricultural equipment and industrial machinery to machine tools and basic electronics.

Now, the economy is again hitting on all cylinders, and the smart money rotates into the basic industry and materials categories. For it is in the middle and late expansionary phases of the business cycle that the demand for commodities like aluminum, chemicals, paper, and steel reaches a zenith.

Of course, at this point, inflationary pressures have already begun to percolate again. And, once again, investors begin to expect the Federal Reserve to start raising interest rates, even as energy prices rocket toward a peak. Under the pressures of rising interest rates and energy prices, the business cycle once again reaches its inevitable peak.

Of course, by this time, the smart money has once again recognized this early bear phase and begun to move back into the defensive sectors of food, drugs, and health care stocks. And the twin cycles repeat!

So what's the broader point of this rather extended example? By understanding the underlying macrowave logic behind these patterns of sector rotation, the savvy macrowave investor can better anticipate movements and changes in both the broad market trend and individual sector trends. The end result will be that the savvy macrowave investor will outperform the typical buy-and-hold investor. The latter investor often winds up back where he or she started in the market over the course of a stock market cycle with *no* profits and perhaps *large* losses. The end result will also be that the savvy macrowave investor will also outperform the pure market timers who make money on the market trends but who miss out on the very lucrative progression of the sectors.

QUESTIONS

1. Stock prices and the broader stock market cycle reflect nothing more than what?

2. Take out a pencil and pad of paper and draw the business cycle. Do the same for the stock market cycle and show the relationship between the two. Compare your drawings to the figures in the book.

3. Which peaks first, the business cycle or the stock market cycle? Which one of the cycles is a leading indicator of the other?

4. What can we say about the duration and amplitude of the business cycle, and what might this mean for your investing and trading strategies?

5. What does the term "sector rotation" refer to?

6. Which sectors do the best in the early bull phase of the stock market cycle?

7. What are some of the so-called defensive sectors that do well in the late bear phase of the stock market cycle?

8. In what phase of the stock market cycle does the energy sector typically peak?

9. Which two sectors generally lead the recovery?

10. At which phase of the stock market cycle is the Federal Reserve likely to begin *raising* interest rates and at which phase is the Fed likely to begin *lowering* interest rates?

EXERCISES

1. Visit www.nber.org. This is the Web site for the National Bureau of Economic Research. Find the appropriate link for reviewing the history of the American Business Cycle. Compare the smallest number of months from the trough of the cycle to the peak with the largest number of months. This will give you an idea of the wide range of the *durations* of economic expansions.

2. Repeat the exercise in question number 1 for the duration of the *contractions*, as measured from the trough from the previous peak. This will give you an idea of how long or short recessions can be. Note that during the Great Depression, the downturn lasted an excruciatingly long 43 months. You should also see that contractions typically are shorter than expansions, which is why bull markets are generally longer than bear markets.

3. At www.nber.org, read about the status of the current business cycle.

4. Go to www.google.com and type in the key words *sector rotation*. Spend some time perusing some of the numerous links. Be careful, however. You will be drawn into a number of paid subscription sites. *I do not recommend any such sites*; some are downright wrong or fraudulent. Always remember, it's "buyer beware" on the Web—particularly for stock market advice. Also note that a number of the "sector timer" Web services still rely on mutual fund sector funds. This is just plain silly in the new age of more flexible and cheaper ETFs like iShares and HOLDRS.

Chapter 10

AS THE INTEREST RATE CYCLE TURNS. . .

As the global economic cycle turns, so the Interest Rate Cycle turns with it. On Tuesday the Fed signaled that its extraordinarily aggressive and successful campaign of interest rate cuts last year may soon be giving way to rate rises to restrain demand.

Financial Times

The typical interest rate cycle begins with a series of rate cuts by the Federal Reserve to fight recession. It progresses to a period in which interest rates hold relatively steady as the economy once again begins to expand. The interest rate cycle then moves to a series of rate hikes by the Federal Reserve to fight the inflationary pressures caused by overexpansion, and then once again experiences a period of relatively steady rates as the economy either downshifts into a nice "soft landing" or falls hard into recession. Over the course of this interest rate cycle, a related "yield curve" describes the relationship between short- and long-term interest rates.

Together, the interest rate cycle and yield curve represent two of the most powerful tools the savvy macrowave investor can use to spot critical changes in market and sector trends. The yield curve tool is especially useful in anticipating a new bear market that might be triggered by the onset of recessionary fears.

In the next two chapters, I will show you how to use the interest rate cycle and the yield curve to your investing advantage. We will also learn about the term structure of interest rates as we master some bond market basics. The overriding point to always keep in mind is that it is very difficult for the stock market to continue an upward bullish trend once the Fed starts a series of interest rate hikes. And it is only a matter of time before the bear retreats once the Fed starts lowering rates. So stay in tune with the interest rate cycle!

Key Macrowave Points

1. The interest rate cycle travels through four clear stages: rate hikes, steady rates, rate reductions, and steady rates.

2. The stock market doesn't like rising interest rates because they choke off growth and earnings. Once the Federal Reserve begins to raise rates, it is only a matter of time before the broad market turns down. Interest rate–sensitive sectors like banking, brokerage, and finance will be particularly hard hit.

3. As interest rates rise, bond prices fall. As rates fall, bond prices rise. This relationship is the most important principle of the bond market.

4. The "term structure of interest rates" describes the relationship between bonds of different risk levels and maturities. Riskier bonds *always* have higher interest rates. Longer-term bonds *typically* have higher interest rates but sometimes the relationship between short- and long-term bonds can reverse, leading to an "inverted" yield curve.

Key Point #1: The Four Stages of the Interest Rate Cycle

The Federal Reserve is preparing for the tightening phase of the interest rate cycle. It is expected that any tightening will initially be modest in order to safeguard the recovery.

UK Newsquest

A typical interest rate cycle goes through four clear stages: (1) a series of rate hikes, (2) steady higher rates, (3) a series of interest rate cuts, and (4) once again steady but lower rates.

The first stage of the interest rate cycle typically occurs in the late expansionary phase of the business cycle. This is when the economy is hitting on all cylinders, unemployment is low, and demand-pull inflationary pressures are building. As key indicators such as the Consumer Price Index, which measures retail price inflation, and the Producer Price Index, which measures wholesale price inflation, begin to reveal inflationary pressures, the Federal Reserve starts to raise interest rates to slow the economy down and fight the inflation. The Fed typically does so in small increments of 25 to 50 basis points over many months, where an increase in interest rates from, say, 7.00 percent to 7.25 percent represents a 25-basis-point move.

In the second stage, the Fed holds interest rates steady as its tight-money "medicine" does indeed slow the economy down and eventually wring inflationary pressures out of the economy. Ideally, the economy won't slow down too much but instead come in for a nice "soft landing." In reality, however, the Fed almost always overdoes it as its rate hikes trigger a hard recession.

At, or sometimes after, such a recession point, the interest rate cycle enters its third stage as the Fed begins lowering interest rates to resuscitate the economic patient it has just killed or wounded. Note, however, that once the Fed begins reducing rates, it does not follow that the economy—or stock market—will immediately recover. This is because it can take a long time—sometimes a *very* long time—for an easy-money policy to revive the economy.

Of course, at some point, the economy *does* begin to recover so that in the fourth stage of the interest rate cycle, the Fed once again "stands pat," that is, it holds interest rates level. Again, however, it will only be a matter of time before the Fed will change rates—either raising them to fight inflation again in an overheated economy or perhaps lowering them to cure the contractionary blues if the economy slips back into a "double-dip" recession.

Key Point #2: Higher Interest Rates Negatively Affect the Market and Sector Trends

> Rising interest rates, brought on by the Federal Reserve . . . have triggered many of this century's bear markets. They make bonds more competitive with stocks for investors' money and they slow economic and profit growth.
>
> *USA Today*

The stock market doesn't like rising interest rates because they choke off growth and earnings. Once the Federal Reserve begins to raise interest rates, it is only a matter of time (although, as we shall soon see, that time period can be many months) before the bulls give way to bears and the broad market trend turns down.

At the same time, Fed rate hikes will hurt some sectors more than others. Key interest rate–sensitive sectors include banking, brokerage, and finance as well as autos and housing. All of these sectors will sell less of their products when interest rates rise because higher interest rates make their products more expensive. This reduction in expected earnings is soon reflected in falling stock prices.

Figure 10-1 graphically illustrates how monetary policy can turn the stock market trend quite literally upside down. It charts the movement of the target "Fed

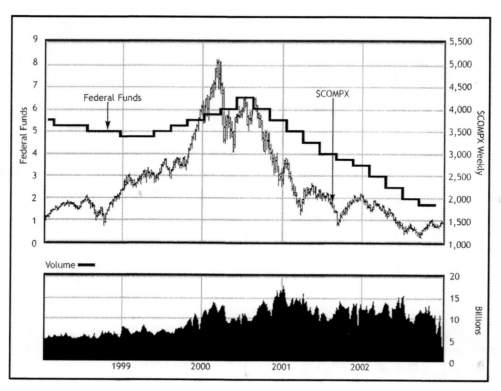

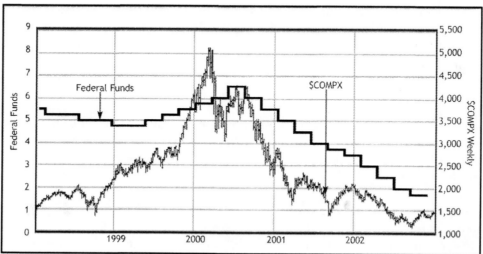

Figure 10-1 The interest rate cycle and stock market trend.

funds rate" against the weekly Nasdaq market index ($COMPX on the right vertical axis) through the interest rate cycle between the period November 1998 and November 2002. Along with the "discount rate," this Fed funds rate is a key interest rate target set by the Federal Open Market Committee (as we discussed in Chapter 6).

In the figure, we see that after a period of stable low interest rates, the Fed started the upward portion of the interest rate cycle with a 25-basis-point hike on June 30, 1999. The stock market's shattered interest rate peace came during the late stages of one of the longest economic expansions in U.S. history, when inflationary pressures had finally begun to brew. At this point, the Nasdaq market had cleared the 2500 mark and would still have a long way to go before reaching its peak of over 5000 in March 2000.

However, from Figure 10-1, we also see that the Fed proceeded to raise rates six times over an 11-month period. Moreover, the last hike in May 2000 was a full 50 basis points. Many economists believe that this last rate hike was overdone and ultimately brought both the stock market and the economy crashing down.

In this regard, you can see quite clearly in Figure 10-1 how the Nasdaq market reached its 5000+ peak coincident with the Fed's fifth rate hike—and thereafter unceremoniously plunged. Moreover, the Fed's hoped-for soft landing never materialized. By March 2001, the economy would officially be in what would become a very prolonged recession.

Another very interesting point about Figure 10-1 is this: Once the Fed started lowering rates in January 2001 to fight the sluggish economy, it would do so a full 11 times in 12 months. However, despite this beneficial policy medicine, the economy would fail to recover strongly. Because of this failure, the stock market would continue its downward trend for many more months—and the Fed would eventually be forced to lower rates again by a full 50 basis points.

As to why Fed policy was not more effective, the likely culprit was the "can't-push-on-a-string" problem that we discussed in Chapter 6. Specifically, the Fed can lower interest rates but it can't force either worried consumers or risk-averse business executives to borrow money.

Having mastered the elements of the interest rate cycle, let's now go over some bond market basics and learn about the all-important term structure of interest rates. This knowledge will position us well for our next chapter, where we will learn about the yield curve as well as how to use the Fed funds futures rate to predict changes in Federal Reserve interest rate policy.

Key Point #3: Some Bond Market Basics

> **Author's Note:** *Please jump to the next chapter if you already understand terms like "par," "discount," "premium," and "current yield" and are familiar with how the bond market works.*

At the mention of the word 'bond,' some peoples' eyes tend to start rolling over.

The Gleaner

To understand how bond prices and bond yields are determined in the market, let's first suppose that you are an investor who wants to purchase a brand new $10,000 10-year Treasury bond at the government's next monthly auction. This auction represents a "primary market," where such new bond issues are sold.

Second, suppose that economic conditions and the level of interest rates are such that this new $10,000 bond will sell at its "par," or face value, of $10,000 with a "coupon rate" of 8 percent. Here, the coupon rate means you will receive $800 per year in interest payments from your bond, which is 8 percent of the $10,000 price. Note also that if you hold on to this bond until it matures, you will receive your full $10,000 back with no capital gain or loss.

Third, suppose that after you buy this new bond, the economy begins to expand at a much faster pace, inflationary pressures start to build, the Federal Reserve begins a new cycle of interest rate hikes, and inflationary expectations rise. The net result is to drive interest rates up *along with coupon rates on new 10-year bonds*— with the new coupon rate assumed to be 10 percent in this example.

Fourth, suppose you need some money and want to sell your old bond rather than hold it to maturity. You can certainly do this in the "secondary market," where previously issued bonds are bought and sold. Your problem, however, is that you will *not* be able to sell your bond for its $10,000 par value. Instead, you will have to lower your purchase price of $10,000 to something below that and sell the bond at a "discount." Why is this so?

As I noted previously, new 10-year Treasury bonds are coming into the market offering coupon rates of 10 percent. Therefore, your old bond is relatively unattractive at its par value because it offers a lower coupon rate for the same par-priced bond. In order for your old bond to compete, its price in the secondary market must *fall*. Specifically, the old bond price must fall by enough to raise its current yield up high enough to equal the 10 percent offered by the new bonds.

Note that I have just mentioned a very important term: the *current yield*. This can be calculated for any bond simply by *dividing the bond's dollar coupon interest paid by its current price*. Using this formula in our example, we can see that the price of your old bond must fall to $8000 in order for the current yield on your old bond to equal the coupon rate of 10 percent on the new bond. To see this, simply divide the new price ($8000) by the old coupon ($800). *It is only at this lower price that an investor will be willing to buy your old bond with an 8 percent coupon rate instead of the more attractively priced new bond with a coupon rate of 10 percent.* And note that if you do decide to sell your old bond at this discounted price, you will incur a capital loss of $2000.

From this example, you can see that *bond prices are inversely related to interest rates.* This is the most important principle of the bond market. *As interest rates rise, bond prices fall.*

Note, too, that this inverse relationship works in reverse: *As interest rates fall, bond prices rise.* For example, suppose that after you had bought your bond in the example above, the economy had fallen into recession instead of robustly expanded. In response, the Federal Reserve would have lowered interest rates, and inflationary expectations would have fallen.

In this deflationary case, the coupon rate on new 10-year bonds may have fallen to as low as 4 percent. So what would that old bond of yours with an 8 percent coupon rate be worth now?

With the coupon rate on new Treasury issues at 4 percent, the price of your old $10,000 bond would have risen to $20,000! This is because the coupon of $800 for your old bond divided by $20,000 provides a current yield equal to the market rate of 4 percent. In such a scenario, you could have sold your bond at a "premium" and realized a capital gain of fully $10,000!

Key Point #4: The Term Structure of Interest Rates

> As yields in the marketplace change, the only variable that can change to compensate an investor for the new required yield in the market is the price of the bond.
>
> *The Gleaner*

The "term structure of interest rates" refers to the relationship between bonds of literally different terms of sale with respect to two key dimensions: *risk* and *time.* To understand this relationship, take a look at Table 10-1. It provides a set of illustrative interest rates or yields for bonds of different risk levels for different lengths of time.

Note that *across the rows*, bonds range from "no risk" to "high risk," where risk is measured by the propensity of the bond issuer to default on paying the interest or principal on these bonds. Such "credit risk" is determined by ratings agencies

Table 10-1   The Term Structure of Interest Rates

	No Risk	Low Risk	Medium Risk	High Risk
Term	Treasury Securities	Aaa to Aa	A to Baa	Ba to C
Short (*1-year or less*)	1.75%	3.43%	3.99%	5.21%
Medium (*1 to 10 years*)	4.36%	4.66%	5.75%	8.19%
Long (*10 to 30 years*)	5.75%	6.36%	6.99%	10.07%

like Moody's and Standard & Poor's that publish "grades" for different bonds. Moody's for example, uses a scale that ranges from Aaa, for high-quality, low-risk bonds, to Ca and C, for very high-risk "junk bonds." From the table, you can see that interest rates clearly rise with credit risk as you move from no-risk Treasury securities to higher-risk corporate and other bonds.

Note that *down the columns*, bonds range from short term to long term and that interest rates clearly rise with time. The higher interest rates bond buyers demand for longer-term bonds may be traced to a number of different kinds of risks. These range from the "event" risk of extreme events like war and terrorism to "inflation" risk—the corrosive effects of rising inflation on a bond's price that we documented in the example in our last key point.

This last observation about inflation risk provides an excellent segue to our introduction of the yield curve in the next chapter. This is because while we can see in Table 10-1 that interest rates typically increase with time, *they do not always do so*! Indeed, there will be times when longer-term bonds have yields that fall *below* shorter-term bonds—thereby "inverting" the so-called yield curve. So, please turn to the next chapter of this stock market thriller and find out why.

QUESTIONS

1. A typical interest rate cycle goes through four clear stages. What are they?

2. When does the first stage of the interest rate cycle typically occur?

3. Why does the Federal Reserve hold interest rates steady in the second stage of the interest rate cycle?

4. Once the Federal Reserve begins to lower interest rates in the third stage of the interest rate cycle, do the stock market and economy immediately recover?

5. Why does the stock market not like rising interest rates?

6. Do Fed rate hikes hurt some sectors more than others? If so, which sectors are hurt most?

7. The Federal Reserve started the upward portion of the interest rate cycle with a 25-basis-point hike on June 30, 1999. How long did it take before the stock market crashed, and how long did it take before the economy went into a recession?

8. What is the par value of a bond? What is the coupon rate?

9. Suppose you buy a bond and then interest rates rise. Suppose further that you want to sell your bond after this increase in interest rates. Will you be able to sell your bond at par, at a premium, or at a discount? Why?

10. How do you calculate the current yield of a bond?

11. The "risk and term structure of interest rates" refers to what relationship?

12. In general, what can we say about the relationship between the credit risk of corporate bonds and their yields?

EXERCISES

1. Visit www.federalreserve.gov. On the "Monetary Policy" link, under "Policymaking," click on the "Federal Open Market Committee" link. Next, click on the "Open Market Operations" link. At this link, you can read about what "open market operations are." More importantly, you can peruse the table called "Intended Federal Funds Rate." This table tracks the changes that the Fed has made in interest rates over time. Specifically, the Fed sets a "target rate" for the Fed funds rate and then uses open-market operations to ensure that the actual rate stays near the target. After you study the table, print it out for use in the next exercise.

2. Go to www.bigcharts.com. Enter the symbol SPX for the S&P 500 Index and specify an interval of three or four years; then click on the "Quick Chart" feature. Compare this chart to the interest rate hikes and cuts that you found in your printed copy of the "Intended Federal Funds Rate" table from exercise 1. Note how the Index reacts to the interest rate changes but

does so with time lags. How long is it before the Index begins to fall after the Fed starts raising interest rates? Does the Index rebound immediately once the Fed starts lowering rates?

3. Use your newly acquired knowledge of "bond market basics" to peruse www.bondsonline.com. Pull up some quotes for different kinds of bonds. Put your knowledge to work of terms like *par* and *discount premium*.

4. Visit www.standardandpoors.com. Peruse the "Ratings" section of the site. Check up on how this leading credit agency rates bonds and what the newly released ratings and listing are. Check out www.moodys.com in a similar fashion.

5. Surf the Web site www.publicdebt.treas.gov to find out a lot more about how the government sells Treasury securities. See what the latest auction results are and compare the short-term rates with the current Fed funds target. If you want to know what a lot of money looks like, click on the link that will tell you what the total public debt outstanding is.

Chapter 11

UNLOCKING THE MYSTERIES OF THE YIELD CURVE

The shape of the yield curve is undoubtedly one of the best predictors of economic growth.

Australian Financial Review

The ever-changing shape of the "yield curve" describes the highly dynamic relationship over time between short-, medium-, and long-term interest rates. The savvy macrowave investor carefully follows the yield curve because it is one of the most important leading indicators of both bearish recessions and bullish expansions. As such, the yield curve is incredibly useful in anticipating changes in two key components of the Three Golden Rules of Macrowave Investing, namely, the broad market and individual sector trends.

Key Macrowave Points

1. The yield curve is determined by the relationship between short- and long-term interest rates. The short end of the curve is determined by the *discretionary* decisions of the Federal Reserve. The long end typically is determined by *inflationary expectations* of investors.

2. The yield curve comes in four key shapes: normal, steep, inverted, and flat. Normal signals a healthy, ongoing, noninflationary expansion. Steep can signal an impending new economic expansion and bull market. A flat curve *can* signal recession, and an inverted curve almost always *does*.

3. Historically, the savvy macrowave investor has used the yield curve to anticipate crucial changes in both the stock and bond market trends and thereby capitalize on many profitable investment opportunities.

Key Point #1: Constructing the Yield Curve

Table 11-1 shows a typical matrix of Treasury securities. Note that the "short end" of the curve begins with 3- and 6-month Treasury bills, moves to 2- and 5-year Treasury notes, and ends at the "long end" of the curve with 10-year notes and 30-year bonds.

Now recall our discussion of bond market basics in the last chapter as you compare columns 2 and 4 in the table. Note how the current yields of the Treasury notes and bonds in column 4 are *lower*, in this example, than the coupon rates in column 2. This implies that interest rates have *fallen* since the time of the securities' issue. Accordingly, bond prices have *risen* in column 3 relative to their par or face value of 100, and the bonds are trading at a premium. This illustrates the inverse relationship between interest rates and bond prices—just as we discussed in the last chapter.

Now, if we "connect the dots" in Table 11-1 between these short-, medium-, and long-term securities, we come up with an associated "yield curve" in Figure 11-1.

The following is a very important point upon which the entire argument for the yield curve as a reliable leading indicator is based: The short end of the yield curve is determined by the *discretionary* decisions of the Federal Reserve with regard to changes in short-run interest rates. That is, when the Fed changes two key short-term interest rates—the Fed funds rate and the discount rate—this has a direct impact on the short end of the curve.

Note, however, that the Fed typically does *not* directly set the long end of the curve.[1] Rather, this long end is determined by *inflationary expectations* in the bond

Table 11-1   A Typical Matrix of Treasury Securities

T-Bills		Current Price	Current Yield
3-Month	—	1.62	1.65
6-Month	—	1.62	1.66
Notes/Bonds	**Coupon Rate**		
2-Year	2.125	100-04+	2.05
5-Year	3.250	100-29+	3.05
10-Year	4.375	102-31+	4.01
30-Year	5.375	108-11+	4.83

[1]Toward the end of the prolonged bear market of 2000–2003, the Fed took the unusual step of buying long-term bonds in the market to lower the long end of the curve. This was both unusual and extreme.

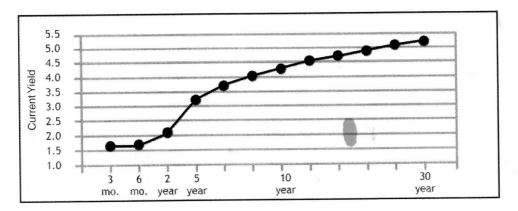

Figure 11-1   Treasury securities and the yield curve.

market. As inflationary expectations rise, so, too, will current yields on the long end of the curve, even as bond prices fall. They do so because inflation erodes the value of existing bonds so that bond prices must fall to reflect this inflation risk. This observation leads us to our discussion of the four key shapes of the yield curve.

Key Point #2: Shapes of the Yield Curve

When the curve flattens, or becomes inverted—with shorter maturities yielding more than long-term ones—the economy contracts. Why? Because banks make money borrowing from depositors at low, short-term rates, and lending it out at higher, long-term rates. "When that spread is wide, they make automatic profits just from doing transactions. When it narrows, banks have to be very careful to whom they make loans. It always narrows at the end of an expansion," UCLA Professor Edward Leamer says.

Last fall, the yield curve became inverted. And sure enough, banks are getting tougher on borrowers.

San Francisco Chronicle

It is in the ever-changing shape of the yield curve that the savvy macrowave investor finds clues of a possible change in market and sector trends and thereby profitable investment opportunities. The four key shapes of the yield curve are *normal, steep, flat,* and *inverted.* These are illustrated in Figure 11-2 for four different periods in our economic history.

The Normal Yield Curve

The normal yield curve defines the halcyon time in the interest rate cycle when bond investors expect the economy to continue to expand at a healthy rate *without* fear of inflation. Such a normal yield curve is typically observed during the middle expansionary period of the business cycle and the early to middle bull phase of the stock market cycle. This is the time when the Fed is holding interest rates steady and there is little or no fear of inflation. It is in such times that the market trend is typically up and specific interest rate–sensitive sectors are performing well.

Just such a time is depicted in the November 1985 normal curve in Figure 11-2—the glorious middle of the Reagan boom. You can see that this normal yield curve slopes nicely upward and is defined by an interest rate spread between the long and short ends of the curve of several hundred basis points.

The Steep Yield Curve

In contrast, we often observe a steep yield curve *at the start of an economic expansion—* just after a recession ends. Such a steep yield curve often augurs a major change in the market trend and the onset of a new bull market. The macrowave logic behind this observation is as simple as it is compelling, and it is all about timing.

At the start of an economic expansion, we will have reached a low point in the interest rate cycle, as the Fed has completed its monetary stimulus. At such a

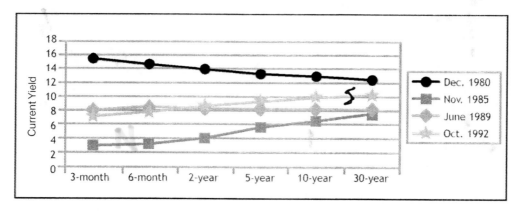

Figure 11-2   Key shapes of the yield curve.

point, with interest rates low and recovery on the horizon, businesses will begin to engage in new capital investment. This increased "capital demand" will be financed largely by corporations taking on more long-term debt. Accordingly, pressure starts to build on the *long end* of the yield curve. This signals the rekindling of healthy capital investment, which will soon be propelling the economy.

At the same time, once long-term bond buyers detect a nascent recovery, they will begin to demand higher interest rates. Bond buyers clearly understand that with any new economic expansion will eventually come the risk of inflation. This is because in an expansion, as unemployment falls and "bottlenecks" begin to emerge in the supply chains of companies, both price and wage inflation pressures will, at some point, begin to build.

These two factors—increased capital demand and the first stirrings of inflationary expectations after a recession—drive the long end of the yield curve up in anticipation of expansion. This happens even as the Federal Reserve is holding the short end steady. The result is a steep yield curve such as is depicted in Figure 11-2 for October 1992. (You may find it interesting that the Fed lowered interest rates in September of 1992 for the last time in that interest rate cycle.)

The Inverted Yield Curve

The inverted yield curve comes about from two interrelated bearish forces. At the short end, the Federal Reserve has begun to raise interest rates to fight inflation. This alone can drive the short end of the curve higher than the long end and invert the curve—even if the long end stays the same.

However, it may also be true that the long end of the curve will start to fall as well—further inverting the curve. Why might this happen? Put another way, why would anyone ever want to buy long-term bonds at a yield lower than short-term bonds?

The answer is simply this: *If* bondholders believe that the Fed's contractionary medicine will trigger a recession, such a recession could be *deflationary*. Bondholders might therefore be willing to *lock in yields that are lower than the current short-term rates*. You can see from this observation why the financial markets interpret the dreaded and infamous inverted yield curve as a strong signal of recession—illustrated in Figure 11-2 for December 1980.

The Flat Yield Curve

A flat yield curve results when the yields are roughly the same for both short- and longer-term securities. This can happen for the same reasons that the yield curve inverts. Either the Fed may be raising short-run interest rates to contract the economy and fight inflation or the long end of the curve may start to fall in anticipation of a recession and possible deflation—or both.

In any case, a flattening of the curve signals slowing economic growth and a possible recession. And of course, every inverted curve must go through a flattening stage on its way to inversion.

Note, however, that *not every flat curve leads to an inversion*. Nor is a flattening curve as reliable a predictor of recession and a new bear market as an inverted curve. Still, once the curve starts to flatten, there is a good chance that it will become inverted, and both the economy and stock market will tank. And that's certainly what happened after the June 1989 flat curve, which is also depicted in Figure 11-2.

Key Point #3: Some Historic Evidence of the Yield Curve's Predictive Powers

> The US economy is heading for recession. Economists might not be telling you this, but the markets are . . . . Yields on 10-year Treasury bonds have fallen 0.6 percentage points below the yield on three-month Treasury bills. Such inversions of the yield curve have been excellent predictors of recession in the past. . . [T]he yield curve flattened or inverted before all of the last seven recessions.
>
> *Investor's Chronicle*

Historically, the savvy macrowave investor has used the yield curve to anticipate crucial changes in both the stock and bond market trends and thereby capitalize on many profitable investment opportunities. Let's examine some of these opportunities by delving a bit deeper into the history behind the key yield curve shapes presented in Figure 11-2. And let's begin by investigating how an inverted yield curve accurately predicted both the stock market collapse of 2000 and the ensuing 2001 recession.

The Stock Market Collapse of 2000 and 2001 Recession

Take a look at Figure 11-3. It documents the changing shape of the yield curve from when the Federal Reserve first began raising interest rates in June 1999 at the late stage of the economic expansion to the inversion of the yield curve in March 2000 and eventual recession of 2001.

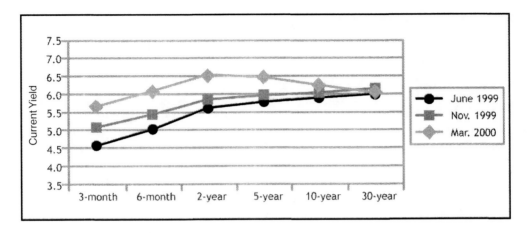

Figure 11-3   An inverted curve signaling a stock market bust.

In the figure, first note the fairly normal shape of the June 1999 curve and the roughly 150-basis-point spread between the short and long ends of the curve. This is the calm before the Fed storm.

Next, observe how by November 1999, as the Federal Reserve continues to raise interest rates to fight growing inflationary pressures, the curve is flattening—with the spread falling to 100 basis points. This is a strong early signal of a possible recession and bear market ahead.

Now take a look at the March 2000 "humpbacked" version of the dreaded inverted yield curve. By now, the spread between the short and long ends has shrunk to less than 50 basis points while the *curve clearly inverts between the 2-year and 30-year range.*

This yield curve inversion is interesting for at least two reasons: *It marks the absolute height of the Nasdaq boom*—and the ensuing bearish crash that will go on for several years. And of course *within exactly a year of this yield curve inversion, the economy would officially be in recession*, just as the inversion forecast.

The broader lesson, of course, is that savvy macrowave investors who observed the March 2000 inversion would have surely cashed out their long positions—and may well have gone short. *Such a strategy would have conservatively prevented huge losses and, in the case of going short, it would have generated huge profits.*

The 1990s Stock Market Boom

Our final example of the predictive powers of the yield curve is offered by Figure 11-4. It illustrates how a steep yield curve in 1992 presaged one of the longest economic expansions in U.S. history—as well as one of the most robust bull markets ever recorded.

Note first the fairly flat yield curve of June 1989 and the virtually nonexistent spread between the short and long ends of the curve. This flat yield curve presaged what eventually would be dubbed the "Bush recession" in caustic "honor" of then-president George Bush.

This Bush recession did indeed officially begin in July of the following year. In the figure, we can see that by that recessionary time, the July 1990 yield curve was already fighting its way back to a reasonably normal shape—with the spread between short- and long-run rates approaching 100 basis points.

With the October 1992 steep yield curve the story gets really interesting. Here, we can see that the spread between the short and long ends of the curve had climbed to over 450 basis points. Clearly, the bond market was anticipating a very strong recovery from the Bush recession—*if* inflationary pressures could be contained.

The August 1995 normal curve provides a good signal that inflationary pressures would indeed be contained. This was in no large part due to a major shift in fiscal policy.

Shortly after taking office in 1993, the newly inaugurated president would raise taxes and cut the growth in federal spending. This would significantly trim the

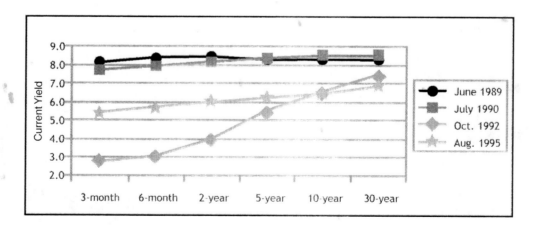

Figure 11-4   A steep yield curve predicting an economic boom and bull market.

budget deficit over the next five years and eventually lead to a surplus. The result was an unprecedented stock market boom. The savvy macrowave investor who correctly read the steep yield curve's bullish signal would have gotten in literally at the bonanza beginning.

QUESTIONS

1. The yield curve is determined by the relationship between what?

2. Why does the savvy macrowave investor carefully follow the yield curve?

3. What is the short end of the yield curve determined by, and what is the long end determined by?

4. What are the four key shapes of the yield curve?

5. In what stage of the business cycle and stock market cycle are we likely to observe a normal yield curve?

6. When do we typically observe a steep yield curve? What is the macrowave logic behind this observance?

7. What are the two major factors that work to steepen the yield curve?

8. With an inverted yield curve, short-run interest rates are higher than long-run rates. What two forces cause the yield curve to invert?

9. In almost all cases, the inverted yield curve signals what?

10. The stock market reached a peak in March 2000. Within a year, the economy was in recession. How could the yield curve have helped you as an investor profit from the market crash?

11. In 1992, the yield curve steepened significantly. What did this presage?

EXERCISES

1. Go to www.google.com and type in *yield curve* in the search window. Check out some of the links. See if you can find some historical examples of how the yield curve accurately predicted a recession or expansion.

2. Visit www.bloomberg.com and see if you can find a picture of the current yield curve as well as a chart of current yields on Treasury securities. (Hint: Try the "Markets" link.) Peruse the site for other information about key interest rates. As an alternative source of current bond information, try www.bondsonline.com.

3. Visit www.stockcharts.com. See if you can find a link for the "Dynamic Yield Curve." It should provide you with an animated "movie" of how the yield curve has changed over time relative to the S&P 500 Index. Alternatively, you can try the "Economy and Bonds" link at www.smart money.com for a picture of the "Living Yield Curve."

PART FOUR

PICKING STRONG AND WEAK STOCKS AND SECTORS

Stage Three: The savvy macrowave investor uses both fundamental analysis and technical analysis to select strong stocks in strong sectors to buy and weak stocks in weak sectors to short.

Chapter 12

IT'S FINGER-LICKIN', STOCK-PICKIN' GOOD

Cheap stocks are cheap for a reason.

William O'Neil

There are a myriad of methods to find potential stock picks. These range from activities like combing magazines and the Internet for hot new ideas to the more systematic application of rules like the proverbial "buy low, sell high" and the more counterintuitive "buy high, sell higher."

This chapter takes a brief tour of some of your very many stock-picking options. In doing so, it sets the stage for the next two chapters that will illustrate how to use both fundamental and technical analysis to perform your "stock screens."

In reviewing these various stock-picking methods, please remember that they represent but a very small sample of search techniques—and I strongly encourage you to find your own ways to uncover diamonds in Wall Street's rough. Please also remember that the initial stock pick—whatever method you use—must be put through both a fundamental and technical screen, as we shall demonstrate in Chapters 13 and 14.

Key Macrowave Points

1. "Buy low, sell high" looks for underpriced bargains. It works well in a trading range market but underperforms in upward-trending markets and can be a recipe for disaster in a downward-trending market.

2. "Buy high, sell higher" looks for stocks that have built a strong base and are about to burst through their "pivot points" to new highs. It works great in an upward-trending market but is very dangerous in bear markets and trading range markets.

3. The "high-volume movers" approach looks for stocks that are moving sharply upward and "breaking out" on above-average

volume—or moving sharply downward and "breaking down." It's usually best to wait for some kind of pullback to enter such stocks rather than plunging right in, provided the stock passes the other savvy macrowave investor tests.

4. Playing the "ratings game" means looking for stocks to buy or short that have been upgraded or downgraded by some major agency. This approach is only as good as the rater. Most of the Wall Street rating agencies are typically behind a stock's curve. Some analysts are downright corrupt.

5. The "buy what you know" approach tries to use one's real-world experience, observing the hottest consumer and social trends to identify what will become the next hot stocks.

6. Comb cutting-edge publications like *Technology Review* for emerging trends and hot new companies. Read investment magazines like *Kiplingers*, *Money*, *Smart Money*, or *Worth*.

7. Run away from "hot stock tips!" Their origins can often be either illegal insider-trading information or scurrilous misdirection by "pump-and-dump" artists.

Key Point #1: Buy Low on the Dips, Sell High on the Peaks

With a new generation of gunslingers driving stock prices higher and higher, how can we find low-priced bargains? By bottom fishing, of course. It's the art of buying low and selling high, and a great way to get rich.

Bart A. DiLiddo

If you liked Cisco at 50 bucks a share, you'll love it at 25.

The Stockbroker as Idiot

As this second quote implies, it was precisely this kind of "buy on the dips" thinking that caused a lot of people to lose money in the last bear market. They bought stocks like Cisco, Lucent, and Oracle on what they thought were "dips" and the damn things just kept heading for the cellar.

This approach is the world of the bargain hunter and so-called cigar butt investors: Find something that looks cheap, load up on it, and sell it dear.

It's easy enough to find such "bargains." Every day in *Investor's Business Daily*, you can find a list of stocks hitting new 52-week lows. Or you can use the stock-screening "engines" at Web sites like www.moneycentral.com and www.wallstreet city.com to find stocks hitting new lows or falling down to their "support" levels.

On the surface, the "buy low, sell high" approach seemingly flies in the face of the First Golden Rule of Macrowave Investing: Buy strong stocks. Still, it is not entirely inconsistent with the rule either. In some cases, strong stocks that operate in weak sectors that get caught in a market downdraft can find their way to an ugly bottom which they will, in fact, bounce smartly up from once the market recovers and the sector finds its day in the sector rotation sun. The following, then, are some basic rules regarding the application of this stock-picking method.

First, the strategy can be a moneymaker if the stock market is in a so-called trading range. As we discussed in Chapter 8, a trading range market, stocks themselves as well as the broad market indices, tend to move up and down within a clearly identifiable range. During such a time, the "buy on the dip, sell on the peak" investor can often eke out a nice little profit exploiting cyclical movements within this range.

Second, however, in a downward-trending market, this approach is a recipe for hara-kiri, at least of your investing capital. It's the "if you liked Cisco at 50 bucks, then you'll love it at 25" problem, where you keep buying on what looks like a dip and the worthless dog just keeps falling.

Third, and most subtly, the buy low, sell high approach can work well in an upward-trending market, if you can find legitimately good stocks to buy low. One problem with this strategy is that if you find a cheap stock in a market moving up, there is probably a good reason why it's cheap, namely, because it is a genuine, bona fide dog that will never again see its day.

Note this most important point of all: Even if you find a cheap stock to buy, you may well wind up selling it at what you think is a "peak" far too soon. Indeed, in an upward-trending market, selling a stock quickly can cause you to miss the real meat of a profit move. That's when a stock breaks through its existing resistance levels, trends upward with the broad market trend, and finds a new peak. In this scenario, the buy low, sell high investor winds up violating one of the most important principles of macrowave investing, which is to let your profits run. That's why the buy low, sell high approach usually underperforms when the market is moving smartly upward.

Key Point #2: Buy High, Sell Higher

Many investors have passed up great stocks because they had reached new price highs. Yet, that's when many of the best stocks begin their major climbs, not when they've bottomed out. That's why buying bargain-priced stocks is often a frustrating experience.

Investor's Business Daily

"Buy high, sell higher" is the investing philosophy made famous by *Investor's Business Daily* founder William O'Neil. Unfortunately, many investors find the idea very counterintuitive. I say "unfortunately" because the buy high, sell higher approach can be a very effective stock-picking strategy, *if* you do so in an upward-trending market.

The basic buy high, sell higher idea is to look for stocks that have set up a solid base of support and are approaching some kind of a high. Then, when such a stock moves above its "pivot point," it's time to buy.

The pivot point is the price where a rising stock faces the final layer of "overhead resistance." Once it passes this point, there's much less of a chance it will succumb to downside selling action and therefore becomes free to break out and hit new highs.

On the surface, the buy high, sell higher method seems very consistent with at least the first part of the First Golden Rule of Macrowave Investing: Buy strong stocks. After all, a stock approaching a new high would certainly seem to be exhibiting strength. Nonetheless, with this approach, it is crucial to remember the last part of the First Golden Rule of Macrowave Investing, namely: *Buy only when the market is trending up.*

In fact, *Investor's Business Daily's* buy high, sell higher approach performs very well in an upward-trending market. In an upward trend, a stock that rises above its pivot point and triggers a buy signal will very often take off on a very nice run.

In contrast, you can get pretty roughed up if you try buying high and selling higher when the market is trading in a tight range. Moreover, you are apt to get absolutely slaughtered if you try this approach in a downward-trending market.

The problem in both cases is the dreaded "failed breakout." As I have said, in an upward-trending market, when a stock clears its pivot point, it has a very good chance of making its own bull run up the charts. However, in a trading range or downward trending market, it is very common for a stock to peek up above its pivot point, levitate for a bit in heavy volume, and then promptly crash a day, a few days, or a week later.

Getting caught in one of these failed breakouts can be very expensive because a stock that falls decisively below its pivot point can often trigger a very violent reaction down. Think of Mr. Market as making a collective judgment along the lines of: "Hey, this one looked like it was going to take off. Oops. Probably not. Let's bail." And as lots of investors run for the exit, the result is a rather bloody "buy high and get the heck out with a small loss" failed breakout.

Key Point #3: High Volume Movers

Sometimes . . . trading volume spikes upward and the price moves higher for no apparent reason. Very often it ultimately turns out that the reason was major purchases of the stock by large institutions, hedge funds, mutual funds or private investors. The stealthy entry of strong players into a stock with enough buying power to boost volume by more than 200% and buoy the price is bullish for current investors.

CNBC

The "high-volume movers" approach looks for stocks to buy that are moving sharply upward and breaking out on above-average volume. It also identifies stocks to short that are moving sharply downward and breaking down on equally high volume. Such movers are featured daily on the *Investor's Business Daily* Web site at www.investors.com. Table 12-1 illustrates a typical *Investor's Business Daily* table.

Table 12-1   The High-Volume Mover Screen

IBDs "Where The Big Money's Flowing Now" These stocks are experiencing unusually high volume.					
Stock symbol	Price (20 min. delay)	Price change	Volume (1000s)	Volume % change	SmartSelect® ratings
Up					
ANT	24.16	+1.16	450	+483	Get ratings
TEVA	78.03	+0.60	1,575	+284	Get ratings
TSCO	39.74	+1.75	279	+228	Get ratings
APPB	24.78	+0.99	609	+184	Get ratings
PIXR	52.82	+1.79	497	+164	Get ratings
WON	36.95	+0.65	641	+162	Get ratings
IRGI	19.99	+0.50	134	+157	Get ratings
Down					
THC	24.21	-4.54	42,260	+2,138	Get ratings
OVER	22.93	-4.60	7,222	+964	Get ratings
LANC	38.95	-6.50	691	+748	Get ratings
SABB	24.35	-2.48	246	+651	Get ratings
AGN	52.80	-1.65	3,326	+647	Get ratings
CYH	22.85	-0.65	941	+512	Get ratings
ABS	21.39	-0.92	4,739	+441	Get ratings

This is a great approach to first put stocks on your radar screen. In fact, I, myself, look at this *Investor's Business Daily* feature daily and put every single stock on it first through a quick technical screen and, if it passes muster, then through an equally quick fundamental screen. (These screens are explained in the next two chapters.)

Be careful, however. Even if a stock passes savvy macrowave muster, *it's often prudent to wait for a pullback of the stock price before buying.* Too often, investors will jump feet first in one of these high-volume movers and get left holding the bag a day or two later as "momentum traders" take some profits and the stock falls back.

Key Point #4: The Ratings Game

> We upgraded our rating to **Outperform** from Neutral after the company reported stronger-than-forecast sales and operating income results across its operating segments. We also raised our target price to 47 from 45.
>
> *R.W. Baird on Parker Hannifin*

The "ratings game" looks for stocks to buy that have been upgraded or stocks to short that have been downgraded. The ratings may be supplied by any one of a number of stock analysts toiling for Wall Street investment banks, Internet Web sites, or financial brokerage firms.

Now here's the big caution: *The ratings game is only as good as the rater.* As a practical matter, the vast majority of the Wall Street rating agencies suffer from either a terminal case of hindsight or outright corruption, or both.

Typically, Wall Street's so-called experts only downgrade a stock months after it should have been downgraded, and they are often equally slow on the upgrade draw. Consider the likes of Jack Grubman at Salomon Smith Barney. He was paid $20 million a year to tout stocks like WorldCom and, allegedly because of obvious conflicts of interest, he refused to downgrade the stock until it had lost 90 percent of its value. Or consider Henry Blodget, of Merrill Lynch. He's the guy the New York Attorney General accused of pumping stocks to the general public while privately circulating memos describing them as "crap" and "junk."

Despite the poor and checkered track record of most Wall Street analysts, the savvy macrowave investor doesn't necessarily have to turn his or her back completely on the ratings game. In fact, every week, I regularly read the section of *Barron's* that lists some of the key upgrades and downgrades for the week. That's also why on a daily basis I always visit one of my favorite Web sites, www.marketedge.com.

Table 12-2 provides a typical list of daily upgrades you might find at the Market Edge Web site. Note that this paid subscription site (which I shall examine in much more detail in Chapter 14) posts two kinds of upgrades. The "Market Edge Upgrades" are based on pure technical analyses. The "Star Changes" are conducted by Standard & Poor's and are based purely on fundamental analysis.

Key Point #5: Buy What You Know

[Peter] Lynch shows that for the average investor, the key to making money in the stock market is sticking with what you know. Instead of investing in a high-tech organization you read about in the press, look around you. Is there a company building a new plant in your area? Has your own company just added a third shift at the warehouse? These are the clues you get before the professionals, the clues that lead to a "tenbagger"—a stock whose value increases tenfold.

Global Investor Bookshop

The legendary Peter Lynch managed the Fidelity Magellan Fund from 1977 to 1990 and was either smart enough—or lucky enough—to rack up enough consistent gains to make his fund the best performer over that period. Lynch fancied himself to be a modern-day mall rat and consumer sleuth. He found his best stock ideas came not from the pages of *Barron's* or the *Wall Street Journal* or even Fidelity's own cadres of analysts but rather from personal observations about a constantly changing modern-day life.

Table 12-2   The Ratings Game

Market Edge Upgrades		
OPWV		Long
ILA		Long
MANH		Long
TIBX		Long
AKAM		Long
Standard & Poor's Star Changes		
	Old	New
COG	***	****
AHC	***	**
CI	***	**
GMCR	****	***

Lynch believed that as an investor, you should know "everything about a company before buying a stock—then follow the story after buying the stock." As a quintessential buy-and-hold investor, Lynch also advised never selling a stock "if the story is still good whether the market is up or down."

As for the tantalizing question as to whether Lynch was actually more lucky than good, at least one Wall Street expert has draped a big question mark over Lynch's success. As the esteemed Professor Jeremy Siegel writes:

> *The most outstanding mutual fund performance over the entire period is that of Fidelity's Magellan fund, whose 19.8 percent annual return from 1971 through June 1997 beat the market by almost 7 percent per year. The probability that this performance was based on luck alone is about one in 200. But this means that, out of the 198 mutual funds that survived the period, there is a very good chance that one would have performed as well as the Magellan fund by chance alone.*

Luck or skill? I don't know. I do know that Lynch would have likely gotten slaughtered in the last bear market just like almost every other fund manager because of his avowed philosophy of holding onto stocks "whether the market is up or down." Still, there is much wisdom in his observation that you can learn a lot just by keeping your eyes open.

Key Point #6: Finding Cutting Edge Tech Stocks

Not even Warren Buffet can save Level 3 Communications.

Despite its waning performance of late, JDS Uniphase has a bright future.

Red Herring Cover Story Excerpts

Go into any major bookstore and browse the magazine rack and your eyes will feast on a veritable sea of investment advice. In venerable magazines like *Forbes, Fortune, Kiplinger's, Money, Smart Money,* and *Worth,* you will find cover articles that tout everything from "the year's best blue chips" and "downtrodden techs ready for a rebound," to "growth stocks for the new millennium" and "Bargain Hunting with a Longtime Bear."

Interestingly, and almost invariably, these "venerables" rarely venture outside the world of the "large cap" knowns. They continually recycle the same big company names we are all familiar with: IBM, GE, Xerox, Dell, Cisco, and other "usual suspects."

Much more adventurous are magazines like M.I.T.'s *Technology Review.* This magazine targets the latest scientific and technological trends in a way that often will point you to new, emerging stocks. Be prepared, however, for some major frustration because a lot of the companies that are featured are not publicly traded yet and many are mere infants in the venture capital stage.

Now here's a note of caution: You may very well find some very good ideas reading the financial press. Just be aware that the stock picks of many of these publications have suffered from the same affliction as the vast majority of Wall Street's money managers who can't even beat the S&P 500 Index. That affliction is continuing to tout stocks during a prolonged bear market where even the best of stocks are more likely to go down than up.

The broader point: As with every source of potential stock picks, put them through the appropriate screens before you take any plunge.

Key Point #7: Ignore Hot Stock Tips

> During the bull market many "insiders" passed along hot stock tips that ultimately didn't pan out. Jeff Lubs, a math and science teacher at a Manhattan Beach middle school, finally bought a telecom stock after being badgered by a friend, whose husband worked for the company . . . Shortly after buying Irvine-based Incomnet at $23 per share, the plunge [of the stock] began. Within a few months, it dropped to $8. A few more months, it was down to $1. . . . "She [Lubs' friend] was like, "Oh, sorry about that."
>
> *Los Angeles Times*

I've given you six different ways to find new stocks. Here's a seventh that I strongly encourage you to eschew—which is a fancy word for "chew up and spit out." Indeed, there is only one thing to do with "hot stock tips" from friends, acquaintances, or even brokers: Run away!

Think about it. If someone has any really good information, it probably has come from the inside. Investing on the basis of such information constitutes insider trading. This practice is illegal, and it can get you into a lot of trouble. Don't you believe me? Ask Martha Stewart.

On the other hand, maybe the information didn't come from any inside knowledge at all. So where did it come from? Was it some pump-and-dump artist seeking to push up a stock's price so he or she could bail as you piled in? And how fresh or old is the information? Are you the second to get it—or the millionth? Enough said.

QUESTIONS

1. What kind of stocks does the buy low, sell high approach look for?

2. In what kind of a market does the buy low, sell high approach work best, and in what kind of a market are you likely to sustain heavy losses?

3. What kind of stocks does the buy high, sell higher approach look for?

4. In what kind of market does the buy high, sell higher approach work best, and in what kind of market does it perform poorly?

5. How does the high-volume mover approach work?

6. Name two of the major problems that arise when you depend on the ratings of Wall Street analysts.

7. Summarize the approach to stock picking of the legendary Peter Lynch.

8. Name some of the magazines that are useful to read when searching for stocks.

9. Why is it wise to ignore the hot stock tips of your friends, acquaintances, or even stockbrokers?

EXERCISES

1. Visit http://finance.yahoo.com, find the "Investing" section, and click on "Screener" at the "Stock Research" link. Review the various "Preset Screens." Find one that corresponds to the buy low, sell high approach, another that relies more on buy high, sell higher, and still another that focuses on high volume.

2. Go to http://investors.com and check out the "High Volume Movers" for the day in the IBD table showing you "Where The Big Money's Flowing."

3. Visit www.moneycentral.com. Click on the "Investing" link and then click on the "Stocks" link. Go down to the "Stock Screener" link and click the "Power Search" link. Try some of the various stock searches they have available, from "New 52-Week Highs" and "Dogs of the Dow" to "Momentum Stocks" and "Distressed Stock Plays."

4. Go to www.bigcharts.com. At this site, we want to develop charts for two particular companies. The first is Barr Labs—an excellent example of a successful buy high, sell higher breakout. In 2000, Barr formed a classic "cup with handle" base. Then, once the stock breached its pivot point, it took off on a tear with a very successful breakout, gaining over 50 percent

in a few short months. The second company is the Willis Group. It suffered a failed breakout during 2002 while the stock market was trending downward.

5. Here's what you do. For Barr, enter the symbol "BRL" in the box and click on the "Interactive Charting" link. Go down to the Time box and choose "Custom." Then enter the dates from 2/01/2000 to 8/30/2000 and click "Draw Chart." Note how the "cup" and "base" form between March and June. Note the downward "handle" for a few weeks in the beginning of June. Finally note how the stock price clears its pivot point and moves up smartly.

6. Now let's do the same thing for the Willis Group, stock symbol WSH. In this case, however, enter the dates 2/01/2002 to 10/31/2002. Note the much more volatile base forming between May and September. Note also the failed breakout in October after Willis's stock jumps above its pivot— and then crashes!

7. Assemble several of the stock symbols for your favorite companies and then visit http://my.zacks.com. Type in one of the symbols in the "Enter Ticker" box and hit Go. Then, click on the link "Estimates for . . . ." You should arrive at a page that summarizes all of the various recommendations for the stock by the major ratings analysts. Try this for several more stocks.

8. Check out the latest issue of M.I.T.'s *Technology Review* at www.technology review.com.

9. Visit www.peternavarro.com and browse the latest edition of the *Savvy Macrowave Investor* newsletter for the stock picks of the week.

Chapter 13

IT'S ABSOLUTELY FUNDAMENTAL

It's amazing to us to think that anyone might study a stock chart, see a particular pattern, determine that the stock is "breaking resistance," and then commit actual money to that proposition. Simply put, *leave technical analysis alone* [emphasis added].

The Motley Fool

With their floppy, three-cornered jester hats and big smiles, [Motley Fool co-founders] Tom and David Gardner . . . offered a message with great appeal: Don't listen to the pompous "wise men" of Wall Street. You can do better investing on your own. . . . Now, more than a year after the meltdown of the tech-heavy Nasdaq Stock Market . . . I found a sadder but wiser Fool . . . *"To look and see your portfolio substantially negative . . . forces you to question your assumptions,"* [Tom] Gardner said. "You naturally hang your head a little bit" [emphasis added].

Copley News Service

Army versus Navy. Motley Fools versus the Wall Street Establishment. Technical analysts versus fundamental analysts. These are some of the great rivalries in history.

In fact, for the savvy macrowave investor, the technical versus fundamental battle is a false dichotomy. Every stock and every sector you consider should go through *both* a technical screen *and* a fundamental screen to determine its relative strength or weakness. Remember our Golden Rules of Macrowave Investing: Buy *strong* stocks in strong sectors in an upward-trending market and short *weak* stocks in weak sectors in a downward-trending market.

As for what fundamental analysts actually do, the fundamental analyst believes that a stock's price is ultimately determined not by the technician's "voodoo charts" and mathematical formulas but by much more down-to-earth factors such as how much money the company is making and how well the company is run. That's why the fundamental analyst focuses on *quantitative* measures of company strength like revenue growth and price-to-earnings and debt ratios. That's also why the fundamental analyst examines more *qualitative* factors like a company's management quality, its labor relations, and its rate of technological innovation.

In contrast, technical analysts focus purely on the price and volume action of a stock, and they care not whether the company sells computer chips or potato chips. They simply use the available price and volume data to build charts and construct a variety of technical indicators like moving averages, oscillators, and Bollinger Bands. They then use these charts and the patterns within them along with the signals of their technical indicators to assess both the likely direction and degree of intensity of a stock price's movement.

Now hear this! From the first quotation leading off this chapter, you can get just a small taste of the disdain that fundamental analysts like the Motley Fools have toward technical analysis. For those of you who have not heard of them, the Motley Fools are self-proclaimed investment gurus who run a popular Web site and who have written a number of best-selling investment books. But from the second, far more humble quote from Fool Tom Gardner, you can also see just how much trouble a fundamentally oriented investor can get into when she or he ignores technical warnings of a market downturn.

The sad fact (and it is a fact that these more idiots than fools have yet to understand to this day) is this: *The Motley Fools never would have had to experience their heavy losses if they had supplemented their sound fundamental approach with even the most rudimentary of technical indicators.* Indeed, they would have seen the train that ultimately ran over their portfolios when it was a mere light at the beginning of the bear market tunnel—and stepped deftly off the track.

With that as our prelude, we are going to explore the fundamentals of fundamental analysis in this chapter. Then, in the next chapter, we will give the technical analyst "devils" their very just due. As we do so, keep in mind that I won't be trying to teach you to *become* fundamental or technical analysts. That is a complicated task that could well take half your life to do properly. Rather, I'm simply going to show you how to apply some very easy-to-use fundamental and technical "screens" to your stocks.

Key Macrowave Points

1. The "efficient market" and "random walk" theories imply that it is impossible to consistently beat the broad stock market index. Instead, you should invest in a broad market index fund or widely diversified portfolio and hang on for the random ride.

2. Fundamental analysts reject the efficient market theory. They believe every stock has an "intrinsic" or "fair" value but that stock prices do not always reflect fair value in the short run. These price discrepancies provide profitable opportunities to buy undervalued stocks or to short overvalued stocks.

3. To determine a company's fair value, the fundamental analyst looks at *quantitative* measures of earnings, growth, liquidity, and leverage, as well as more *qualitative* aspects such as management quality, product innovation, and the marketing network.

4. Fundamental analysis has its roots in the work of value-investing scholars like Benjamin Graham and David Dodd and leading practitioners such as Warren Buffett.

5. Fundamental analysis is very time consuming. However, performing a fundamental screen is not. The savvy macrowave investor uses a variety of Internet resources to conduct fundamental screens on every potential stock pick.

6. The fundamental analyst who ignores the technical side of the stock-screening equation invariably falls into two kinds of traps: (1) buying fundamentally strong stocks in *weak sectors*, and (2) buying fundamentally strong stocks in a *downward-trending market*.

7. While technical analysts and fundamental analysts fight like cats and dogs, both camps have much to offer. Use both a fundamental and technical screen!

Key Point #1: An Efficient and Random Market? Not!

In a "perfect" stock market, going by the Random Walk theory, no individual investor will have an advantage over any other as all material information will reach everybody equally and at the same instant. Consequently, share price movements will be totally "unpredictable" or "random," and there will be no room for speculation, let alone manipulation, because all new information would instantly be factored into each stock's price. But in real life, stock markets, or any other market for that matter, are far from perfect.

Business Times

In order to understand the philosophy behind fundamental analysis, we must first examine two of Wall Street's most enduring fallacies: the alleged existence of a totally "efficient market" and the mistaken description of stock price movements as a totally "random walk."

According to the efficient market theory, stock prices always reflect all available information. That means that at any point in time stocks are always fairly valued. It is therefore impossible to ever find any bargains to buy or overpriced stocks to short.

According to the "random walk" theory, stock prices move for totally unpredictable reasons. That means that at any point in time, it is useless to try to pick "winning stocks."

Together, the efficient market and random walk theories imply that it is impossible to consistently beat the broad stock market index with savvy stock picking except by sheer luck. The clear implication of these two myths is that investors should not even try to beat the market. Instead, they should simply invest in broad market index funds. Alternatively, they should pursue a buy-and-hold strategy. That is, they should buy a highly diverse portfolio and then simply hold on for the random ride.

Perhaps needless to say, if you really swallow the efficient market-random walk line, you should stop reading this book right now. Instead, go throw your money in an index fund, and forget about it.

If, however, you are interested in joining the legions of hedge funds, savvy portfolio managers, and active investors who regularly do beat the market, then read on!

Key Point #2: Exploit Price Deviations from "Fair Value"

> There are portfolio managers who have better track records than others, and there are investment houses with more renowned research analysis than others. So how can performance be random when people are clearly profiting from and beating the market?
>
> *Reem Heakal*

The fundamental analyst embraces three key assumptions that sharply contradict the efficient market and random walk theories. The first assumption is that every stock has an "intrinsic" or "fair" value. This can be uncovered by carefully analyzing the firm's earnings, growth, management structure, and other such quite literally fundamental statistics.

The second assumption is that stock prices do not always reflect a firm's intrinsic value *in the short run*. This is because the market is not perfectly efficient as the efficient market theorists' claim. Rather, because of imperfections in the flow of information and other uncertainties, the markets are only "weakly efficient."

The third key assumption is that while the short run price of a stock may deviate significantly from its intrinsic value, *over the longer run, a stock's price will gravitate toward its fair or intrinsic value*. That means that if you can uncover an undervalued stock to buy or an overvalued stock to short sell, you will eventually profit handsomely.

The powerful implication of these three assumptions should be clear: The fundamental analyst who conducts careful research should be able to find strong stocks to buy that are undervalued and weak stocks to short sell that are overvalued.

Key Point #3: Many Fundamental Analysts Are "Value Investors"

Buy dollar bills for 50 cents.

Warren Buffett

It is perhaps worth a short digression here to explore the relationship between fundamental analysis and the so-called value-investing style. The relationship exists because fundamental analysis has its roots in the work of value-investing scholars like Benjamin Graham and David Dodd as well as leading practitioners such as the Oracle of Omaha himself, the esteemed Warren Buffett.

Perhaps the best way to see the relationship of fundamental analysis to value investing is to examine how Buffett picks stocks. To Buffett, a company to buy must meet all of the following criteria:

- Products or services and a method of making money that are easy to understand. (This is a key tenet of Buffett but not necessarily of fundamental analysis.)

- A history of earning a high rate of return for investors, not just the potential to do so. (Note that these first two criteria kept Buffett completely out of the dot-com boom.)

- Some form of strategic advantage that will allow the company to continue to earn an above-average return over time—for example, barriers to entry, patents, exclusive access to natural resources, or some other kind of monopoly power.

- Healthy profits not just on heavy volume but also from high profits per unit of sale.

- No excessive debt levels or leverage.

- Trustworthy management acting in the best interests of shareholders. In other words, no Enron or Tyco CEOs allowed.

- A stock price selling below Buffett's calculation of intrinsic value.

Note that most of these factors relate to the ability of a company to earn money with little risk and flow earnings through to shareholders. Using this fundamental approach in conjunction with his buy-and-hold philosophy, Warren Buffett has compiled one of the most enviable investing records in financial market history.

Note further, however, that primarily because of criteria number 1 and number 2, the Oracle from Omaha missed out on one of the great gold rushes in Wall Street history. That history involved going long in tech stocks during the Nasdaq boom and going short on those same stocks during their dramatic bust.

The broader point of this digression is simply this: In today's swiftly moving modern stock market, the fundamental analysis of gurus like Warren Buffett need not be the end of our education as savvy macrowave investors but rather simply an excellent beginning. Let's turn, then, in our next key point to some of the fundamental analyst's major tools.

Key Point #4: The Fundamental Analyst's Tools

The "trick" of course is to figure out how to confidently estimate the "true" value of the shares as opposed to the market price.

Shawn Allen

To determine a company's fair or intrinsic value, the fundamental analyst begins first with *quantitative* measures of a company's financial health and prospects. Such measures include such income statement data as sales, operating costs, net profit margins, return on equity, cash flow, and earnings per share. On the balance sheet side, quantitative measures also include various asset and debt ratios as well as the capital structure of the company.

As I indicated earlier, my goal here is *not* to teach you how to conduct such fundamental analysis but rather simply how to use it in a fundamental screen. Toward that end, it is important to always see the Big Picture. In this case, what the fundamental analyst is trying to do by combing through this sea of accounting data is to answer these kinds of questions—note the kinship of these questions to many of the Buffett criteria posted in the last key point:

- Has the company consistently earned a profit and is it likely to continue to do so in the future?

- Is the company's revenue base growing?

- Does the profit it earns before taxes flow through to the shareholder?

- Has the company borrowed so much money that it is likely to get into a cash crunch in an economic downturn?

- Does it have plenty of cash on hand to weather any storm?

The *qualitative* measures that a fundamental analyst looks at span a wide range. In fact, in many cases, the importance of a given factor can be very much dependent on the sector or industry the company is in.

For example, while the fundamental analyst will always be looking at every company to see whether it is well managed, some sectors like the airlines and coal industries are much more prone to labor strikes and shutdowns than others. By the same token, a company's rate of technological change and innovation is much more important in New Economy sectors like computer software and biotechnology than in Old Economy industries like chemicals, paper, and steel.

Key Point #5: Use the Internet to Simplify Your Fundamental Screening

Figuring out the fair value of a company is the tough part. There are no magic formulas, and a complete understanding of the entire process could take an entire career to develop (and for some analysts, it seems that two lifetimes wouldn't be enough).

Andrew Greta, The Street.com

It should be obvious from our discussion so far that fundamental analysis can be both very time consuming and very tedious. While I certainly won't discourage you from rolling up your sleeves and digging deep into a company's data and methods, I will, however, point out here that there are a number of quick and easy-to-use "fundamental screens" available on the Internet. *Using such screens, you will be able to analyze literally hundreds of stocks in far less time than it would take you to conduct your own in-depth fundamental analysis of a single company.*

As for which fundamental screen on the Internet you should use, I will let you find the one(s) that work best for you—and more fully explore this universe in some of the exercises at the end of the chapter. However, in the meantime, I want to show you how to conduct a fundamental screen using one of my favorite screening tools: *Investor's Business Daily*'s Web site, Investors.com, at www.investors.com.

In this regard, you must be a subscriber to the *Investor's Business Daily* newspaper in order to gain free access to the Web site's stock-picking search engines. I highly recommend subscribing! *Investor's Business Daily*, or *IBD*, for short, is simply required reading for every investor interested in intelligently speculating in the market.

That said, let's take a look at a typical *IBD* stock screen, which is illustrated in Figure 13-1 for the Internet router king Cisco. (To view such a screen, subscribers can simply go to the "*IBD* Power Tools" box at www.investors.com and type in a stock symbol.)

Note first that *IBD* provides an overall rating for the stock—in the case of Cisco, a 56 on a scale of 0 to 100, or a grade of C- on a scale of A to E. Note also that *IBD* provides both technical and fundamental ratings for *both* the stock itself and its sector or "group." Finally, note that there are both technical and fundamental ratings for the *individual stock*.

Reviewing this table, your first impression might be that this is a reasonably strong stock. However, at this time, it appears to be in a very weak sector. Indeed, both the technical and fundamental group ratings are a flat-out flunking E.

Overall Rating: (56 = C-)

The Overall Rating incorporates the five Stock Diagnosis Ratings and then compares the results to all other stocks. This is not an average of the five ratings and they are not weighted equally.

Stock's diagnosis			
Technical rating	(54 = D+)	*Group's technical rating*	(22 = E)
Fundamental rating	(77 = B-)	*Group's fundamental rating*	(25 = E)
Attractiveness rating	(69 = C+)		

Cisco Systems Inc.'s rank within the Computer-Networking Group

worst ████████████████████████████ 91% best
Overall Rank: 5th out of 47 stocks

worst ████████████████████████████ 87% best
Technical rank: 7th out of 47 stocks

worst ████████████████████████████ 89% best
Fundamental rank: 6th out of 47 stocks

worst ████████████████████████████ 93% best
Attractiveness rank: 4th out of 47 stocks

Figure 13-1   The *IBD* Fundamental Stock Picking Screen.

Now, let's look more closely at the fundamental rating. According to *IBD*, this rating is based on four factors:

1. Annual and quarterly sales and earnings growth rates
2. Sales and earnings acceleration
3. Earnings stability and profit margins
4. Return on equity (ROE)

In other words, the analytical gnomes at *IBD* take very seriously a statement oft repeated in this book: Stock prices reflect nothing more than an investor's expectations about a future stream of earnings. Therefore, *IBD*'s fundamental screen is a very limited but powerful one that focuses exclusively on earnings.

Note in the table that Cisco gets a B- for its fundamentals. The question you might ask at this point might be: Is that a good enough score to pass a fundamental test if you are thinking about buying Cisco?

I can't give you a hard and fast answer to that question. What I can say is that after you conduct a bunch of your own fundamental screens using *IBD*'s rating system, you will be able to establish your own thresholds of what you find fundamentally acceptable. It may, for example, be B+ and above for buying a stock. It may also be D and below for shorting a stock. Or you may want tighter or looser criteria. The points are: The thresholds will be up to you but please do a fundamental screen.

As a final comment, note that while I consider *IBD*'s fundamental screen to be an excellent tool, I will *not* suggest in the next chapter that you rely solely on *IBD* for a technical screen as well. It's not that *IBD*'s technical rating is necessarily wrong. For me, it just doesn't provide as much ready information as several other preferred technical screening engines that can be found on the Web. That's why in the next chapter on technical analysis, I will offer several alternative Web sites to conduct your technical screen.

Key Point #6: The Fundamental Analyst's Traps

To look and see your portfolio substantially negative . . . forces you to question your assumptions. . . . You naturally hang your head a little bit.

Motley Fool Tom Gardner

Okay. Maybe I'm rubbing it into the Motley Fool's face a bit by repeating these words from the opening quotation to this chapter. But I do want to drive home this key point: It is important to conduct both a fundamental and a technical screen. Otherwise, the fundamental analyst is likely to fall, as the self-proclaimed investment gurus Motley Fools did, into at least one of two types of traps.

To illustrate these traps, first recall from key point number 2 that, according to the tenets of fundamental analysis, a company's stock price may be above or below its fair value *in the short run* but that the stock price always gravitates toward fair value *in the longer run*. But just how "long" might the long run be before a stock price finds its fair value?

The unfortunate answer is that *the long run can certainly be long enough for the fundamental analyst to sustain heavy losses over a period of months or perhaps even years.* The following paragraphs, then, describe the two most common traps of the fundamental analyst both of which the Motley Fools fell into as they continued to tout tech stocks in a bear market.

Trap #1: Good Stocks in Bad Markets

The fundamental analyst will invest in a fundamentally strong company but do so in a bad overall *market*. And, of course, he or she will lose money because very few stocks can rise above a downward market trend—a downward trend, I might add, that would be easily detectable with technical analysis.

Of course, you might say that if the fundamental analyst were to hold on long enough, both the market and the stock might come back. Yes, you *could* say that. But why, for example, would you have wanted to hold onto a fundamentally strong stock between, say, March 2000 and August 2002—and in the process lose 50 percent to 80 percent of your investment? No, we can do much better than such buy-and-hold Motley Foolishness with our savvy macrowave investing approach!

Trap #2: Good Stocks in Bad Sectors

The fundamental analyst will invest in a great company in a bad market *sector*. The relevant fact here is that over half of a stock price's movement is related to the movement of the sector it does business in *rather* than how the company manages its own operations. That's why I have said that you can buy the best-managed company in the world with the best-looking balance sheet and still lose a ton of money if you pick the wrong sector at the wrong time.

Key Point #7: Use Both a Fundamental and Technical Analysis Screen!

The battle between fundamental and technical analysis is a thing of the past. . . .Smart traders . . . increasingly use a combination of technical and fundamental analysis to get better results.

Shares Magazine

Technical analysts and fundamental analysts fight like cats and dogs, with fundamental analysts accusing the technicians of a bunch of chartist witchcraft while technicians often rightfully ridicule the fundamental crowd for picking stocks with great fundamentals that drop like a stone.

So who's right? Both camps are! Any stock or sector you buy should be both technically and fundamentally strong. And any stock or sector you might want to short should be both technically and fundamentally weak. And that's our segue to our next chapter on technical analysis.

QUESTIONS

1. Every stock you consider should go through what two types of screens?

2. According to the efficient market theory, stock prices always reflect what? What does this imply for the possibility of finding any stock bargains?

3. According to the random walk theory, stock prices move for what kinds of reasons? What does this assumption imply for trying to pick stocks?

4. If you believe in the efficient market and random walk theories, what should your investment approach be?

5. Fundamental analysts reject the efficient market theory. What is their alternative belief about stock prices?

6. A stock market analyst is looking for companies that make products that are easy to understand, that have a history of running a high rate of return, that are not burdened by excessive debt levels, and have a trustworthy management. What famous stock market guru is this stock market analyst likely trying to emulate?

7. Name several quantitative and qualitative measures that fundamental analysts look for when evaluating a stock.

8. To use the method of the savvy macrowave investor, is it important that you know how to conduct your own fundamental analysis, or is it sufficient that you simply know how to conduct a fundamental screen?

9. What are the two traps the fundamental analyst typically falls into? How can these traps be avoided?

10. Technical and fundamental analysts often fight like cats and dogs. So which camp is right?

EXERCISES

1. Visit www.peternavarro.com, click on the "Macrowave University" link and find the article entitled "The Efficient Market Hypothesis & The Random Walk Theory." It's an excellent background piece for the curious.

2. Go to www.google.com and type in the words *intrinsic value investing* and conduct a search. Peruse some of the entries to get a better sense of how the whole idea of value investing—essentially a fundamental analysis approach—works.

3. If you want to learn some more about fundamental analysis, visit www.stocks.about.com and click on the "Fundamental Analysis" link.

4. Visit www.theonlineinvestor.com and type in *Warren Buffett* in their search box. Hit Go and read some of the latest missives on the Oracle of Omaha.

5. Visit http://my.zacks.com. Click on the "Screening" link. Then check out "Zacks Predefined Screenings." These include such screens as "Top Value," "Top EPS Growth Stocks," and "Highest Dividend Yields." Try using one or more of the screens for "Any Size" companies and then "Small Cap" companies. Jot down several of the names for use in Exercise 8.

6. Wall Street City's search engines run like Ferraris when it comes to stock screening. Go to www.wallstreetcity.com and click on the "ProSearch" link. Then go to "ProSearch Engines." Perform a fundamental screen that searches for companies with a "5-year cash flow growth" that is as "high as possible" and a debt/equity ratio that is as "low as possible." Peruse the resulting companies, and jot down a few of the stock symbols for use in Exercise 8. Then, try a few more searches using other criteria of fundamental analysis like "Dividend Consistency," "Earnings Per Share," and "Gross Profit Margin."

7. Exercises 5 and 6 showed you how to do your own fundamental screens. However, a much quicker method to quickly and simply check the fundamental rating of a stock is to use the ratings systems at sites like www.standardandpoors.com and www.investors.com. In this exercise, please visit the

Standard & Poor's site. At the "Equity" heading, click on the "Top Buys/Top Sells." This is a list of stocks that have been rated using fundamental analysis on a star system. Jot down a few for use in Exercise 8. [*Note*: These same ratings are available at www.marketedge.com along with technical ratings for stocks. I will show you in the next chapter how to use market edge as a tool to quickly do both a fundamental and technical screen.]

8. Using the stocks you jotted down in the last several exercises (and maybe the list of every stock in your portfolio), go to www.investors.com. Log in to the site and use *IBD*'s "Power Tools" to do an "*IBD* Stock Checkup" to check the "Fundamental Rank" and "Fundamental Rating" for each of the stocks. [*Note*: You must be a subscriber to the paper. If you aren't, you can try a free trial subscription. Doing so is highly recommended!]

9. Historically, General Electric has had a very good fundamental rating. But even a stock like GE can fall into the fundamental analyst's trap of being a good stock in a bad market. To see how a stock like GE dropped during the bear market of 2000–2002, go to www.bigcharts.com. Type in *GE* in the "Enter Symbol or Keyword" box and click on the "Interactive Charting" link. Then go down to the "Time" box, set to "Custom," and put in the dates 1/1/2000 to 12/31/2001. Finally, click on the "Compare to" box and pick the S&P 500 Index. Hit "Draw Chart." Notice how the Great GE tumbled with the rest of the market over much of the time period.

Chapter 14

TECHNICALLY SPEAKING

Technical analysis by itself, although necessary, is not sufficient. It is the combination of technical and fundamental valuation techniques that provide a powerful investment tool. By identifying turning points ahead of time coupled with the assessment of whether the stock or market is over or under-owned, we can build scenarios around the turning point dates that will act as triggers for a change in trend. These scenarios are then changed, altered and new scenarios added as the turning dates approach. Although we never know for sure until the aftermath of the event, it always pays to anticipate the move.

Simon Koh, Business Times

"Gap ups" and "gap downs." "Resistance" and "support." "Double bottoms" and "head and shoulders tops." This is just some of the "lingo" of technical analysis.

To become truly successful macrowave investors, we must first come to understand this language. We must next become familiar with the various tools in the technical analyst's box, from price charts and volume indicators to measures of momentum and investor sentiment. Finally, we must learn, as we have done with fundamental analysis, how to apply some very basic technical analysis "screens."

We must do all of this because the savvy macrowave investor uses technical analysis on a daily basis to identify the trends, momentum, and sentiment not just of the broad market but also of the market's individual sectors and stocks. Through the use of technical analysis, the savvy macrowave investor is able to bring much more clarity to the flow of information from the four dynamic factors as well as a much more forward look to the fundamental information being taken in daily from the media and Wall Street.

Importantly, in this chapter, we are not just going to learn the "basics" of technical analysis. We shall also see that virtually every technical indicator and chart may be explained in terms of basic investor psychology and human behavior. That means that technical analysis is not "chartist voodoo," as some of its critics claim. Nor is it even sterile "black box" mathematics—as it may appear to be at first glance. Rather, technical analysis provides a very powerful graphical and mathematical *reflection* of the ever-changing "moods" of the market.

Macrowave Key Points

1. The language of technical analysis has its roots in basic investor psychology and human behavior.

2. Technical analysis begins with the basic "price chart," which quite literally paints pictures of the market trend, sector trends, and individual stock trends.

3. The technical analyst looks for tell-tale patterns that historically have been helpful in predicting trend reversals or a continuation of the trend. Some familiar patterns include the head and shoulders top or bottom and the cup-with-handle.

4. The technical analyst uses raw buying and selling volume together with various "volume indicators" to confirm the direction of the market, sector, and individual stock trends that are revealed by price charts.

5. "Moving averages" are used to amplify the direction of the trend and smooth out the "noise" that can come from price and volume fluctuations. The "crossovers" of shorter- and longer-term moving averages are particularly valuable in timing your entries and exits from the market.

6. Momentum indicators like the RSI and the MACD are used to better pinpoint what stage the current trend is in and likewise are useful in generating buy and sell signals.

7. "Sentiment" indicators reveal whether investors are feeling bullish or bearish. They are "contrarian" indicators; when too many investors become bullish, that's a bearish signal, and vice versa.

8. As with fundamental analysis, the savvy macrowave investor does *not* have to master technical analysis. Rather, the goal is to understand enough to intelligently apply some basic technical analysis "screens."

9. Some of the tools of technical analysis work better—and some worse—when the market is trending up or down rather than trading sideways.

Key Point #1: Learn the Lingo and Underlying Psychology

The head and shoulders pattern is a classical sort of technical pattern that shows a failure of confidence on the part of the investor. Remember, when people are talking about support and resistance, they're just talking about areas where people decided that it was good to buy and where it was good to sell. So when you've broken through the bottom of a head and shoulders pattern, you've broken through a point where twice before investors thought this was a good spot to buy this stock and all those people now have a loss in the stock and that puts pressure on it on the downside.

Ken Tower, Cybertrader on CNNFN

In this key point, I want to briefly explain some of the most common and useful terms of technical analysis. These include: the "gap up" and "gap down," "support" and "resistance," "breakouts" and "breakdowns," "overbought" and "oversold" conditions, "pullbacks," and "relative strength." More importantly, I also want to explain some of the underlying investor psychology and human behavior behind these terms. Understanding such psychology is important to understanding the many moods of the market.

Gaps Up and Down

The major U.S. stock markets open Monday through Friday at 9:30 A.M. Eastern time and close at 4:00 P.M. The price at which a stock is first sold "at the open" is defined as its opening price while the last price of the day represents its "close." The price range includes the stock's high and low prices for the day.

In a gap up, the stock price jumps up so that its low price for the day is higher than its previous day's high price. Conversely, with a gap down, its high price for the day is lower than its previous day's low price. Such gaps are very important to understand because if you are caught holding a stock in a gap down, you are in for a big loss—while a gap up can provide an unexpected windfall.

The behavioral explanation for these gaps is simple. Investors are simply reacting to some new information from one of the four dynamic factors and inflating or discounting the price of a stock accordingly. This information may have come the previous day after the close. Or it may have hit the wires in the early morning hours preceding the open.

In some cases, it may be a piece of company- or sector-specific news relating to the first dynamic factor of corporate earnings: Intel announces unexpectedly low earnings, a judge rules against Sun Microsystems in an antitrust case, or one of Amgen's prize new drugs in trial fails a test. This bad news triggers a gap down as investors suddenly revise their expectations and bid down the stock price.

The information may also be related to the flow of macro data—the second dynamic factor. For example, an unexpected fall in jobless claims raises the expectation of a robust economic recovery, and the stocks of cyclical paper, chemical, and steel companies gap up, perhaps with much of the rest of the market.

Resistance and Support; Breakouts and Breakdowns

The concepts of resistance and support are very useful, particularly when it comes to your initial entry into a stock. You can think of resistance as a price ceiling above which sellers begin to outnumber buyers and which is very difficult to break through. Conversely, support is a price floor below which buyers begin to outnumber sellers.

To understand resistance from a behavioral point of view, think of a stock that you might have bought that is now selling significantly *below* your buying price. From your point of view, this stock is a real loser, and you can't wait to get rid of it. But you don't want to take a loss either. So what do you do? You decide that you will sell this worthless piece of garbage as soon as its price rises back up to your original buying price.

Now, if there are a lot of folks just like you thinking exactly the same thing—sell as soon as the stock hits a certain price—that's resistance. This is because at that price, the stock is going to get hit with a wave of selling which will beat it back down.

As for support, there's a similar behavioral explanation. A support level is simply some price at which more buyers than sellers think the stock has become a bargain. So when the stock's price falls, it can only go so far down until a wave of buyers swoops in to pick the stock up at the bargain price and thereby quite literally lend support.

In general, you want to buy stocks much closer to support than resistance. You also want to wait patiently for a stock that is near a key resistance level to see if it can break through it and make its next move up.

In fact, that's exactly what a breakout is; it happens when prices move up sharply through an important layer of resistance. And of course a breakdown occurs when prices move down sharply through a key support level.

Overbought and Oversold Conditions; Pullbacks and Bounces

Once a stock starts to get really hot, it can move very quickly upward. With some stocks, it's almost like a feeding frenzy, as buyers pile into the market thinking they are going to strike it rich.

However, when a stock moves too quickly, it can move into an overbought condition. This is a condition in which it is very likely that the stock will at least temporarily pull back.

The behavioral explanation is again pretty simple. When a stock moves quickly up in price, at some point, some shorter-term traders are going to begin selling to take some profits off the table. Once some selling begins, it can trigger more selling. At least temporarily, sellers overwhelm buyers, and this leads to a pullback. That's why you don't typically want to buy a stock that technical analysis is telling you is in an overbought condition and may be ready for a pullback. Rather, you wait for the pullback to occur and then enter on the pullback at a nicely reduced price.

As for an oversold condition, it is just the opposite kind of situation. Investors are dumping a stock much too quickly, and it will be due for a nice little "bounce." When a stock is oversold, you can often enter the stock at a good price.

Relative Strength, Outperforming, and Underperforming

Relative strength is a very important term for the savvy macrowave investor because the savvy macrowave investor is always looking for strong and weak stocks and sectors. But strong and weak relative to what? That's where the idea of relative strength comes in.

Suppose, for example, that the broad market is in an up trend. In such an up trend, a given market sector like autos or housing or technology may be moving up faster or slower than other market sectors as well as the broad market. A sector moving up faster is said to be outperforming the market while one that is moving slower is underperforming. So, too, is it for individual stocks within sectors. Some stocks in a sector may be outperforming others in the sector. "Relative strength" analysis measures how a stock or sector or specific index is performing relative to another stock or sector or broader market index.

All of this can be measured by using relative strength analysis. Simply divide one index, sector, or stock by the one you wish to measure it against, and plot the ratio. For instance, divide the auto sector by the S&P 500 (broad market). If the relative strength line is rising, the auto sector is outperforming the market; if it's falling, it's underperforming.

You may then want to individually divide Ford, GM, and Chrysler by the auto sector to see which of these companies is outperforming or underperforming in its sector. If the auto sector is outperforming the broad market, you would buy the strong stocks that are outperforming in the sector. If the auto sector is underperforming the broad market (and the market trend is down), you would short the stocks that are underperforming in the sector.

Key Point #2: Price Chart Patterns Identify Trends!

Imagine you own a stock that has been rising steadily for 18 months as investors anticipate increased earnings for six consecutive quarters. A trend line can be drawn with a ruler connecting the troughs in prices as a stock moves higher. If you maintain the chart every day, eventually the price will close below this significant upward trend. To a technician, this is a signal that the trend of the stock price has shifted from upwards to sideways, or possibly downwards.

Bruce Kamich, Financial Times

In Chapter 8, we learned that the market trend and the sector trends are the savvy macrowave investor's very best friends. In that chapter, we also took a rather cursory stab at using price charts to illustrate the three basic trending patterns: up, down, and sideways in a trading range. Let's look at the use of "price chart patterns" for trend tracking a little more closely now.

When analyzing the trend of the broad market, an individual sector, or a specific stock, the crucial first step is to look at its price chart. For example, for the broad market, you can look at the price chart of SPY—the exchange-traded fund for the S&P 500, or QQQ, the ETF for the Nasdaq 100 Index. Similarly, for the individual sectors, you can look at the price charts of SMH for semiconductors, BBH for biotechnology, or PPH for pharmaceuticals.

Figure 14-1 illustrates the price chart for SPY. From Figure 14-1, we can see that the up trend consists of a series of ascending peaks and troughs. Note that

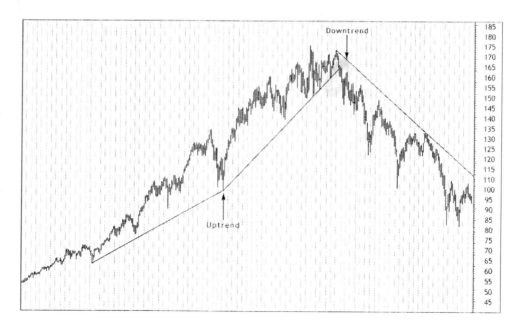

Figure 14-1   The broad market trending up, then down.

prices are making higher highs and higher lows, with pullbacks along the way up. This is precisely the type of market you would be looking to buy into (or "go long"). Note also in the figure, that I have drawn a "trend line" beneath the lows of the up trend. This serves as a "support" line of the up trend.

Now take a look at the down trend illustrated in the same figure. You can see that a down trend is a series of descending peaks and troughs, with prices making lower lows and lower highs along the way down. This is the type of market you would look to sell out of or "go short." A trend line is drawn on top of the highs of the down trend to serve as a resistance line of the down trend.

Now let's switch gears and see how this works for a specific stock rather than the broad market. Take a look at Figure 14-2. It illustrates the trend of Coca-Cola, with the stock symbol KO.

Note in the figure that Coke is trading sideways in a trading range during the period. Note further that the sideways trend is defined by a series of horizontal peaks and troughs, with prices moving back and forth in a horizontal "channel." Finally, note the trend lines are drawn across the top of the highs of the channel, which serves as a price resistance line, and beneath the lows of the bottom of the channel, which serves as price support.

Figure 14-2 Coca-Cola trading sideways in a trading range.

According to the Third Golden Rule of Macrowave Investing, it's best to stay out of such a sideways market and in cash. The underlying logic of such a neutral position is that the intelligent speculator is better off waiting for the trend to declare itself rather than trying to guess whether the eventual trend will turn up or down.

Note, however, that some more aggressive short-term traders will pursue a buy low, sell high strategy. That is, they will buy low as prices approach the bottom of the channel, and then sell, or go short, as prices approach the top of the channel. That's fine if you are an experienced trader. But understand that you can get absolutely slaughtered trying such a channeling strategy if the market starts trending down and you don't realize the trend has shifted.

Key Point #3: Some Common Chart Patterns Can Be Helpful

> Generally, to reverse a strong long-term downward trend, the market needs to find a Support level, rally a bit and then come back to test that Support level, forming what we like to call a "W-shaped double bottom." So, assuming the Nasdaq doesn't break below the April lows. . . , this short-term setback might be, in fact, good news for the longer term and make a base that we can build on to get a new bull market going later in the year.
>
> *Nick Glydon, Sunday Business* (London)

When you look at a price chart, don't limit yourself to simply trying to spot the general trend and trend lines. Instead, also keep your eyes open for some very telltale patterns that historically have had some nice predictive powers for determining a reversal or continuation of the current trend. Some of the more familiar of these patterns include the head and shoulders top or bottom, the double top or double bottom, and the cup-with-handle and saucer formations.

The Head and Shoulders Top or Bottom

Figure 14-3 illustrates a typical "head and shoulders top" for the stock of the utility company Consolidated Edison. This is a very bearish picture of a stock that has met some heavy resistance, meekly tried to break through it, and broken down with little conviction. When you see a head and shoulders top forming, it's usually a very bad sign, for the stock is almost certainly headed for the down side. Conversely, a "head and shoulders bottom" can be very bullish.

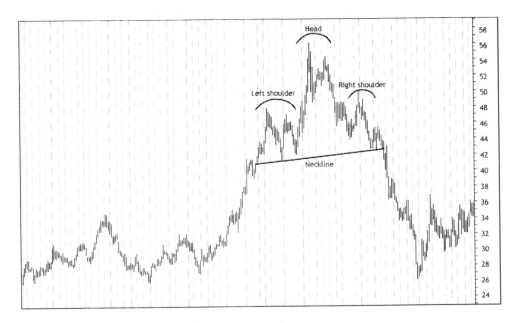

Figure 14-3   A bearish head and shoulders top for Consolidated Edison.

The Double Top or Double Bottom

Figure 14-4 illustrates a similarly bearish "double top" for the Nasdaq Composite Index along with a bullish "double bottom" for Microsoft.

The Nasdaq's double top is simply a variation on the head and shoulders theme. Behaviorally, once a stock or index has taken a crack at breaking through resistance twice and failed, buyers are likely to give up. Conversely, when we see a double bottom pattern such as is illustrated for Microsoft in the lower portion of Figure 14-4, prospects are bullish because it indicates that support is holding.

The Cup-with-Handle Formation

We've touched briefly on this pattern in Chapter 12 in our discussion of the buy high, sell higher philosophy of stock picking. This pattern is illustrated in Figure 14-5 for the stock of Autodesk, along with an example of a gap down in price. You can see from the figure why it's called a "cup with handle."

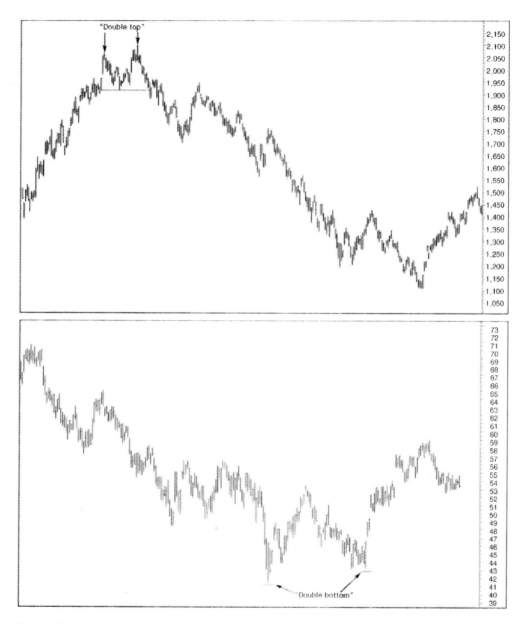

Figure 14-4   A bearish double top and bullish double bottom.

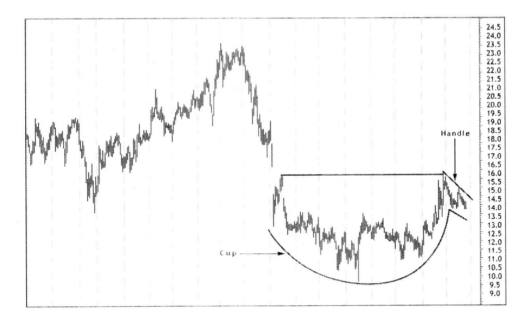

Figure 14-5 The cup with handle.

The underlying behavioral idea behind the cup (also called a saucer) is that the stock or sector is laying a foundation for a future runup. At this point in the stock price's movement, investors don't have enough conviction to bid the stock up quickly. But they do have enough confidence in the stock not to cut and run. That confidence allows the stock to put in a nice base over a longer period of time, anywhere from 7 to 65 weeks. It will be from this base which the stock can hopefully take off or "break out."

Note further that the trigger for such a break out may be the emergence of a "handle" on the cup that has a slight *downward* drift. This downward-drifting handle reflects the last selling pressure that will come from the people who bought the stock at the old high. It represents the final layer of resistance the stock must break through to make its breakout. If the stock overcomes this final resistance, it's on its way up!

Key Point #4: Volume Speaks Volumes

There seems to be heavy accumulation of Urethane's shares in recent days, and they have been rising on increasing volume—a very positive signal. Our charts indicate that the stock could rise as high as 22 over the short-term.

Mark Leibovit, BusinessWeek

Once you've used a price chart to identify the trend and reviewed the basic chart pattern, you can begin to look more closely at the *volume* of the shares traded as well as various volume indicators. What you are looking for is some confirmation of the prevailing trend or some signal of an impending reversal of the trend. Specifically, you will find a confirmation of either an up trend or down trend *if the volume of shares being traded is increasing in the direction of the trend*. This is illustrated in Figure 14-6, which includes "volume bars" at the bottom of the chart to accompany the corresponding price bars in the top of the chart for the stock price of Sara Lee.

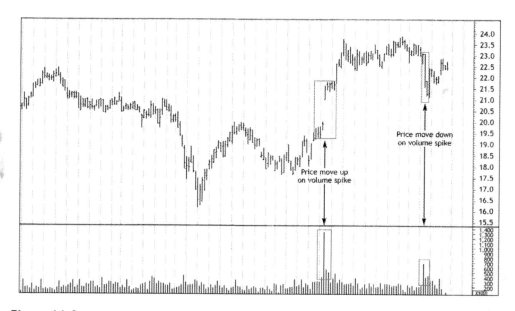

Figure 14-6   Raw volume pointing the way for Sara Lee.

Note in the figure how the volume of shares traded "spiked" at the beginning of the stock's up trend and then showed increasing volume. Note also the volume spike that triggered the down trend.

On Balance Volume, Accumulation versus Distribution

Beyond mere raw volume, there are also a variety of volume indicators that give us further insight into the strength of the price trend. By far and away, my favorite is "On Balance Volume (OBV)."

This powerful indicator was originally developed by the legendary Joseph Granville. He was looking for an early warning system that the big mutual funds and institutional buyers might be piling into a stock—or bailing out. It is precisely these large buyers that account for over 70 percent of a stock price's movement up or down, and their buying habits are therefore very important to track.

Granville's idea was elegantly simple: He figured that if more volume was going into a stock on the days that its price was going up than on the days the price was falling, the stock must be under "accumulation" by the Big Buyers, and that would be very bullish. Of course, just the opposite is true when the stock is under "distribution." That's when volume is higher on down days than up.

Now here's the punchline! The savvy macrowave investor tracks On Balance Volume very closely and *never* buys a stock that is under distribution and *never* shorts a stock that is under accumulation. Respect these two rules and you will go a long way toward protecting your portfolio.

Key Point #5: Moving Averages Clarify the Trend!

> Last night after the close, officials at Novellus Systems (NVLS) backed previous fourth-quarter earnings estimates of 11 cents per share. The firm also raised its booking projection for the reporting period. NVLS shares are subsequently enjoying a rally of eight percent today. Since bottoming in early October, the stock has risen 90 percent. This impressive rally has taken the stock above its 10-week and 20-week moving averages, which have recently completed a bullish crossover.
>
> *Schaeffer's "Herd" on the Street*

Technical analysts often use a set of "simple moving averages (SMAs)" to help time their entries and exits into the market. The set of moving averages typically includes three or four time periods, with the 10-day, 20-day, 50-day, and 200-day being commonly calculated SMAs. Such *moving averages are used to clarify and amplify the direction of a trend and smooth out the "noise" that arises from price and volume fluctuations.*

To calculate a 10-day SMA, for example, a computer simply adds the closing prices for the past 10 days, divides by 10, and plots that number on a chart. Then, as the stock price moves forward in time, the computer drops the oldest closing price and adds the most recent, again divides by 10, and plots that number. This process continues, forming an "SMA line." If a stock is moving up in price, so, too, will its moving average lines.

Figure 14-7 illustrates the movements of the 10-day, 20-day, and 50-day SMAs for the stock of Wellpoint Health.

In the figure, note the points where the shorter-term averages cross over the longer-term averages. Technical analysts love to use such "crossovers" to generate buy and sell signals.

In particular, when the shorter-period SMAs begin to cross above the longer-period moving averages, the price trend is on its way up. This is a bullish buy signal. On the other hand, when the shorter-period moving averages cross *below* the longer-term moving averages, this generates a sell signal, as the trend is turning down.

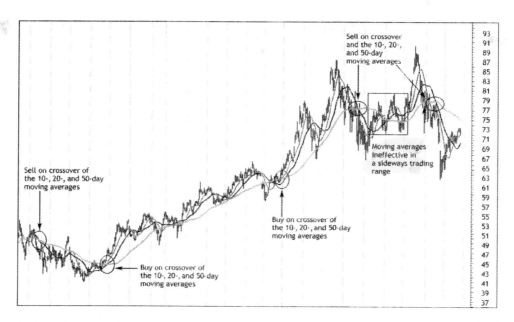

Figure 14-7 Moving average crossovers generating buy and sell signals.

Note how these entry and exit crossover points play out in the chart. As you study them, try to think intuitively as to why these moving averages behave the way they do relative to one another.

Key Point #6: The Signals of Momentum Indicators

We are witnessing a clear up trend in progress with higher tops and bottoms being made. RSI, has reached the overbought zone. This indicates that a correction downwards is due. However, it could remain in the overbought zone for a while before the correction actually starts. In strong markets, RSI remains in an overbought situation for quite a while before turning downwards.

MACD cross over did not take place last week and therefore the danger of prices going downwards remains less. MACD is comfortably above the zero line in the indicator denoting a positive momentum again. Even if prices correct downwards next week, and the MACD remains above zero level there is no cause to worry.

Global News Wire

Various "momentum indicators" like the RSI oscillator and the Moving Average Convergence/Divergence (MACD) indicator can be used along with moving average analysis to confirm the current trend, warn of an impending stall, or signal a trend reversal. Such momentum indicators are likewise helpful in timing one's entries and exits from the market.

The RSI Oscillator

The Relative Strength Index (RSI) is in a general class of momentum indicators known as "oscillators." It measures the relative price strength of a stock, sector, or market index *against itself*. It does so by taking a general length of time (for example, 14 days) and measuring the average price advances to declines over that period. The result is an indicator that quite literally "oscillates" between 0 and 100.

When the RSI reads above 70, technical analysts consider the stock to be in the kind of overbought condition we talked about in key point number 1. In contrast, when the RSI is under 30, the stock is oversold. Moreover, a reading turning up above 30 is considered bullish and a buy signal, while a reading turning down below 70 is considered bearish and a sell signal.

Moving Average Convergence/Divergence (MACD)

The "Moving Average Convergence/Divergence (MACD)" is a very complicated indicator. It uses an average of the differences of two moving averages called the "MACD line" together with an exponential moving average of the MACD line called the "signal line."

While I know that may all sound like gobbledygook to the mathematically challenged, don't worry about it! All you have to know is that when the MACD line crosses above its "trigger line," it's a buy signal while a MACD line crossing below its signal line is a sell signal.

This use of technical indictors like OBV, the RSI, and the MACD to improve the timing of one's market entries and exits is illustrated in Figure 14-8. Please study this figure closely. Notice how the changes in the trend of each of these RSI, OBV, and MACD indicators did an excellent job in signaling the changes in trend in the Nasdaq price chart.

If your eyes are starting to glaze over with all of this discussion, not to worry. I will show you soon how to use this somewhat complicated information in a very easy-to-use and simple technical screen. So please be patient! We've got one more set of indicators to go.

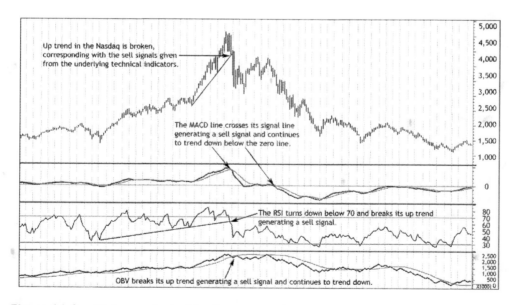

Figure 14-8   Using technical indicators to time entries and exits.

Key Point #7: Au Contrarian! The Logic of Market Sentiment

> Market pundits view investor sentiment as a contrarian indicator because if a person is willing to tell a survey they are bearish, they have likely already sold.
>
> The latest Investors Intelligence data put bears at 39 percent and bulls at 31 percent. The S&P Investment Policy Committee said that is the most bears versus bulls seen since September 2001.
>
> Meanwhile, the committee cautioned that while sentiment readings are "again" giving investors hope that a bottom is near, "it is always wise to wait for strong price and volume numbers before turning bullish."
>
> *Marketwatch.com*

Sentiment indicators measure exactly what the name implies, the sentiment or overall "mood" of the majority of investors in the market. And here's the most important point: Sentiment indicators should be looked at with a *contrarian* view! That is, if the majority of investors are bullish, most likely it is time to become bearish! And if a majority of investors are bearish, it's time to be a bull!

If we look once again at the underlying psychology of the market and the resultant human behavior, this contrarian conclusion makes eminent good sense. Just think about it this way: If too many people are already bulls, there won't be enough cash still sitting on the sidelines to continue to propel the market up! Conversely, if there are a lot of bears sitting on the sidelines in cash, that's money that could eventually be pumped into the market. Got it?

Here, then, are several useful indicators that can be regularly found in *Barron's* magazine or *Investor's Business Daily* newspaper. They are well worth paying attention to.

Investors Intelligence and the VIX

Investors Intelligence is a subscription newsletter service. It compiles three numbers on a weekly basis that are closely watched on Wall Street: percent bulls, percent bears, and the percent of those that are bullish, but expecting a short-term correction. Bullish readings over 55 percent are viewed as too much optimism, and should be viewed as a bearish sign. Bearish readings under 35 percent represent too much pessimism, and should be viewed as a bullish sign.

The Market Volatility Index (VIX) is a second contrarian indicator. It measures the sentiment of options traders by gauging the level of volatility in the prices of options traded on stocks in the S&P 100 Index.

When the VIX is trending up, that's usually a bearish sign, and when it's trending down, that's a bullish sign. In addition, relatively high readings in the VIX should be viewed as too much pessimism and likewise a bullish sign. That's because such high readings usually indicate an intense *panic* in the markets and typically, after a wave of panic selling, the market recovers.

In contrast, relatively low readings should be viewed as too much optimism and as a bearish sign. That is because complacent investors are likely to be whopped upside the head by a wave of selling triggered by the smart money, which senses that there isn't much cash left on the sidelines to sustain the rally.

Figure 14-9 contrasts the movements of the weekly VIX versus that of the weekly S&P 500. Note how the broad market moves in the opposite direction of the VIX-ergo; it's a contrarian indicator.

Key Point #8: Use a Technical Screen!

Most investors will probably never use such esoteric technical tools. But even novice stock watchers should be aware of the basics of technical analysis.

Riverside Press Enterprise

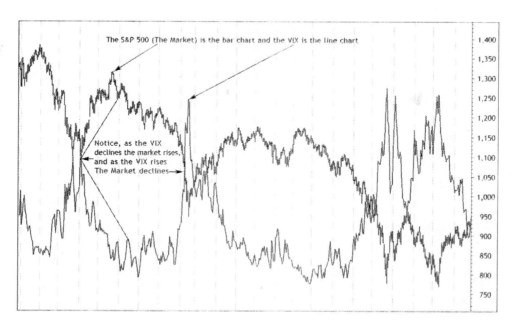

Figure 14-9   The vexatious and contrarian VIX.

Well, you've really done a good job plowing through all of that technical analysis information. I know it's all a bit complicated. But my philosophy here is to simply give you an overview of the technical analyst's tools and the underlying investor psychology as a way of preparing to conduct your own, much more simple technical screens.

As with fundamental analysis, the savvy macrowave investor does *not* have to master all of the techniques of technical analysis. Rather, all you have to do is simply *learn how to apply some basic technical analysis screens.*

As for how you can do this, there are a relatively large number of technical screening services available on the Internet to assist you. One slightly more labor-intensive option is to go to a site like www.bigcharts.com and generate your own technical charts and indicators. (I will show you how to do this in several exercises at the end of this chapter.)

The second option, which is much faster and much less labor-intensive, is to use a paid subscription site like www.investors.com, www.wallstreetcity.com, or my favorite, www.marketedge.com.

For example, at the Market Edge site, you can just type a stock symbol into a box and out will pop a very detailed technical analysis screen, complete with a buy, short, or avoid signal. Such a technical screen, which has been edited slightly for length, is illustrated in Table 14-1 for the stock of IBM. The neat thing about this table is that we can take a walk through it and find a match for many of the technical tools and indicators we discussed earlier in the chapter.

The table begins under the heading "Trading Activity" with a summary of the close, open, change, high, low, and volume for that trading day for IBM. For starters, compare the daily volume in the upper-right-hand portion of the table to the "Ave Volume" or Average Volume in the middle column lower in the chart. In this case, the day's volume was slightly below the average volume as the stock fell. It would have been a much more worrisome sign if the stock had fallen on significantly above-average volume.

Note also the underlined Web link "Technical Terms Explained" in the upper-right-hand corner of the table. I will ask you to explore this link in an exercise at the end of the chapter. That said, please now take a look under the "Opinion" heading. You can see that Market Edge rates IBM "long," or a buy. Note also that the "Score," "C-Rate," and "Power Rating" are all *proprietary indicators* that I will have you read more about in an exercise below.

Next take a look at the "Recommendation" box. We see that the stock is a buy but Market Edge is warning that the stock is overbought and that you should wait for a pullback to buy the stock. Do these terms sound familiar to you from key point number 1?

One row farther down, Market Edge elaborates on its recommendation for IBM in the "Comments" section, which provides a summary of the key

Table 14-1   Market Edge's "Second Opinion" of IBM

Second Opinion® - INTL BUSINESS MACHIN (IBM)
Exchange: NYSE
• In S&P 500

Trading Activity				Technical Terms Explained	
Close	84.43	Change	-0.47	Volume(00)	89902
Open	83.95	High	85.17	Low	83.80

Opinion					
Opinion	LONG	Opinion Date	10/23/02	Opinion Price	74.49
Score	0	C-Rate	17.8	Power Rating	82

Recommendation
Stock is a Buy; Overbought; Wait for pullback to initiate new position.

Comments
Moving Average Convergence/Divergence (MACD) indicates a Bullish Trend.
Chart pattern indicates a Strong Upward Trend.
Relative Strength is Bullish.
Up/Down volume pattern indicates that the stock is under Accumulation.
The 50 day Moving Average is rising which is Bullish.
The 200 day Moving Average is falling which is Bearish.
Price is Under Support of 85.98 which is Bearish.
Stochastics indicate stock is Overbought.

Price Analysis				Volume Analysis			Technical Analysis	
Yr. High			126.39	Ave Volume(00)	100448		Alpha	0.00
Yr. Low			54.01	MO Chg.(%)		-19.4	Beta	1.20
MO Chg.(%)			13.2					
Trend Line Resistance			N/A	U/D Ratio		1.0	MACD ST	BL
Trend Line Support			85.9	U/D Slope		UP	MACD LT	BL
Resistance Range		84.92-85.17					STO(Fast %K)	90
Support Range		77.84-79.08		On Balance Volume		BL	STO(Slow %K)	95
SELL STOP			76.2	Positive OBV		BR	50-Day R.S.	1.12
Volatility(%)			2.7	Negative OBV			Wilders RSI	78
Position			93				OBOS	-1
ADXR			30	Money Flow(MF)		46	B.BANDS	11
MA	Price	%	Slope	MF Slope		DOWN	RSV	38
10 Day	80.41	105	UP					
21 Day	79.65	106	UP					
50 Day	70.95	119	UP					
200 Day	80.41	105	DOWN					

indicators. You can see how this chapter has prepared you very well to understand these comments as they refer to our by-now-familiar terms like "MACD," "Chart Pattern," "Relative Strength," "Moving Average," and "Support." Note also that the Comments make reference to the "stochastics," indicating that the stock is overbought, just as we discussed in key point number 6.

The remainder of Table 14-1 provides some additional information about the price and volume action of the stock as well as a more detailed summary of the relative bullishness and bearishness of the technical indicators. Note how the

10-day, 21-day, and 50-day moving averages are all stacked up nicely above one another, indicating a nice upward trend—but that the 200-day average is still down and bearish.

Note also that in the table, there are many of the terms you are now familiar with like the MACD and On Balance Volume, while "STO" refers to the oscillators we discussed. However, there are also a number of terms that we did not discuss like beta, money flow, and B. Bands, which is shorthand for Bollinger Bands. I will urge you to more fully acquaint yourself with these terms in the Market Edge scorecard in some of the exercises below. I will also explain more fully about the beta measure in our next chapter on risk management.

In the meantime, the *broader* point of the table is that by using a technical screen like that of Market Edge or *Investor's Business Daily*, you can quickly assess the technical strength or weakness of a stock or sector. The savvy macrowave investor never buys a technically weak stock and never shorts a technically strong one. To do so would be to gamble against the odds rather than to intelligently speculate.

Key Point #9: Some Tools Work Better Than Others, Depending on the Market Trend

> Before rushing to buy or sell a stock on the basis of one [technical] signal, you must use a number of them. . . . You'd have to see the same signal in a number of indicators. For instance, if price is going up, it should be confirmed by volume. If prices are going up, but volume is going down, that could tell you there is insufficient strength. It might be best to ignore a buy signal that appears in the price trend but not in the volume trend.
>
> *The Hamilton Spectator*

As a final and very important point about technical analysis, it is a simple fact of life that some of its tools and indicators work better—and some work much worse—when the market is trending up or down rather than trading sideways.

For example, during a sideways market, indicators of overbought and oversold conditions perform very well. However, during a strong upward trend of the market, technical analysis will often flash false signals of an "overbought" condition. These false signals will discourage entry and may prompt an over-early exit from a profitable stock.

Similarly, in a downward-trending market, technical "oversold" readings may flash a false buy signal. In such a case, you might buy the stock at what you think is a bargain price. Then you watch it continue to fall with the downward trend.

Figure 14-10 illustrates some of the pitfalls of using the wrong technical indicators for given market conditions. Please study these charts well before moving on to the questions and exercises at the end of this chapter.

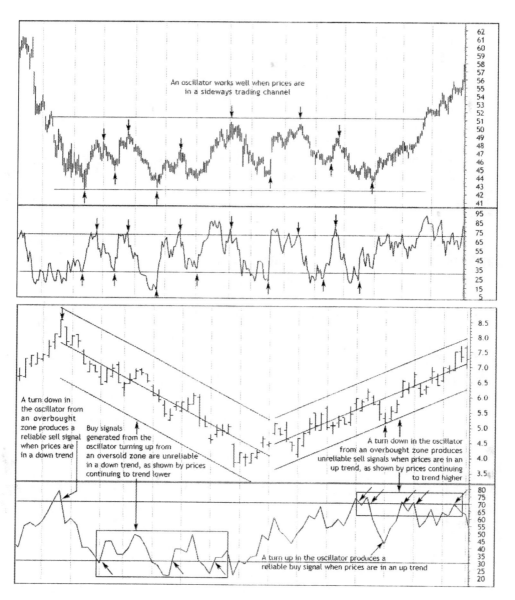

Figure 14-10   When bad things happen to good technical indicators.

QUESTIONS

1. The savvy macrowave investor uses technical analysis on a daily basis to do what?

2. Name some of the most common and useful terms of technical analysis.

3. Technical analysis has its roots in underlying investor psychology and human behavior. Why is this important?

4. What is the crucial first step in analyzing the trend of the broad market, an individual sector, or a specific stock? By taking this first step what are we able to accomplish?

5. If you look at a price chart and see a series of ascending peaks and troughs characterized by prices that are making higher highs and higher lows, what kind of trend are you observing?

6. When you see a double top chart pattern, is this bullish or bearish? What is the underlying behavioral explanation for this pattern?

7. Once the technical analyst has used the price chart to identify the trend and reviewed the basic chart pattern, the analyst typically does what next? Why?

8. If the On Balance Volume indicator indicates that a stock is under "distribution," is that bullish or bearish?

9. Moving averages are used to clarify and amplify the direction of a trend. How can they do that?

10. When the technical analyst sees a shorter-period moving average begin to cross above a longer-period moving average, what does that say about the price trend and is this a bullish buy signal or a bearish sell signal?

11. The RSI oscillator and the Moving Average Convergence/ Divergence indicator are what kind of indicators? How can they be used?

12. If the majority of investors are bullish, most likely it is time for you to become what? Why is this so?

13. I do not expect any of you reading this book to become technical analysts. I do, however, expect you to be able to do what after reading this chapter?

14. Technical analysis is often used to uncover both overbought and oversold conditions. In which kind of market are these signals likely to be more valuable, a sideways market or an upward-trending market?

EXERCISES

1. At the time of this writing, www.prophet.net was a free Web site that required registration. It's offered free at least in part because they hope you will subscribe for the premier services. At any rate, it's a site with very powerful tools. Go to it now and consider filling out the free registration. Then, log on to the site and go to the "Java Charts" link. Look for the link offering instructions on how to use the site. Click on the link and read the instructions in preparation for the next exercise.

2. Go to the "Java Charts" link at www.prophet.net and type in the symbol *QQQ* for the Nasdaq 100. Hit Go and study the price chart. Now use the feature that allows you to draw "trend lines" on the chart and draw in the various trends for QQQ over the one-year period. Look for any familiar chart patterns like a double top or bottom that preceded a change in trend. Use this feature to examine other stocks for other time periods. The goal is to become familiar with spotting trends and drawing trend lines.

3. Visit www.stockcharts.com. This is a paid subscription site but, at the time of this writing, it had some free features. Start with the link "Chart School." Spend some time at this link reading up on some of the myriad of chart patterns that technical analysts use. These include "Reversal Patterns" that signify a change in trend like the "Double Bottom" we discussed and the "Head and Shoulders Top" as well as "Continuation Patterns" like the "Cup with Handle" and various "Flags" and "Pennants." This exercise will better familiarize yourself with the whole idea of chart analysis.

4. At www.stockcharts.com, click on the "Free Charts" link. Then find one of the "Free Charting Tools" called "Technical Scans." In the "Select a Scan Summary" box, click on the "Technical Indicator Scans" option. Then, try any one of a number of scans such as "Bullish MACD Crossovers," "Gap Ups," and so on. The goal here is to put our theoretical discussion of the various technical indicators into real practice on real stocks.

5. Visit www.marketedge.com and take a cruise around the Web site. Be sure to read about "Second Opinion Performance." It provides a discussion of the profit performance of its stock picks. Please also consider trying a free trial subscription as Market Edge may eventually become a valuable tool when you conduct your stock screens.

6. You can only do this exercise if you have become a trial subscriber to Market Edge. If you have, please log on to the site and go to the "Stocks" link. Then type in the stock symbol for IBM and compare it to Table 14-1 in the book. Note how the table is different for the different time period in which you are looking at the stock. Technical analysis provides ever-changing patterns.

7. As a continuation of exercise number 6, click on the link "Technical Terms Explained" that appears in the upper-right-hand corner of the Second Opinion report for IBM. This link will take you to a very detailed explanation of each of the components of the Market Edge scorecard. I *strongly* urge you to spend a good bit of time systematically working your way through all of the various definitions. It will be time very well spent, especially if you decide to use Market Edge as part of your regular technical screening activity.

8. The use of momentum indicators and moving averages can be enhanced by using Bollinger Bands. These are volatility bands that are placed 2 standard deviations above and below a 20-period simple moving average of a market or securities price. To read more about Bollinger Bands, go to my Web site at www.peternavarro.com, click on the "Macrowave University" link, and read the article "Bollinger Band and Exponential Moving Average Primer." As you do so, also note the difference between the Simple Moving Average (SMA) and the Exponential Moving Average (EMA).

9. After you finish reading the article in exercise number 8, please go to www.bigcharts.com and use the "Interactive Charting" link to graph some Bollinger Bands and the 3-line EMA for your favorite stock. (You'll find the EMA in the "Moving Averages" box and the Bollinger Bands in the "Upper Indicators" boxes in the "Indicators" link.)

10. Take a spin around www.investorsintelligence.com and the related site www.financialnewsletters.com to learn a bit more about the origins of the *Investor's Intelligence* sentiment indicator. You will see that it dates all the way back to 1963 and has had a pretty good track record.

11. Go to the "ProSearch" link at www.wallstreetcity.com and click on the free "Quick Search." Click on "All Stocks" in the "Quick Search" Box and go to "Technical Analysis." Then use the feature to run some "breakout" searches based on movements in the MACD, Moving Averages, and Stochastics. Jot down some of the names of these stocks and then go back to www.marketedge.com. Type in the names of these stocks in the "Second

Opinion" stock box and compare the results of Wall Street City and Market Edge.

12. Visit www.channelingstocks.com to view a Web site that offers a very seductive but dangerous promise for a pretty hefty monthly free. I offer up this site as a warning *not* to get hooked into expensive sites that may wind up losing you more money than they make you. The obvious problem with a site like this is that "channeling" strategies may work pretty well in a sideways market but are likely to fail miserably in a downward-trending market. So go ahead and read some of the information on the site, including the sappy "testimonials," just to get a flavor of the kind of "marketing pitch" you will encounter on the Web. Remember, it's caveat emptor: Buyer beware!

PART FIVE

BUYING, SELLING, AND SHORTING STOCKS

Stage Four: The savvy macrowave investor uses solid risk management, money management, and trade management tools together with direct access investing to strategically enter and exit positions so as to cut losses and let profits run.

Chapter 15

MANAGING YOUR RISK

The biggest risk is not taking one.

AIG Insurance

The dumbest risk is taking a big one for the prospect of a little reward.

Ron Vara

Managing your risk and protecting your trading capital are the two very most important keys to successful long-term investing. There are some great stock pickers who still blow up simply because they don't know how to manage either their money or their risk. That's why *before* you actually go about the risky business of investing your money in speculative stocks, you must first come to better understand the nature of risk and then arm yourself with a set of very basic risk management, money management, and trade management rules. In this chapter, we'll tackle the risk issue. In Chapter 16, it will be money management's turn. Then in Chapter 17, we discuss trade management.

Key Macrowave Points

1. Because risk exists, there is also the possibility of reward. The savvy macrowave investor uses an awareness of the four dynamic factors to continually monitor risk and exploit its many opportunities.

2. Dimensions of risk include market risk, sector risk, and company risk. The savvy macrowave investor reduces *market risk* by investing with the trend, *sector risk* by buying into strong sectors and shorting weak sectors, and *company risk* by "basket trading."

3. Sources of risk range from credit risk, country risk, and exchange rate risk to interest rate risk, liquidity risk, political risk, and regulatory risk.

4. Each of us is "risk averse," but there are wide differences among us. Every savvy macrowave investor must choose a level of acceptable risk and seek rewards accordingly—but do so within the

confines of a strict reward-to-risk ratio. The savvy macrowave investor never enters into an investment unless the risk/reward ratio is favorable.

5. The beta tells us how risky a stock is relative to the broad market. The Sharpe ratio exposes the difference between the "lucky gambler" who may win by assuming excessive risk and the successful speculator who minimizes risk for a given level of reward.

6. The traditional investor is wrongly taught that a well-diversified portfolio includes stocks from *many* different sectors at *all* times. In contrast, the savvy macrowave investor focuses on just a *few* sectors at any *one* time and regularly changes sectors according to the "patterns of sector rotation."

7. The savvy macrowave investor embraces risk management rules: Don't put all your eggs in one basket. Never bet the farm. When in doubt, go flat. Do your research.

Key Point #1: Risk Represents Both Danger and Opportunity

Understanding risk and reward is at the very heart of trading but few traders formally assess these relationships. One of the first steps to market survival is to understand how risk is defined by the potential downside of any planned trade or investment. What could go up could also go down.

Daryl Guppy, Global News Wire

You can hurt yourself in the shower just as badly as in a car. But the chances of injury in the shower are significantly less than that of in a car. That makes cars more risky than showers.

So, too, in a stock market context, you can lose just as much money in a blue chip stock as you can with a dot-com high-flyer. But the chances of GE stock plummeting are a lot lower than Amazon's. That means you should expect a higher rate of return and capital appreciation when you plunk your money down on Amazon than when you buy GE shares. The greater the risk, the greater should be your reward!

In fact, without risk, there would be no reward in the stock market. That's why, as the Chinese symbol for crisis conveys, risk represents both danger and opportunity. The danger comes from the possibility that you will lose money on the stocks you buy or short. The opportunity comes from the reward you receive if you speculate in the right direction.

The savvy macrowave investor monitors the flow of information from the four dynamic factors precisely because these factors are the primary source of volatility in the market, making them the vehicle that transports risk to the investing table.

Key Point #2: The Three Dimensions of Risk

The stock market does not like instability.

Joel Naroff

The savvy macrowave investor visualizes risk in three dimensions: market risk, sector risk, and company risk—and follows the Three Golden Rules of Macrowave Investing accordingly.

Market risk revolves around the basic question: Is the stock market going up, down, or sideways? It is the purest kind of macrowave risk because, if we've learned anything so far, it is that market trends are, by and large, determined by emerging macroeconomic news and conditions about recession, inflation, war, terrorism, rising interest rates, and so on. *The savvy macrowave investor greatly reduces market risk by always investing in the same direction as the market trend*—long in an upward trend, short in a downward trend, out of the market in a sideways movement.

As for *sector risk*, it comes from any kind of event that affects a specific industry or sector. For example, when the OPEC oil cartel announces an increase in oil prices and a cutback in production quotas, fuel-intensive sectors like the airlines, autos, and utilities are all exposed to increased energy cost risk that can translate into lower profits and stock prices. Similarly, when the Fed raises interest rates, banks, brokerage firms, and mortgage processors suffer. *The savvy macrowave investor reduces sector risk by only buying stocks in strong sectors and shorting weak stocks in weak sectors*.

Note also that sector risk typically accounts for at least 50 percent and, perhaps as much as 80 percent of an individual stock price's movement. That's why the savvy macrowave investor is very careful to diversify *first* by *sector* rather than by company. In this regard, buying five different stocks in the same sector does *not* diversify sector risk.

As for *company risk*, it may involve *management* risk—the chief operating officer is discovered to have looted the company. It might involve *regulatory* risk—Genentech gets a favorable decision on a key patent. It might involve an exogenous shock like a storm—and an Exxon oil tanker runs aground. It might even involve unfavorable news coverage—*Barron's* does an exposé on the flawed business model of J2 Global Communications.

One way to minimize company risk is to trade at the sector level. For example, instead of buying Merck or Pfizer, you can buy the pharmaceutical exchange-traded fund PPH. The preferred approach for the savvy macrowave investor to reduce company risk is, however, to "*basket trade.*" If you find a strong sector to buy stocks in, buy the top two to four stocks. Exit *all* of the positions if the investment goes against you and cut your losses. If the trade goes in your direction, only exit one or more of the stocks that perform least well over time while maintaining or increasing positions in the others.

Key Point #3: The Myriad Sources of Risk

Citigroup and JP Morgan Chase, two of the biggest lenders, have already written off millions of dollars in bad debts from the Argentina crisis this year. The economic woes in Latin America have been a strong factor in the slide of world stock markets.

Africa News

When something new happens that is good or bad in the economic, political, or regulatory arena, that's called "event risk." It's a broad umbrella term for all of the good and bad things that can happen to strong and weak stocks and strong and weak sectors as well as to the broader market. The following is a useful taxonomy of some of the different sources of risk:

- *Credit risk.* This is a type of company risk. Virtually every company borrows money to undertake capital improvements and to manage their cash flow. From a lender's point of view, the perennial question is whether the company will be able to pay the loan back. The bigger the concern, the bigger the credit risk. Such risk not only affects a company's bond rating but its stock price as well.

- *Country risk.* When Argentina or Brazil defaults on loans, the stock prices of companies like Citigroup which made those loans suffer. This suffering can spread to the entire financial sector and even the broader market.

- *Exchange rate risk.* If McDonald's sells a bunch of burgers to Muscovites and the Russian ruble falls, the corporation takes a hit. This is because when McDonald's goes to repatriate its profits back to the United States, it has to exchange weak rubles for strong dollars, shrinking its effective profits. That's exchange rate risk. So if you are buying the stock of a company with substantial operations abroad, it's useful to know whether they hedge such risk.

- *Interest rate risk.* We've talked a lot about how when the Federal Reserve raises or lowers rates it ripples through interest rate–sensitive sectors like banking and brokerage as well as the broader market so you know all about this one.

- *Liquidity risk.* This is a nasty little problem for a lot of stocks. There simply are not a lot of shares of some companies that are traded on the market. This means that when it comes time to get out of the stock, it may be difficult to do so at a decent price. That's because with a stock that trades in low volume or is "illiquid," the spread between the "ask price" that you want to sell for and the "bid price" that someone might be willing to buy the stock for is typically large. In order to sell, you may have to settle for the much lower bid. And that costs you money. Never trade in illiquid stocks! *If the average daily volume is below 300,000 shares, forget about it!*

- *Political risk.* Companies that do business in foreign countries have to worry about everything from typhoons and famine to military coups and terrorism. If you have bought the stock of one of those companies, you have to worry about these things too.

- *Regulatory risk.* The government giveth, with favorable tariffs to steel companies, lucrative subsidies to the housing industry, or patent protection for drug companies. It also taketh away, with antitrust proceedings against a software monopoly, new taxes on Internet commerce, or price controls on "Big Pharma" (the pharmaceutical sector). The savvy macrowave investor has a keen awareness of companies and sectors that are exposed to higher levels of regulatory risk.

Key Point #4: The Reward-to-Risk Ratio

On Tuesday, Morgan Stanley downgraded shares of the beer behemoth to "equal-weight" from "overweight." While acknowledging that "everything is playing right" for Anheuser-Busch, the brokerage also feels that its risk-reward tradeoff seems largely discounted at current levels.

Marketwatch.com

Some people love to take risks, and they jump out of airplanes and ride motorcycles. Others who are more "risk averse" are quite content to play golf or fish. So, too, is it with stock market investors.

Some people like to invest in highly volatile tech stocks looking for a big profit while willing to incur a heavier loss. But others prefer the relative safety of blue chip stocks, quite willing to sacrifice the possibility of a big gain in exchange for a lesser chance of a big loss.

While each person must look into his or her heart—and perhaps stomach—to determine just how much risk he or she wants to bear, *all* savvy macrowave investors follow one very important rule: They never risk more money on an investment than they can possibly make. This is the "reward-to-risk ratio," and it is one of the most important concepts in macrowave investing.

The savvy macrowave investor *never* enters into an investment unless the reward-to-risk ratio is favorable. At a minimum, this means risking no more than one dollar of investment capital for every $3 or more of potential profit. If you follow this rule, you can be wrong in your speculations more than half of the time and still make a profit!

Key Point #5: Some Useful Yardsticks to Measure Risk

> The Sharpe ratio is the brainchild of Nobel laureate William Sharpe, a Stanford University professor. . . . Sharpe's formula measures the extra return investors receive for each unit of risk they take.
>
> *BusinessWeek*

The "Sharpe ratio" is one very useful yardstick to measure risk. It calculates a "risk-adjusted return" on your portfolio based on the volatility of the stocks that you have invested in. The beauty of the Sharpe ratio is that it *exposes the difference between the "lucky gambler" who may win in the markets by assuming excessive risk versus the successful speculator who earns rewards without assuming undue risk.*

In one of the exercises below, I will show you where you can learn more about the Sharpe ratio—and perhaps even calculate that ratio for your own portfolio. You can use the Sharpe ratio to determine whether you are bearing too much risk for the returns you are making.

A second useful measure of risk is a stock's "beta." It measures the level of risk of an individual stock *relative* to the broad market.

Note that you were first introduced to the term in the last chapter. It appeared as part of the technical analysis of IBM performed by Market Edge, as illustrated in Table 14-1. If you were to flip back to that table now, you would see that the beta for IBM is 1.20. But what exactly is this beta measuring?

Put simply, it is measuring how much IBM's stock price is likely to go up if the broad market is moving up and how much it is likely to go down if the market is moving down. In this case, a beta of 1.20 means that IBM's stock price is 20 percent more volatile than the overall market.

In contrast, the stock price of a relatively "safe" water or gas utility might be less than 1.00, say, at 0.8. In this case, the company's stock price would go up 20 percent less when the broad market moves up but it would also go down 20 percent less when the broad market is moving down. In other words, the stock is much less volatile than the broader market and therefore entails relatively lower market risk.

Key Point #6: What Does "Well Diversified" Mean?

To reduce risk, investors should own a cross section of companies with representation in an array of industries.

Capital Investment Services of America

Please don't buy into the bad advice just given. In this regard, the traditional investor is taught that a well-diversified portfolio includes stocks from *many* different sectors at *all* times. In contrast, the savvy macrowave investor focuses on just a *few* sectors at any *one* time.

To the savvy macrowave investor, the traditional investor's strategy of broad "sector allocation" is merely a recipe for very mediocre returns. This is because the traditional investor is always holding, at any one time, numerous weak sectors that are underperforming.

In contrast, the savvy macrowave investor looks for strong sectors to buy in an up market and weak sectors to short in a down market. *That means holding only a few of the best-performing sectors at a time.* Moreover, the savvy macrowave investor regularly changes sectors as the stock market moves through the patterns of sector rotation that we discussed in Chapter 9.

Key Point #7: Some (More) Risk Management Rules

Mr. Stupid, why risk everything on one trade?

Paul Tudor Jones

We've learned in this chapter so far to basket trade, trade only liquid stocks, always pursue a favorable risk/reward ratio, and diversify narrowly by outperforming sectors. The following are just a few more risk management rules that the savvy macrowave investor lives by:

- *Don't put all your eggs in one basket.* Never put more than 10 to 20 percent of your investment capital into any one stock or sector.

- *Never bet the farm.* Never put yourself in a position where you can lose all of your money—or more! That means you must be very careful about trading on "margin." Margin buying allows you to at least double your buying power in the market but it also means that your losses can quickly mount.

- *When in doubt, go flat.* The savvy macrowave investor is very patient. If you are unable to clearly determine the trend, and market risk is very high, the best place for your cash is on the sidelines. That's the risk-basis for the Third Golden Rule of Macrowave Investing: Stay in cash when there is no discernible trend.

- *Do your research.* As the Holiday Inn commercial once said: "The best surprise is no surprise." In an investing context, this means that the more research you do, the less risk you face. But you must do the right kind of research. Here are some of the things every savvy macrowave investor knows:

  - The strong and weak sectors and the strong and weak stocks within them.

  - How and why your stocks move in relation to the four dynamic factors and the three key cycles.

  - The technical characteristics of your stocks: the price chart patterns, the volumes, the support and resistance levels, the moving averages, and the patterns of accumulation and distribution.

  - The fundamentals: earnings growth, price performance, management structure, institutional ownership, and so on.

  - The macroeconomic event and earnings calendars. Don't open a major new stock position before a major economic report unless you are specifically speculating on the direction of the report. Don't buy or short a stock just before its earnings announcement unless you are specifically trading on the earnings news.

QUESTIONS

1. What are two of the very most important keys to successful, long-term investing?

2. Risk represents the chance you will lose what? Because such risk exists, there is also a possibility of what happening?

3. Name the three *dimensions* of risk. Explain how the savvy macrowave investor reduces each kind of risk.

4. Name at least four *sources* of risk.

5. When it comes to the reward-to-risk ratio, the savvy macrowave investor follows what rule?

6. What does the Sharpe ratio reveal?

7. What does the beta tell us?

8. Contrast the approach to sector diversification of the traditional investor versus the savvy macrowave investor.

9. List at least five risk management rules.

EXERCISES

1. In the next several exercises, we are going to put together a lot of what we have learned in the last several chapters. In this exercise, I will specifically show you how to use www.bigcharts.com to find all of the major companies in a sector. Our goal is to reduce company risk by finding only strong stocks to buy. So start by going to the "Industries" link at www.bigcharts.com, and click on "Health care" in the left-hand column. Next, click on the "Pharmaceuticals" link. Scroll down to the bottom of the page and click on the link "Show All Stocks in This Industry." This will give you a list of publicly traded pharmaceutical stocks. Note that there are close to 200 stocks on this list. Scroll through the list and see if you can find a few recognizable names. Then *print the list out.*

2. Now let's do a technical screen of all of the pharmaceutical stocks on the list from the previous exercise. As we do this, we shall also check for the "liquidity" of the stocks. And yes, this will be a bit laborious—but I never promised you a rose garden, just a better investing approach. So log on to your account at www.marketedge.com and begin to type in the stock symbols from your printed list of pharmaceutical companies. (Note that many of the stocks on the list won't be covered by Market Edge. No worries. They are too small to bother with.)

3. Now as you go down this list, put a checkmark by any stock that is rated a "Strong Buy" *or* that has a "Long" recommendation and a "C-Rate" greater than 5. Note that to receive a checkmark, the stock must also pass a liquidity test. Specifically, it should also have an "Ave Volume," or Average Daily Volume, of at least 300,000 shares.

4. In this exercise, we will put all those pharmaceutical stocks that passed Market Edge's technical screen and liquidity test through the *Investor's*

Business Daily fundamental screen. So log on to *IBD*, go to the "IBD Power Tools" feature, check the "IBD Stock Checkup" category, and start feeding your stock symbols from the previous exercise into the box. To pass *IBD*'s fundamental screen, the stock should have a fundamental rating of B+ or higher. By the time you finish this exercise, you should have a nice little list of strong stocks in the pharmaceutical sector. By doing so, you will have significantly reduced company risk."

5. Now we are going to switch gears and see what we can do to reduce sector risk. Specifically, we are going to return to www.marketedge.com and use the Second Opinion's Technical Screening tool to assess the strength of the pharmaceutical, semiconductor, telecom, software, and wireless sectors. You can do this by putting the stock symbols PPH, SMH, TTH, SWH, and WMH, respectively, into the "Enter Symbol" box. These are the exchange-traded funds for the sectors. If the rating is long, then the sector is showing some strength.

6. Now here's a more systematic way to assess sector strength using Market Edge. Go to the "Advanced Tools" link and click on "Industry Group Analysis." Using the "All Groups" link, rank the industries from strongest to weakest. You can use this feature in your regular technical screen for strong and weak sectors—and thereby further reduce sector risk.

7. Go to the "Macrowave University" link at www.peternavarro.com and read more about the Sharpe ratio at the "Sharpe Ratio" link. Then go to www.google.com or www.yahoo.com and type in *Sharpe ratio* in the search box. See if you can find a Web site that has a Sharpe ratio calculator that will allow you to evaluate your own portfolio.

8. Return to www.marketedge.com and compare the betas for Cisco (CSCO), Dell (DELL), and Sun Microsystems (SUNW) versus General Dynamics (GD), Johnson & Johnson (JNJ), and Procter & Gamble (PG). You will see that in the first group of much more volatile tech stocks the beta is greater than in the second one. However, with a defense industry stock like General Dynamics and "defensive" noncyclical drug and food stocks like J&J and Procter & Gamble, the beta is significantly less than 1.

Chapter 16

MANAGING YOUR MONEY

Author's Note: *This may be the most important chapter in the book. It is also one of the more difficult. Please stick with it. I promise you it will all be worth it!*

Traders and investors spend all their time in search of the ultimate trading method. They have no clue that the road to stock market riches ultimately lies in sound money management!

David W. Aloyan

Let's assume you are holding a $100,000 cash portfolio and that you are going to begin your savvy macrowave investing by buying a basket of two strong stocks in three different strong sectors. This will give you a total of six stocks or "positions." The questions you will want to answer include:

- How many shares of each stock should I buy? How much of my total cash should I allocate to all of the trades?

- At what point should I sell any one of the stocks to *cut my losses* if the trade goes against me?

- How much of my total portfolio of $100,000 am I willing to lose if *all* of these trades go against me?

- If a trade is successful, how long should I *let my profits run*? Put another way, when should I liquidate my shares to lock in my profits?

- Lastly, if I am successful in my investing and my $100,000 portfolio grows, will this change the amount of cash I am willing to risk and commit to each trade?

These are crucial, "rubber-meets-the-road" questions, and they can all be easily answered once you have mastered the *Five Steps of Successful Money Management*. The goal of money management is to preserve and expand your investing capital within acceptable risk limits. Figure 16-1 provides a schematic overview of the five steps.

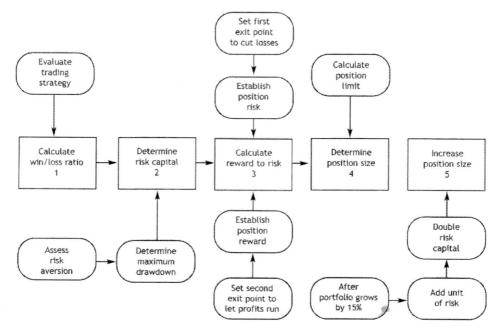

Figure 16-1   The money management process.

As you review this diagram, it may seem a bit complicated. You may also encounter a number of terms that may well be new to you—terms like reward-to-risk ratio, maximum drawdown, and risk capital. Please don't be daunted. This money management process all will soon be very easy to understand. Once you have mastered it, it will become your Holy Grail of investing.

The Five Steps of Successful Money Management

1. Your "Win%" constitutes your investing "batting average" and reveals the effectiveness of your investment strategy. If your strategy, on average, is correct on 6 of 10 trades, that's a 60 percent Win%.

2. Your risk capital is the amount of money you are willing to lose at any one time on all open positions if all of those trades go against you. The maximum drawdown is the most money you are willing to lose if you lose 10 times in a row. It is calculated by multiplying 10 times your risk capital. Your maximum drawdown is ultimately determined by your risk aversion.

3. The savvy macrowave investor always establishes two exit points for a trade *before* entering any new position. The first exit point "cuts your losses" and defines the dollar value of your "position risk." The second exit point *locks in your profits* should the trade work out; it defines your "position reward." Dividing position reward by position risk yields the reward-to-risk ratio. A 3-to-1 reward-to-risk to green light a trade is a good rule of thumb.

4. To determine how many shares of each stock to buy or short sell, divide your total risk capital by the total number of positions. This is your position limit—the most you will lose on any one position. Next, divide this position limit by your position risk; this gives you the number of shares to hold. Note that the number of shares does *not* depend on the price of each stock but merely on the amount of money you are willing to lose on each position.

5. Once you have made some profits, you can add another "unit of risk" to your stop losses. By adding this unit of risk, you can double your stop losses and risk capital. This allows you to buy more shares and opens the door to exponentially growing rewards.

Step #1: Calculate Your Investing Batting Average or Win%

You can give anyone the best tools in the world and if they don't use them with good money management, they will not make money in the markets. . . . We're convinced that a person could make a profit simply by buying and selling the markets according to the dart board if they followed all of the right things as far as money management is concerned.

Welles Wilder

The first step to effectively manage your money is to evaluate the effectiveness of your overall investing strategy. The best way to do this is to calculate your "winning percentage," or "Win%." This is simply a "batting average" for your trades.

For example, if your stock picks are typically right 6 out of 10 times, your Win% is 60 percent. If you are right only 4 out of 10 times, your Win% is 40 percent. This investor's batting average is very important because, in conjunction with your "reward-to-risk ratio" which is discussed in key point number 3 below, it can help guide your money management decisions.

Now please note: You can still make money even if you are right less than half of the time, that is, if your Win% is less than 50 percent. This will be true, however, only *if* you adhere to strict money management rules.

So how do you calculate your Win%? The formula is simple: You simply tally up your winning trades and divide these winning trades by your total trades.

One way to get the data to do this is to look at your historical investing record. In fact, if you've been investing for a while, all you will likely have to do is pull out your income tax forms and look at your trading activity.

Alternatively, you may want to calculate your Win% prospectively based on your next 50 trades. I actually prefer this forward-looking approach for one very simple reason. After you have finished reading this book and begin to put the principles of macrowave investing into practice, your Win% is likely to improve dramatically over your historical average.

In this regard, I strongly recommend that you do *not* use real money while you are learning to master the savvy macrowave investing method. Instead, as I shall explain in more detail in Chapter 20, you should consider using STOCK-TRAK software to simulate your stock trading for at least several weeks and perhaps several months before putting any of your capital on the line. And as you do so, you can calculate your Win%.

Step #2: Determine Your Risk Capital

The second step of the money management process is to determine your "risk capital." We will see that this will depend on your own unique level of "risk aversion" and the "maximum drawdown" that your level of risk aversion will tolerate.

Your risk capital is the amount of money you are willing to lose at any one time on all of your open positions, *if all of these trades go against you*. Note that your risk capital is *not* the total amount of your portfolio you have in stocks. It is simply the amount of money that you are willing to lose on your open positions before you sell them and cut your losses.

For example, on a $100,000 portfolio, you may be willing to lose no more than $2000 at any one time. Thus, your risk capital would be $2000.

Now, your maximum drawdown represents a *"worst-case scenario" in which you lose your risk capital 10 times in a row on a series of bad trades*. Thus, if your risk capital is $2000, your maximum drawdown will be $20,000—10 times your risk capital.

As to what dollar amount you should use for your risk capital, it will depend on your own level of "risk aversion." Specifically, you must ask yourself these questions:

- Do you want to be a highly risk-averse, relatively more conservative investor risking little of your cash for a smaller reward?

- Or do you want to be more aggressive, risking more of your cash in exchange for a bigger return?

I can't answer these questions for you. I can, however, give you some parameters within which to make your choice. As an upper bound, you should *never* risk losing more than 5 percent of your portfolio at any one time. Setting your risk capital at more than 5 percent crosses the line from intelligent speculating to reckless gambling. However, on the other end, risking less than a 2 percent loss at any one time is a needlessly conservative approach that will make your investing rewards hardly worth the effort. Within these constraints, here, then are some choices for you to consider based on your sense of your own risk aversion.

Choosing Your Own Unique Level of Risk and Risk Capital

Suppose you consider yourself to be a conservative investor. We will take this to mean that you are willing to risk no more than 2 percent of your capital at any one time. This level of risk aversion exposes you to a maximum $2000 loss on a $100,000 portfolio *if all of your open positions went against you and you exited the positions when they triggered your "stop losses"* (more about stop losses below).

Now suppose alternatively that you are moderately aggressive and would risk 3 percent. Or perhaps you are very aggressive and would risk 4 percent. In the moderately aggressive case, your risk capital would be $3000 while in the very aggressive case, it would be $4000.

Now let's go back to the idea of maximum drawdown because it ultimately becomes the litmus test for choosing your own unique level of risk aversion—and by implication your risk capital.

The maximum drawdown for the conservative investor case is $20,000 (10 times $2000) while for the aggressive investor, it is $40,000. Thus, in the worst-case scenario of 10 losses in a row, the conservative investor would be left with a portfolio of $80,000 while the aggressive investor's portfolio would shrink to $60,000.

Now here is where the idea of the maximum drawdown litmus test for choosing your risk capital comes in: If the size of a $40,000 loss frightens you and will likely keep you up all night with worry, then you have simply chosen a risk level that is too high. So ratchet it down to, say, a more conservative level of 3 percent—or to whatever point that you can sleep like a baby, without waking up in the middle of the night screaming like one. And once you've done that and chosen your maximum drawdown, you have chosen, by implication, your level of risk capital. Now you are ready for Step 3 of the money management process.

Step #3: Determining Your Reward-to-Risk Ratio

In Step 3, you determine your "reward-to-risk ratio." Your reward-to-risk ratio defines how much money you are willing to lose in exchange for the expectation of a possible gain or reward on each of the stocks or positions in your portfolio. As you will also see, the reward-to-risk ratio acts as your investing traffic cop. For any given trade, it will give you either a green light to buy or short sell or a red light to hold on to your cash.

To understand why, we must start with the two overarching principles of money management: You must ruthlessly "cut your losses." You must also confidently "let your profits run."

You ruthlessly cut your losses because you *never* let your emotions come into play. You are confident enough to let your profits run because you have done your research and analysis and have speculated intelligently on the upside potential of any given trade. It follows from these principles that the savvy macrowave investor always establishes two possible exit points for a trade *before* entering any new position.

The purpose of the *first exit point* is to cut your losses should the trade go against you. This first exit point is your stop loss. If the stock hits that price, you're out!

As to where you set the first exit point, it will be determined in one of several ways. As we talked about in the last chapter, it might be by a fixed rule such as "I will not lose more than 10 percent" in a stock. Alternatively, you can use a technical indicator, for example, a key support level for a long position or a key resistance level for a short position.

Regardless of how you set your stop loss, once you have set this exit point, this exit point defines your "position risk." This is the dollar value of the "risk" part of the reward-to-risk ratio for that particular trade. For example, if you buy a stock at $20.25 and set your "cut your losses" exit point at $17.25, your position risk is $3.00.

As for the second exit point, its purpose is to lock in your profits should the trade work out the way you had planned. In so doing, this exit point defines your "position reward." This is the "reward" part of the reward-to-risk ratio. So if you buy a stock at $20.25 and believe it will go up to $26.25 where you will then sell it, your position reward is $6.

Now here's the punchline: *To calculate the reward-to-risk ratio for a given trade, you simply divide the position reward by the position risk*. In this example, it is $6 divided by $3 for a reward-to-risk ratio of 2. The following is a more extended example:

A Reward-to-Risk Ratio Example

Suppose the Nasdaq market is in an up trend, but that it has pulled back recently. However, after reviewing your price charts and the broader macro fundamentals, you strongly believe that the Nasdaq will soon head back up. In this case, your strategy will be to go long the Nasdaq using the "Cubes"—the Nasdaq 100 Exchange-Traded Fund QQQ.

At present, the Cubes are trading at $21.60, and you have observed that every time QQQ has fallen to this point, it has hit a key support level and bounced back up to its first major level of resistance at $27.60.

Thus far, based on your observations, you have determined that *your position reward is likely to be in the $6 range*. This is the difference between the price of $27.60 at resistance and the likely support level for QQQ at $21.60.

Now that you have calculated your position reward, what about your position risk? Well, in further studying the price chart of QQQ, you might next determine that the next layer of support below $21.60 is $19.90 That means that if QQQ falls below $21.60, it will likely drop quickly to $19.90.

Accordingly, if you place your stop loss "loosely" below $19.90 to, say, $19.60 (I will explain why you should use such a "loose" stop in the next chapter) *you would have a $2 position risk*. The end result is a reward-to-risk ratio of 3: $6 divided by $2.

The next question you must ask yourself is whether this reward-to-risk ratio is acceptable. The answer to that question *depends on your Win%!* This point is illustrated in Table 16-1.

This table shows you what your reward-to-risk ratio must be to break even for a given Win%. For example, if you have a Win% of 40 percent, you only need a reward-to-risk ratio of 1.5 to 1 to break even whereas if your Win% is a very meager 20 percent, you will need a reward-to-risk ratio of at least 4 to 1 to break even.

Now looking at this table, you may be scratching your head a bit. This is because it clearly illustrates something that may be very counterintuitive: You can be wrong *much more* than half of the time with your stock picking and still *not* lose money if you adhere to very strict money management principles! That's precisely the power of effective money management.

**Table 16-1   Your Winning Percentage
Helping to Determine Your Reward-to-Risk Ratio**

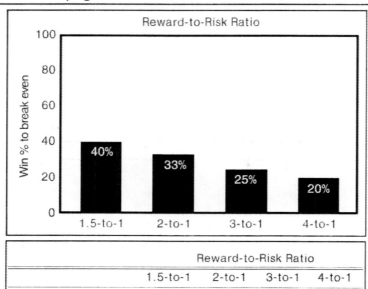

	Reward-to-Risk Ratio			
	1.5-to-1	2-to-1	3-to-1	4-to-1
Win % to break even	40%	33%	25%	20%

Choosing Your Own Reward-to-Risk Ratio

I cannot choose for you your own acceptable reward-to-risk ratio. However, I can again give you some parameters as I did earlier in helping you choose your own level of risk aversion. In particular, anything below a 2-to-1 reward-to-risk ratio is probably too low even if you have a high Win%. If you can't find stock picks with better ratios, you shouldn't be in the game.

On the other hand, it is very difficult to find stocks that offer reward-to-risk ratios that are 4 to 1 or higher. The market is simply too efficient to provide an abundance of such opportunities. Accordingly, a decent compromise may be a 3-to-1 ratio. Perhaps start with that and see how it works.

Of course, the idea will be that any stock that offers you the promise of at least a 3-to-1 ratio is one that you should "green light" while any trade with less than a 3-to-1 ratio gets red lighted or stopped by your traffic cop reward-to-risk test.

In summary, in this key point, I have showed you how to use the concept of the reward-to-risk ratio to green light or red light a trade. The next step in the process is to show you how to determine how many shares to buy or short of a stock should your money management light be green. This fourth step takes us into the critical realm of determining your "position size."

Step #4: Determining Your Position Limit and Position Size

Let's return now to where we started in this chapter, to the assumptions that you have $100,000 in cash, you have done your savvy macrowave investor due diligence, and you are ready to buy a basket of two strong stocks in each of three strong sectors in an upward-trending market. Your next question must be:

> What should be my "position sizes?" That is, how many shares of each stock should I buy?

This is a very easy question to answer using the tools of money management you have now acquired. To illustrate, let's make the following specific assumptions:

- You are moderately aggressive, which means that you have chosen a risk capital of 3 percent, or $3000.

- You have chosen a reward-to-risk ratio of 3 so that for each of the six positions you intend to hold, you will risk no more than $1 for a $3 reward.

- For simplicity, each of the six stocks you have chosen to buy will have a position reward of $6 and a position risk of $2, which means that you will risk no more than a $2 loss on each individual stock.

To determine how many shares to buy of each stock, you must first divide your risk capital of $3000 by 6, where 6 is the number of positions you intend to hold. This gives you $500, which is your "position limit." This is the most you will allow yourself to lose on any one stock or position.

Next, to arrive at the actual number of shares to buy, you simply divide the $500 by your position risk of $2. In this example, this gives you 250 shares.

Now here's an important point: The number of shares you buy will *not* depend on the price of each of the stocks but merely on the amount of money you are willing to lose on each!

Table 16-2 provides a concrete example of this very simple case. The first and second columns of the table list the stocks and their symbols. These are your three baskets of two stocks in three strong sectors.

Note that Kraft Foods and Dole Food are in the food and beverage sector, PacifiCare and Health Net are in the health services sector, and Corinthian Colleges and University of Phoenix Online are in the education and training sector. These sectors generally outperform in an early bear to middle bear market because food and health services are basic necessities, and people seek out education and training to be competitive in a slowing work environment.

Table 16-2   Money Management in Action

Company	Symbol	Current Price	Target Price	Position Reward	Position Risk	Reward to Risk	Position Limit	# of Shares	$ Invested
Kraft Foods	KFT	$33.00	$39.00	$6.00	$2.00	3	$500.00	250	$8,250.00
Dole Food	DOL	$26.00	$32.00	$6.00	$2.00	3	$500.00	250	$6,500.00
PacifiCare Health Systems	PHSY	$18.00	$24.00	$6.00	$2.00	3	$500.00	250	$4,500.00
Health Net	HNT	$22.00	$28.00	$6.00	$2.00	3	$500.00	250	$5,500.00
Corinthian Colleges	COCO	$20.00	$26.00	$6.00	$2.00	3	$500.00	250	$5,000.00
University of Phoenix Online	UOPX	$22.00	$28.00	$6.00	$2.00	3	$500.00	250	$5,500.00
							Risk Capital $3,000.00	Total Cash Used	$35,250.00

Next, note the current price of each of the stocks in column 3 and our associated target price in column 4. The difference between the two columns is your position reward, which we see in column 5 is $6 for each stock.

In column 6, we see that the position risk is $2 for each stock so that dividing column 5 by column 6, we get the reward-to-risk ratio for each of the six stocks. From column 7, we see that the reward-to-risk ratio is 3 so that each stock meets our reward-to-risk test and is a "go" to buy.

Now, in column 8, we have the position limit of $500 for each stock. We arrived at $500 by dividing our moderately aggressive risk capital of $3000 by the number of positions, namely, 6.

Finally, dividing our position limit in column 8 by our position risk or stop loss in column 6, we come up with the number of shares to buy of each stock in column 9. This equals 250 shares for each company, and we see in the last column what each of these shares has cost us plus the "Total Cash Used" from our portfolio.

In this regard, please note this important fact: As long as we stay within the portfolio budget and do not lose more than our risk capital, the amount of cash that we actually use from our portfolio is irrelevant!

Step #5: Increasing Position Sizes by Adding Units of Risk

We come now to the fifth step in the money management process and our final money management question:

> If I am profitable in my investing and my portfolio grows, will this change the amount of risk capital I am willing to commit to each trade?

The answer is a very definite yes! To more specifically answer this question, we must introduce one final money management concept: "units of risk."

The idea behind units of risk is that *only after you have made some profits will you begin to take on more risk in order to gain more reward.* Interestingly enough, most investors do just the opposite! They actually *increase* their risk when they are *losing* money. That is, rather than cutting their losses, they try to "average down their losses" by buying more shares. As I shall explain in more detail in the next chapter, this maneuver is dead wrong, as they are throwing good money after bad.

In contrast, savvy macrowave investors only increase their risk when they have earned the right to do so—that is, after they have earned some profits and are playing with the house's money! Specifically, savvy macrowave investors systematically add "units of risk" to increase their risk capital as their profits grow. Here's how this works:

You first set the value of an additional unit of risk equal to your initial risk capital. In the case of a moderately aggressive investor, this next unit of risk will therefore be 3 percent, or $3000 on a $100,000 portfolio.

Next, you use this simple rule of thumb: After you increase the value of your portfolio by 15 percent through profitable trading (in this case you must increase it by $15,000), you then add this next unit of risk. This allows you to increase your risk capital to $6000, which is simply your initial risk capital multiplied by 2.

If we return to our example in the last key point, this would mean that rather than using $3000 of stop losses or risk capital, *you can double those stop losses to $6000. This allows you to buy more shares. In doing so, you open the door to greater rewards.*

Table 16-3 illustrates how this might work. In the table, we assume that you have already made $15,000 in profits and that your account has reached $115,000.

Table 16-3 How to Increase Your Risk Capital

Company	Symbol	Current Price	Target Price	Position Reward	Position Risk	Reward to Risk	Position Limit	# of Shares	$ Invested
RF Micro Devices	RFMD	$6.00	$9.00	$3.00	$1.00	3	$1,000.00	1,000	$6,000.00
Cree	CREE	$12.00	$18.00	$6.00	$2.00	3	$1,000.00	500	$6,000.00
RSA Security	RSAS	$3.00	$6.00	$3.00	$1.00	3	$1,000.00	1,000	$3,000.00
Network Associates	NET	$12.00	$18.00	$6.00	$2.00	3	$1,000.00	500	$6,000.00
Adtran	ADTN	$18.00	$27.00	$9.00	$3.00	3	$1,000.00	333	$5,994.00
Nextel	NXTL	$6.00	$12.00	$6.00	$2.00	3	$1,000.00	500	$3,000.00
					Risk Capital		$6,000.00	Total Cash Used	$29,994.00

You now add an additional unit of risk, bringing you up to 2 units of risk. This equates to $6000 of stop losses.

In the table, first note that we are again purchasing three baskets of two stocks in three different sectors. RF Micro Devices and Cree are in the semiconductor sector, RSA Security and Network Associates are in the security software and services sector, and Adtran and Nextel are in the telecommunications sector. These sectors generally outperform in an early to middle bull market, as businesses have a demand for more and better technology.

Note, also, in the table that I have relaxed the assumption in our last example in Table 16-2 of a *uniform* reward of $6 and *uniform* risk of $2. Instead, I have allowed these rewards and risks to vary by individual stock, as they would in the real investing world. By relaxing this assumption, I can show you how to use our money management method to determine the position sizes of stocks with differing dollar amounts of position risk and position reward.

For example, while RFMD has a target price of $9 and a position reward of $3, Cree has a target price of $18 and a position reward of $6. Note, however, that in both cases, the stocks pass the 3-to-1 reward-to-risk test. More to the point, note how these different position risk levels lead to different position sizes—for RFMD it's 1000 shares but for Cree, it is only 500 shares.

Well, there you have it! You've done a great job working your way through some very difficult material. In one of the exercises below, I will lead you to a place where you can learn to add additional units of risk as your portfolio grows. From that exercise, you will see how that as you make your profits, *your portfolio will grow exponentially as you play more and more with the house's money*. Then, once you have finished the questions and exercises, it will be time to turn to the next chapter and complete our "Trifecta" of risk, money, and trade management tools.

QUESTIONS

1. How do you calculate your Win%?

2. What is the definition of your risk capital? What about your maximum drawdown, and how is it calculated?

3. What does your actual level of risk capital depend on?

4. If you are a moderately aggressive investor, what percent of your portfolio should you use as your risk capital? How about if you are a very aggressive investor?

5. The savvy macrowave investor always establishes at least two possible exit points for a trade *before* entering any new position. What are these two exit

points, what does each define, and what is their relationship to the reward-to-risk ratio?

6. What is a good rule of thumb to use for your reward-to-risk ratio? How is this ratio used?

7. To determine your position sizes, what two steps must you take?

8. Generally speaking, when does the savvy macrowave investor begin to add position risk? How does this strategy differ from the typical investor?

9. What is a good rule of thumb for adding your first unit of risk after you have increased the size of your portfolio through profit-making? What does adding this unit of risk do to the size of your risk capital and stop losses?

EXERCISES

1. With this exercise, we'll catch two fish with one net. You'll learn to calculate a Win% *and* get some perspective on the effectiveness of the Market Edge buy and short sale recommendations. So log on to your account at www.marketedge.com, click on "Analysis Tools," go to "Money Runner," and then click on the "Current Buy List." Calculate the Win% for all of the open trades on this list. Then, do the same for Money Runner's "Current Short List." Compare the two lists. Does Market Edge have a better Win% on its long positions or its short positions? Hold that thought—and keep this data—as you move to Exercise 2.

2. The purpose of this exercise is to see how the market trend influences the Win%. As a general rule, Market Edge should have a better Win% for its "Current Buy List" than its "Current Short List" when the market trend is up. That's because the system is trading with the trend. Alternatively, it should have a better Win% for its current short list if the market trend is down. To check this, go to www.bigcharts.com, take a look at a price chart for the S&P 500 and the Nasdaq, and try to determine which way the market trend is moving. Then go back to the Market Edge data and see if the Market Edge has a better Win% for the list that is on the same side as the market trend.

3. With this exercise, it's time for a little introspection. Specifically, I want you to try and answer the question of how risk averse you are and what your maximum drawdown is. As you think about this, be sure to include your spouse or partner, if the question is applicable.

4. This exercise will show you how to use the support and resistance levels revealed by technical analysis to calculate position risk, position reward, and the reward-to-risk ratio. So please return to *www.marketedge.com* and use the "Second Opinion" feature to look at the technical analysis of 10 of your favorite stocks. Calculate the risk-to-reward ratio for each of these stocks by using the lower-bound of the "Support Range" as your position risk for a long position and the upper-bound of the "resistance range" for your position reward. Note that in some cases, Market Edge may not provide both support and resistance so you won't be able to calculate the ratio.

5. Suppose you want to enter a short position in McDonald's and further assume that you have a position limit of $1000. Assume the stock is currently trading at $20. Use the 52-week low of $16 as your support level to determine your position reward. Assume the recent price resistance is at $22. How many shares should you short sell? What's the reward-to-risk ratio? Would this be a good trade?

6. Go to the "Macrowave University" link at www.peternavarro.com and click on "David W. Aloyan's Money Management Rules." This article will explain in more detail how to add units of risk as your portfolio grows.

7. Fill in the blanks in Table 16-4 below. Assume a 4 percent risk capital for an initial portfolio value of $100,000 and no profits have yet been earned. (*Hint*: If you have any trouble doing this, look at Table 16-3 in the text. The major differences between the table in this exercise and the table in the text is a different risk capital assumption, a smaller number of stocks, slightly different position risks, and no additional units of risk.)

Table 16-4   Fill in the Blanks to Test Your Knowledge

Company	Symbol	Current Price	Target Price	Position Reward	Position Risk	Reward to Risk	Position Limit	# of Shares	$ Invested
Cree	CREE	$12.00	$18.00		$2.00				
RSA Security	RSAS	$3.00	$6.00		$1.00				
Adtran	ADTN	$18.00	$27.00		$3.00				
Nextel	NXTL	$6.00	$12.00		$2.00				
					Risk Capital		Total Cash Used		

Chapter 17

MANAGING YOUR TRADES

Author's Note: *More experienced traders may want to quickly skim the material in this chapter or simply move on to the next. However, even experienced traders will benefit from this "refresher course" on trade management.*

Plan your trade and trade your plan.

A Wall Street axiom

To become a truly savvy macrowave investor, it is not enough to efficiently manage your risk and money. When it comes to the day-to-day tending of your portfolio, you must also know how to effectively manage your trades. This requires mastering not just the "tools" and "rules" of trade management. It also means coming to grips with some basic—and oft-times very dangerous— "investor psychology."

On the *tools* front, it is crucial to know the difference between market and limit orders and when to use each. It is equally critical to know how to use stop losses, trailing stops, and buy stops, each of which are essential to achieving your goal of cutting losses and letting your profits run.

On the *rules* front, we must abide by such maxims as "never turn a winner into to a loser," "never average down a loss," and "never overtrade." And on the *investor psychology* front, we must look in the mirror and see whether we are prone to trading on emotion rather than with a plan, treating our portfolio as a form of entertainment rather than a business, or susceptible to the outside influences of "the herd."

In this chapter, we are going to cover all of this trade management ground— and perhaps just a little bit more.

Macrowave Key Points

1. The debate over market versus limit orders centers around the risk of capturing *the spread* between the ask price and the bid price versus *the price movement*. Use a limit order if the market is trading sideways and/or the stock is in an overbought condition. Use a

market order if the market is strongly up and/or your technical analysis indicates momentum.

2. Many investors set their stop losses at places where they will be accidentally stopped out. To set intelligent stops, avoid "round numbers" and key technical analysis "decision nodes" like "support" and "resistance." Set "loose stops" outside the range of a stock price's normal volatility.

3. Use "trailing stops" to ensure that you "never turn a winner into a loser" and to lock in profits.

4. Use "buy stops" to play breakouts. Be careful not to run "naked" without a stop loss after your buy stop is triggered, particularly in a volatile market.

5. Never average down a loss in an attempt to lower your breakeven point! This is a sucker's bet. Most trades that move in the wrong direction *will continue to do so.*

6. In the past, charlatan stockbrokers used to "churn" the portfolios of their clients, trading stocks simply to generate commissions. Today, many online investors do this to themselves out of boredom, greed, inexperience, or an addiction to trading. Don't do this!

7. "Don't try to pick tops or bottoms," "don't meet margin calls," and "don't chase fast markets" are just a few of some very valuable insider tips.

8. Forget David Letterman. David Aloyan's Top Ten List on investor psychology includes such gems as "never invest on impulse, emotion, or hope," "never trade to pay your bills," "don't be impressed by hot money," and "put your personal life first; it will reflect positively in your trading."

Key Point #1: Market versus Limit Orders

When it did open and I was about to place my usual limit order, the stock was moving up, so I placed a market order. When stocks are on the move, you must do that or miss the boat.

The Market Pro

You've done your savvy macrowave investing homework, you've located a strong stock in a strong sector, and you are ready to buy 100 shares. So you log on to your online brokerage account, and you get ready to place your order. The question is: Should you use a *market* order or a *limit* order?

As I shall soon explain, the answer will depend primarily on the direction of the current market trend, as well as some important technical indicators. Before I offer that explanation, let's first come to better understand the "market-versus-limit debate and the "*spread*" which is really at stake over the choice of which to use.

Table 17-1 shows a current quote during a typical trading day for the stock of the fictional company Elvis Creations—stock symbol KING. Please note four things.

First, the "Last" of $9.75 shows the actual price someone just paid for the stock at 2:30 P.M. in the trading day. Second, the "bid" of $9.50 shows the *highest* price at least one bidder is willing to pay. Third, the "ask" of $10 shows the *lowest* current asking price of a seller. Finally, you can calculate the "spread" simply by subtracting the bid from the ask price. It is this spread that is really at stake when it comes time for you to decide whether to use a market order or a limit order.

With a *market* order, you will instruct your online broker to buy your desired 100 shares of KING at the current market price. Typically, this will mean that you will pay at or close to the "ask" of $10 and thereby forfeit all or most of the spread to the seller. To avoid surrendering this spread, alternatively you can put in a *limit* order at or near the "bid."

Suppose, then, you put in a limit order that instructs your online broker to buy 100 shares of KING for a price *no more than* the bid of $9.50. If you get filled at this limit price, you will have paid $9.50 and saved a nice little fifty bucks by not having to pay the asking price!

That sounds pretty good. But the problem with using such a limit order is that you *have no guarantee that your order will actually be filled at your limit price*. This is because, in a rapidly moving stock market, the bids and asks are constantly changing, and there simply may not be a willing seller at your limit price.

Table 17-1   Current Quote for Elvis Creations (KING)

	Last	Bid	Ask	Volume	Time
KING	$9.75	$9.50	$10	375,000	2:30

Now here's the worst-case scenario: The stock that you want to buy because you think it is going to go up, *does just that*—immediately! In this case, because you were not filled at your limit order price, your attempt to *capture the spread* backfires because it prevents you from *capturing the price movement* that you would otherwise have enjoyed if you had simply placed a market order and been filled at the original ask of 10 bucks.

To see this even more clearly, let's do an example. Suppose the ask of KING moves up another dollar to $11 as you are impatiently waiting for your limit order to fill and that the new bid is $10.50. Suppose further that at this point, you put in a new limit order of $10.50 and actually get your order filled at the bid. In your effort to capture the original 50-cent spread, you wind up losing not only that spread. You also pay $50 more for your shares above what you would have *had* to pay if you had used a market order to begin with and been filled at the original ask.

Now here's an even more subtle consideration: If, in your frustration that your original limit order did not get filled, you put in a *market* order at the higher price, you would have wound up paying an extra $100 in your effort to capture the $50. So what the heck should you do: *Try to capture the spread with a limit order or focus more upon capturing the price movement with a market order?*

The answer is very straightforward, and it will depend on two things: the current market trend and a technical analysis of the price and volume action of the stock you are seeking to buy or short.

Rule #1

Use a limit order if the market is trading in a sideways range and be patient enough to wait for the order to be filled. More subtly, you can set your limit order even *below* the current bid and try to "bottom fish" a little bit if your technical analysis shows any strong indication that the stock is "overbought" and due for a little pullback. In either case, you still run the risk of not getting filled, but the risk is fairly minimal.

Rule #2

If the broad market is in a strong upward trend and/or your technical analysis indicates that the stock price of the company in question is showing very strong momentum, please don't be pennywise and dollar foolish: *Use a market order!*

In this regard, if you closely follow the methods of the savvy macrowave investor, you will only be buying strong stocks in strong sectors in an upward-trending market and shorting weak stocks in weak sectors in a downward-trending market. *Almost by definition, this kind of stock picking will favor the use of market orders for your initial entry position!*

And let me put that point one other way to drive it home: The best time to use limit orders to buy stocks is in a sideways market. That's typically the *worst* time for you to even be in the market.

Key Point #2: Set Intelligent Stop Losses—Don't Be Shaken Out!

> It is essential to use stops to ensure losses are limited in the event the market moves against you. However, avoid setting them at fixed amounts, either too close to the current price or on obvious support and resistance levels.
>
> *Man Financial Australia*

In the last two chapters on risk and money management, we talked a lot about how important it is to cut your losses. I also introduced you briefly to the stop loss and described a stop loss as either a physical or mental price level at which you sell a stock (or cover a short sale) to cut your losses.

In the case of a mental stop loss, you must sit by your computer, constantly watch the price action, and if you see the price dip below your stop loss, then you fire off an order to close your position. In the case of a physical stop loss, you simply send an order in to your online broker that directs your broker to close your position if the price of the stock hits your stop loss. Either way, setting intelligent stops is a lot more difficult than you may think. Indeed, *far too many investors set their stops at places where it is highly likely that they will be stopped out, even on what should otherwise be a most excellent trade.* There are three problems.

First, you might decide to set your stop around a "round number" like 30 or 50 or 100. Unfortunately, such round numbers draw stop losses from other investors as chili dip attracts nachos. If you place your stop at a round number, you are *much* more likely to get stopped out. Accordingly, if your stop loss rule says "set it at $50," lower your stop slightly to, say, $49.79, or better yet, to $49.47. Avoid round numbers!

Second, you should also avoid setting your stops around well-traveled technical analysis "decision nodes." Remember: Millions of very smart technical traders are out there charting things like support and resistance levels to generate both buy and sell signals. In fact, in the last chapter, we talked precisely about how to use a stock's support level to determine where to place your own stop losses.

Now here's the implication of this observation: *Setting a truly intelligent stop loss means staying well out of the way of these technical analysis decision nodes.* As a practical matter, this means if you identify a level of support that would serve as a trigger for a stop loss, *adjust your stop a little bit downward* away from the support level (and be sure to adjust your reward-to-risk ratio accordingly). Why do you want to make this adjustment? To avoid this frustrating scenario:

The stock price falls not just to the support level, but, because of some strong downward momentum, it falls just a little below that support level. In this case, you get stopped out because you placed your stop *at* support. Then, you watch in frustration as the stock bounces quickly back up—maybe even within seconds or minutes—and then never looks back. The result: You've not only lost some money but also missed a great opportunity to turn some profit. *Avoid technical decision nodes!*

The third challenge you face in setting intelligent stops is that you might unwittingly set your stop loss *within the range of a stock's normal volatility.* For example, the share price of a highly volatile stock may regularly swing $2 to $3 in a day. If you set your stop loss within this normal daily trading range, you could get stopped out on an *intraday dip* even on an up day for the stock. *Therefore, you must set "loose" stops that give your portfolio plenty of room to breathe.*

Key Point #3: Use Trailing Stops to Lock in Profits

Move your stops up to break even as soon as possible.

David W. Aloyan

One of the most important trade management rules in the savvy macrowave investor's handbook is to "never turn a winner into a loser." There is nothing more frustrating than watching a stock that first moved up smartly in price for a hefty paper profit fall back below your original buying price *before* you exit the stock. The injury to that insult comes, of course, when you wind up selling what could have been a big winner for a very real cash loss.

To avoid turning your winners into losers, you must learn to use "trailing stops." For example, suppose you wound up buying KING at $10.50 a share with a limit order. Initially, you set a stop loss of a little below the support level of $8.50, say at $8.29.

Now suppose further that KING moves smartly up to $14. *At this point, you should move your stop loss up to above your original purchase price of $10.50.* That way, the worst that can happen is that you get out with no gain.

More broadly, using the most sophisticated "direct access investing" platforms that we shall talk more about in Chapter 18, you can place real-time and constantly moving "*trailing stops.*" In our example, you might, therefore, specify a trailing stop of $1.75 to your online broker. That way, if the price of KING ever falls by $1.75 *from whatever high it achieves*, your shares will be sold. In this way, the trailing stop helps you lock in profits.

Key Point #4: Use Buy Stops to Play Breakouts

Use a buy-stop order. While not fail-safe, it can help you buy shares at or close to the pivot.

Investor's Business Daily

Suppose you want to use the buy high, sell higher strategy for a particular stock. As we learned in Chapter 12, this means you will buy the stock only *after* it clears its pivot point and last layer of resistance.

One way to do this is to hang around chained to your computer screen and online broker waiting for a stock price to clear the magic pivot. However, a much, much easier way is to simply send your online broker a "buy stop" order.

A buy stop simply tells your broker, "if the price of KING increases to $$x$, then buy y shares of KING at the market price," where x is your buy stop price and y is the number of shares you want.

Note, however, that you must be very careful using a buy stop order. The problem is that between the time your buy stop is triggered and the time you come back to your computer and realize that you have actually bought the stock, you will be holding a "naked" position without a stop loss. If the stock price merely peeks above its pivot point and then quickly crashes below it, you can lose a lot of money very quickly. And that's not uncommon with stocks that are trying to break out of their bases in a volatile market. So use the buy stop judiciously.

Key Point #5: Never Average Down a Loss

Never average down a losing position. This may be tempting to many traders, as the ego wants so badly to be proven right that it looks appealing to average down your cost. But in reality what you are usually doing is throwing more money at a bad idea.

Price Headley

Averaging down a loss simply means buying more shares of a stock that you have bought when it goes down—instead of selling the stock to quickly cut your losses. The suckers who do this see it as a means of lowering their "breakeven" price on the stock. Here's how it works:

Suppose you pay a price of $50 each for 1000 shares of Mediocre Industries, stock symbol AVG. Immediately, however, the trade goes against you as AVG falls to $44.

Rather than cut your losses, however, you buy another 1000 shares. This "averages down" the price of your total 2000 shares to $47. Your thinking is that AVG only has to rebound to $47 to get you back to your breakeven point on the trade.

That may be sound mathematical logic. But it is *horrible* investor psychology. What you are saying to yourself is that my trading boat has now sprung a leak. So the best way to bail the boat out is to punch another hole in it.

The fact is: Most trades that move in the wrong direction *will continue to do so.* This is because there are good reasons why stock prices fall or rise. And once they begin to fall, they often gather momentum. So please: Never average down a loss!

Key Point #6: Don't Churn Your Own Portfolio!

> Don't overtrade. Don't be shaken out of a trade based on intraday noise if it still looks good overall.
>
> *David W. Aloyan*

Today, many investors use the Internet and an online brokerage account to actively manage their own portfolios, and stockbrokers never get involved. This is a very good thing for most of us because, in the past, it was quite common for scurrilous brokers to "churn" the portfolios of their clients. Specifically, *these charlatans would execute trades, not to improve the profit potential or diversity of the portfolio, but simply to generate commissions.*

Now here's one of the highest ironies of what otherwise should be the Investor's Golden Age of the Internet: Today, many online investors do to themselves what stockbrokers used to do for them—they churn their *own* portfolios!

Why do many of today's investors overtrade? The reasons are many and varied. They range from boredom, greed, and inexperience to an even more insidious addiction to trading. My advice to you, then, is this: Do a little introspection and make sure none of these reasons applies to you. Don't churn your own portfolio!

Key Point #7: Some Inside Tips

These tips have been culled from the collective consciousness of some of the best traders and investors in the world. They speak for themselves and therefore are offered without explanation.

1. Don't try to pick tops and bottoms.
2. Buy dips in an up-trending market; sell bounces in a down-trending market.
3. Don't meet margin calls. Why throw good money after bad?
4. Look at all time frames before making a decision: daily, weekly, and monthly charts. Use intraday charts to time entry and exit points.
5. Don't chase fast markets (gaps up and gaps down). Wait for them to come back to you.
6. If a position doesn't look as good as the day you put it on, close it out.

Key Point #8: David Aloyan's Top Ten Investor Psychology Tips

Talk show host David Letterman is not the only one to have an impressive Top Ten List. When it comes to addressing important issues in investor psychology, David Aloyan's Top Ten List is equally compelling. Here it is in all its self-explanatory splendor:

1. Trade or invest because you love it. Don't do it as a form of entertainment.
2. Never invest on impulse, emotion, or hope. Have a plan.
3. Never invest more than you can afford to lose.
4. Never trade to pay your bills.
5. Make your trading decisions away from the outside noise and ignore conventional wisdom. Learn to be a confident minority; when most people agree, they are generally wrong.
6. Don't be impressed by hot money. Traders that ramp up big returns quickly are most likely to fall big!
7. Always believe you will win, and reward yourself for doing so.

8. Analyze your losses to ensure that you are following your rules and methodology.

9. Always take breaks from the market to reflect.

10. Put your personal life first; it will reflect positively in your trading.

QUESTIONS

1. The debate over using market versus limit orders centers around what?

2. When should you use a limit order and when should you use a market order?

3. What are the three major rules of setting intelligent stop losses?

4. What are the two main reasons why you use a "trailing stop"?

5. When is a good time to use a buy stop? What should you be careful of?

6. Why do some investors try to average down a loss? Under what conditions should you do this? Why is averaging down a loss generally a very a bad idea?

7. What is the traditional definition of portfolio "churning"? Why do some online investors today effectively churn their own portfolios?

8. Name at least three valuable insider tips of effective trade management.

9. Name at least five of David Aloyan's Top Ten Investor Psychology Tips.

EXERCISES

1. Go to www.schwab.com or any one of a number of Internet sites that provide current stock quotes and calculate the spreads from the current bid and ask for a number of New York Stock Exchange big cap stocks like GE and GM. Do the same for a number of smaller cap Nasdaq stocks like MKSI and INVN. Do you see any pattern to the spreads? (Interestingly, while the spreads should be smaller for large cap NYSE stocks, the Nasdaq is a more efficient market because it trades electronically and directly links buyers and sellers rather than using a market maker like the NYSE.)

2. Go to www.bigcharts.com and use the Interactive Charting function to call up charts of QQQ and SPY. Use these price charts to assess the status of the current market trend—is it up, down, or moving sideways? Then,

check the latest Technical Analysis for Cisco (CSCO) at www.market edge.com, looking for signs of any upward momentum as well as any over-bought signals. Based on this assessment, determine whether you would use a limit order or market order to immediately buy some CSCO shares.

3. After you have completed the tasks in exercise number 2, check the current stock quote for CSCO at any one of a number of Internet sites. (Try www.schwab.com again if all else fails.) Write down the current bid, ask, and last price. Then keep checking the quote *every minute for the next 10 minutes*. Write down the bid, ask, and last price. Are there any cases where the clearing price has fallen to the original bid? If so, a limit order would have gotten you in. If not, has the price risen? If so, if you had used a limit order, you likely would have surrendered some upward price movement in your attempt to successfully buy the stock.

4. Visit www.marketedge.com and examine the technical characteristics of your favorite stock. Note both the current price and the support level. Assume that you already own shares of this stock and wish to place a stop loss at the support level. What price would you specify for your stop loss? (*Hint*: This level would be enough below the support level so that you are not stopped out.) Try this exercise for some other stocks in your portfolio or on your watch list.

5. Look at the current price of a number of your favorite stocks and assume that you bought the stocks at these prices. Then calculate what a 10 percent stop loss would be. Do this for at least five different stocks. Does your calculated stop loss come too close to a round number? If so, how would you adjust it?

6. These next four exercises are all interrelated. Go to http://finance.yahoo.com, type in the symbol of your favorite stock in the "Enter symbol(s)" box, and hit "Get." Click on the "Historical Prices" link and use it to get the last 30 days of price data. Scroll down to the bottom of the page and click on "Download Spreadsheet Format" to download the data. Save the data in an Excel spreadsheet and move on to exercise number 7.

7. Look at the data in your spreadsheet. Specifically "eyeball" the intraday highs and lows for the past 30 days and try to guesstimate the stock's daily volatility. Write your guesstimate down as well as what your stop loss would have to be to avoid normal intraday volatility. Then move on to exercise number 8, keeping your spreadsheet open.

8. Now let's approach the task in exercise number 7 a bit more systematically. What we want to do is calculate an *average* for the daily intraday volatility.

So, in a new data column, use the functions of Excel to subtract the daily high from the daily low to arrive at this daily intraday price swing. At the bottom of this new column, use Excel to calculate the *average* of price swing as well as its *maximum*. And here's the punchline: The safest way to avoid being stopped out on an intraday move is to put your stop loss *outside* the maximum price swing. Alternatively, if that stop seems a bit too loose, you can use the average price swing *plus* one standard deviation, where the standard deviation can also be calculated using Excel functions.

9. Compare your guesstimates of a reasonable stop loss in exercise number 7 to the more systematic calculations in exercise number 8.

Chapter 18

EXECUTING YOUR TRADES

What do capital punishment and profitable stock market investing have in common? They both depend on the execution.

Ron Vara

In this important chapter about trade execution, let's start off with two assumptions. First, let's assume that you have successfully used your savvy macrowave investing skills to pick out a portfolio of great stocks in strong sectors to buy. Second, let's further assume that you have meticulously used your risk management, money management, and trade management tools to prepare for an efficient entry into your positions. That means that all you have left to do now is to actually buy your stocks. That should be a piece of cake, right?

Wrong! In fact, at the pinnacle of the pyramid of risks that every investor faces there sits one last but very important kind. This is the "risk of trade execution." As we shall soon see, this kind of risk wears many faces.

It can be your traditional broker on the phone who charges you premium rates for the slowest trades on Wall Street. Alternatively, it can be the "cheap" online broker that offers very low commissions but fills your orders at the worst possible prices. And it can even be more expensive online brokers who unscrupulously "front run" your trades.

The purpose of this chapter is to show you how to avoid all of these risks of trade execution. We will see that the key to eliminating every single one of them is to use a direct access, Level II trading platform.

Key Macrowave Points

1. There are three ways to execute a trade: Phone your broker, use a Level I online broker, or most preferably, use a direct access, Level II trading platform.

2. Level I trading lacks "market transparency." You only see the "current bid," "current ask," and the "last price." In contrast, with a Level II trading platform, you see the whole market. Such transparency can help you greatly improve the timing of your trade executions.

3. Level I online programs are prone to slippage, which occurs when your order is not filled at the best possible price. Sources of slippage range from slow execution to more unscrupulous broker practices like "payment for order flow," "front running," and "internalization."

4. Commission costs for a direct access, Level II trading platform can be slightly higher but the savings from increased market transparency and better trade execution more than outweigh any higher costs.

5. Besides eliminating slippage and providing market transparency, direct access platforms arm you with a much more extended set of risk, money, and trade management tools as well as much more sophisticated "programmed ordering."

Key Point #1: The Three Methods to Execute Your Trades

1. "He can't come to the phone right now. He's on the ledge."

2. "He's meeting with the SEC as we speak."

From The Top 10 Signs Your Broker Was Affected by the Stock Market Crash

There are three basic ways to execute a stock trade. You can phone the order in to your stockbroker. You can place the order yourself on the Internet using a Level I online broker. Or you can use a direct access, Level II online trading platform.

Of these methods, the old-fashioned, slowest, and by far most expensive way is to phone your broker. Your broker will, in turn, either phone somebody else with the order or, more likely, go online and place the order directly. In the process, two things happen.

First, you pay a significantly higher commission for phone orders than online orders. Second, by the time the broker gets around to actually placing your order, you may get a worse price. Together, these are two very compelling reasons to execute your own trades online instead of by phone. But which kind of online broker should you use, Level I or Level II?

To answer that question, we must first understand the critical difference between Level I versus Level II trading. Then, we must closely examine the problem of "slippage" that can arise with Level I brokerage firms.

Key Point #2: Level I versus Level II Trading

Level II quotes give you the kind of detailed financial data professional traders have long relied on.

The Street.com

Table 18-1 illustrates a typical Level I online quote for the telecom gear maker JDS Uniphase (JDSU). The term *Level I* comes from the fact that on this screen all you can see are the "top-line" market results—the last price paid, the current bid price, the current ask price, and the volume. So what is missing from this Level I picture? "Market transparency!"

To understand the powers of market transparency, take a good look at the Level II screen in Figure 18-1. Note that you can see the same current bid, current ask, and the last price paid just as in Level I. But, in the lower left column of the figure, you can also see *all* of the underlying bids ranked in descending order—that's the *demand* side of the market equation. In the lower middle column, you can likewise see the underlying asking prices or "offers" ranked in ascending order—that's the underlying *supply* situation. And in the lower right column, you can also see a "ticker" that ticks off in real time the "last prices" as sales occur in real time.

This list of bid and ask prices together with the "last price ticker" of market clearing prices gives you a much better picture of the underlying supply and demand conditions in the market as well as any upward or downward momentum. But these are not the only clues Level II provides about momentum and conditions in the market for a particular stock.

Look even more closely now at the Level II screen. In both the bid and ask columns, you can also see both the names of the actual market participants *and* the number of shares each of these market participants are seeking to buy or sell.

For example, in the figure, the ever-wily market maker Goldman Sachs, or GSCO, is providing the current bid or offer of $17.27 for 700 shares of JDS Uniphase. (You arrive at 700 shares by multiplying the 7 in the column times 100.) At the current ask, market titan Merrill Lynch, or MLCO, wants $17.31 for 500 shares.

Table 18-1   The Level I Stock Quote

	Last Price	Bid	Ask	Volume
JDSU	$17.31	$17.27	$17.31	14,692,600

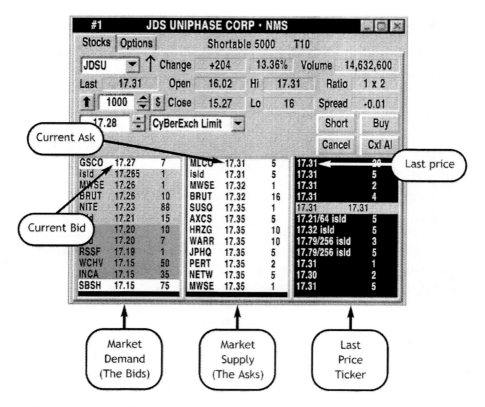

Figure 18-1   The market transparency of a Level II stock box.

Looking farther down the bid list, you can also see some of the biggest names in the business—Wachovia (WCHV), InstiNet (INCA), and Smith Barney/Shearson (SBSH). Each of these Big Dogs appears to be doing some "bottom fishing" for JDSU. They all have low bids of $17.15 for quite large share sizes, thereby providing the stock with some apparent support in this bid range. More broadly, this kind of information about market participants is particularly important because when large brokerage firms enter the market offering to buy or sell large share sizes, this knowledge can exert considerable upward or downward pressure on price.

It follows from these observations that the transparency of a Level II platform provides a much more complete market picture. By seeing this Big Picture, the savvy macrowave investor can greatly improve the timing of trade executions as well as more efficiently apply risk management, money management, and trade management tools.

For example, you may observe a "thin" market with just a few bids that quickly fall in price as you move down the bid queue. The last price ticker may also indicate that the market is clearing on the soft side—at or near the bid price rather than the ask price. And you may even detect the presence of one or two market makers with very large share sizes breaking in to the ask column at or near the ask price seeking to dump shares. These three conditions are all signs of a weakening stock and strongly suggest a strategy of waiting before entry to benefit from a lower price.

Alternatively, a market quite literally thick with bids and prices that are consistently "hitting the ask price" in the last price ticker coupled with the presence of market makers with large share sizes on the bid size all suggest hot demand. In such a market, there may be no time to lose in making one's entry, lest you wind up paying a significantly higher price than you intended to.

The broader point: Level II trading platforms clearly trump Level I brokerages on the market transparency front. Note, however, that there is an equally important advantage of Level II over Level I trading, and it has to do with our next topic—the controversial issue of "slippage."

Key Point #3: The Slippage Problem with Level I Brokers

> Of the 29 firms the Securities and Exchange Commission investigated, 17 "improperly emphasized payment for order flow in deciding where to send orders." The regulators said the firms did not even try to assess the prices available from trading firms other than those that were paying them. Indeed, most routed orders to traders whose execution quality was well below industry averages.
>
> *The New York Times*

Slippage occurs when you send an order to your online broker and it is not filled at the best possible price. Figure 18-2 illustrates how the trade execution process works together with the major sources of slippage. Specifically, the figure illustrates five possible paths your order can follow and the four sources of slippage.

For all five paths, the process begins on the left-hand side of the figure when you place an order with your broker either by phone or online. In this regard, you may be surprised to know that even with an online broker, you are *not* necessarily connected directly to the market. Instead, many online brokers are simply

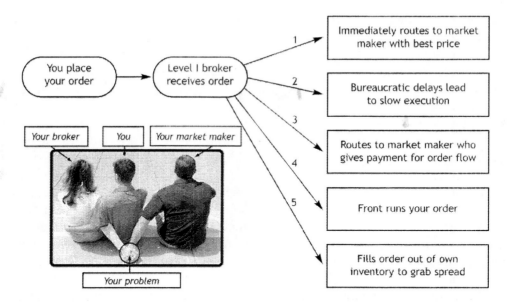

Figure 18-2 The trade execution path and four major sources of slippage.

"middlemen" who will take your order and then route it to a "market maker" that will actually execute the trade.

The "best-case" scenario is illustrated in Path 1 at the top of the figure. Here, your fast and managerially efficient broker immediately routes your order to the market maker offering the best price.

In Path 2, however, your brokerage firm, no matter how noble its intentions, may be mismanaged or lack sufficient resources to quickly process orders. In the seconds—or even minutes!—that your order is delayed, a market can move a few cents, 50 cents, or even several dollars. The resultant slippage can be quite costly, particularly as you increase the number of shares you are buying or selling.

Beyond just slow order execution, there is, however, a second and much more ignoble set of problems. These include "payment for order flow," "front running," and "internalization."

The payment for order flow problem is illustrated in Path 3 and caricatured in the picture inserted into the lower left-hand corner of the figure. The picture depicts the cozy relationship that can arise when an online broker receives a payment from a market maker for routing a customer's order to that market maker for final execution. The obvious problem with such payments is that they provide your broker with a strong financial incentive to route orders based on which market maker is going to give them the biggest "kickback," not the quickest fill at the best price.

Now what about "front running"? This problem is illustrated in Path 4, and frankly, it is a problem that is even worse than payment for order flow. At least with payment for order flow, you still have some small chance of getting routed to a market maker with a decent price. With front running, however, you are simply being fleeced. Here's how it works.

You, along with hundreds of other clients, send your broker an order for a particular stock at roughly the same time. Sitting in his catbird seat, the broker is able to observe all this action. So rather than immediately executing all of the necessary trades on behalf of all the clients, the broker lets these trades start to accumulate even as he begins to buy enough stock for himself to eventually fill the orders. Meanwhile, the broker's purchases of shares start to push up the market price. At this point, the broker then takes the shares he just bought and turns around and sells them to his clients for a profit at this higher price. And note, this front running can take just minutes or even seconds!

The final source of slippage, which is illustrated in Path 5, is "internalization." This occurs when your broker is not just a middleman routing your order but also a major buyer and seller in the market holding large inventories. The problem here is simply that when your broker holds a large inventory of stocks, she has both the incentive and the means to fill your order at a price that allows her to capture some or all of the spread that might otherwise go to you.

Because of the four major sources of slippage—slow execution, payment for order flow, front running, and internalization—that "cheap" Level I online broker you may be using may not be "cheap" at all. Consider this example.

Suppose your discount broker charges you a nominal $8 a trade and you go ahead and purchase 1000 shares of Amazon at $20.29. The only problem is that when you placed your market order the current ask was $20.21. But because your broker routed the order so as to capture some payment for order flow or engaged in front running, you got filled at $20.29. That's an extra 8 cents on 1000 shares, and it means your "effective" commission on the trade actually doubled to $16—$8 bucks for the commission and $8 for the slippage (that is, $1000 times the 8-cent differential).

Key Point #4: Direct Access Trading Eliminates Slippage

Approximately 85% of market orders executed on Nasdaq today are routed to markets that are **not** quoting the best price.

Former SEC Chairman Arthur Levitt

The good news is that you can totally eliminate any and all slippage by trading in your inept or unscrupulous Level I online broker for a shiny new direct access, Level II platform. Such platforms are readily available from a wide variety of companies that range from CyberTrader and TradeStation to RushTrade, TradeCast, and RealTick.

Note that in most cases, you will pay a bit more for your commissions than you will with the cheap discount brokers. But these higher commission costs will be much more than offset both by the advantages of market transparency provided by the Level II features as well as by the speed and directness of your trade executions. Figure 18-3 illustrates the two different paths that are available to you when you buy and sell stocks on a direct access platform.

Note first that for both order paths, you totally bypass the "middleman" broker. Instead, you become your own broker choosing your own market routing.

Specifically, in the first path traced along the top of the figure, you can route your order to a "smart market" computer program that searches for the best available price. In the second path traced along the bottom of the figure, you can route directly to a particular market maker of your choice that you identify from your Level II snapshot of the market.

For example, in Figure 18-2, GSCO was bidding $17.27 for 700 shares of JDSU. With a direct access platform, you can choose to "hit this bid" directly for 700 shares or less.

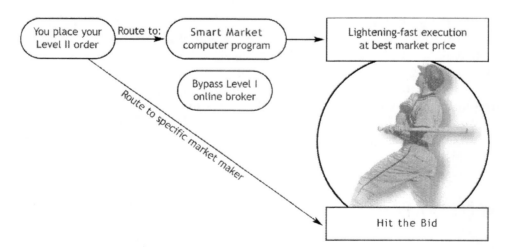

Figure 18-3   The trade execution paths for direct access investing platforms.

Most importantly, for whichever path you take, the speed of execution is lightning fast. Indeed, *you* are directly wired right into the market with exactly the same status as a market participant like Goldman Sachs or Merrill Lynch *or* any Level I online broker like Ameritrade or E*Trade.

Key Point #5: The Virtues of Programmed Ordering

> With TradeStation, you can transform your PC into an interactive trading assistant that can actually watch the markets for you—tick-by-tick—in real-time, and send your buy, sell and cancel orders automatically. . . . Whether you're waiting for a buy or sell opportunity for one— or a dozen—of your favorite stocks, you won't have to stay glued to your screen trying to monitor each security at once.
>
> *TradeStation.com*

The final nail in the Level I online broker coffin is this: Besides eliminating slippage and providing greater market transparency, direct access platforms arm you with a much more extended set of risk, money, and trade management tools. Such tools go far beyond the simple buy stops and sell stops that are available from the Level I discount broker crowd and extend to much more sophisticated "programmed ordering."

Let me illustrate the power of some of these tools with a very simple example that draws directly on our discussions in Chapters 16 and 17. In particular, in key point number 3 of Chapter 16, I explained why the savvy macrowave investor always chooses at least two possible exit points for every trade—one exit point to cut losses and the other to lock in profits. In key point number 3 of Chapter 17, I also extolled the virtues of "trailing stops" to lock in profits, where a trailing stop is easily a third possible exit point that floats with market conditions.

Suppose, then, that I have used both technical analysis and fundamental analysis to identify Adios, Inc. as a strong stock in a strong sector. I look further at the stock's price chart and see that it is currently trading just below a key level of resistance at $50. My technical analysis also reveals downside support of $46 and the next layer of significant resistance at $62.

In this particular case, I clearly do not want to buy the stock until it clears the first resistance point at $50. But if it does clear that point, I can clearly see a possible $12 position reward ($62–$50) with only a $4 position risk ($50–$46). This gives me a reward-to-risk ratio of 3, which clearly passes my money management test.

So what do I do now? Do I sit around chained to my computer all day long and wait to see if the stock sticks its head above $50 and then buy it? Of course not! Using a direct access platform, I can enter a buy stop order at, say, $50.25 and then go wherever I darn well please.

But wait! You might know that I could also place the very same kind of buy stop order with any Level I online broker. That's certainly true. But let's now assume that my buy stop was indeed triggered, and I've become the proud owner of 500 shares of Adios. It's now time for me to put my three money management stops in place. With a direct access platform, I can use some programmed ordering to easily do this. Here's what I program my direct access platform to do:

- ORDER ONE: If the price of Adios decreases to $45.89 *or* if the price of Adios increases to $61.90, then close all shares at the market price.
- ORDER TWO: Set a $2 trailing stop for Adios.

With Order 1, I have established a rule for closing my position if either of my pre-arranged exit points is reached. Moreover, per our discussion in key point number 2 in Chapter 17, I have studiously avoided setting both of my exit points at either "round numbers" or exactly at key technical analysis decision nodes—in this case support and resistance levels.

With Order 2, I have also added a trailing stop. I do this to ensure that I will lock in at least some profits should the stock suddenly lurch down well below its normal intraday range of volatility of $1.89. (I have determined this intraday volatility to be $1.89 by comparing the difference between the intraday lows and highs of the stock.)

Of course, these are very simple rules that I have programmed into my orders. In addition, at least with some trading platforms like TradeStation, you can also program much more sophisticated buy and sell strategies that are based on factors such as MACD crossovers, moving average behavior, and so on. In one of the exercises below, I will help you explore this larger world of programmed ordering.

In the meantime, the broader point I'd like you to take away here is that by being able to program your orders using your direct access platform, you can much more efficiently apply your risk management, money management, and trade management tools. By doing such programmed ordering, you will also be freed up to go about the business of your life rather than being chained to your computer and online broker. Such freedom is a very good thing, particularly for folks like myself who also have a "day job," mine being a business professor at the University of California.

QUESTIONS

1. What are the three ways to execute a trade? Which is the best and cheapest?

2. What are the three most important pieces of information about a stock price that are provided by a Level I view of the market?

3. What additional pieces of information are provided by a Level II view of the market? What do you gain with this Level II information and why is this important?

4. If you see GSCO, MLCO, and NITE on a Level II screen, who are they?

5. What is slippage? What are the four major sources of slippage?

6. Why might you be willing to pay slightly higher commission costs for direct access trading?

7. Besides eliminating slippage and providing market transparency, what is the other major advantage of direct access, Level II platforms?

EXERCISES

1. Visit www.tradingacademy.com/level2login.htm for a Web streamed "webinar" that discusses the "Dirty Little Secrets" of Wall Street along with some excellent content on the use of Level II in a direct access environment. At www.tradingacademy.com, you can also find information on some additional and very useful hands-on training on direct access platforms.

2. Visit www.rushtrade.com and find "Free Demos." At this link, you can download and use a free direct access execution platform to better understand the concepts of self-control order routing and execution speed. Before you leave the Web site, check out the different types of platforms available to you and the associated commissions, charges, and account minimums.

3. Visit the Web site of another major player in the direct access platform business, www.cybertrader.com, and compare the commissions, charges, and features to that of RushTrade. Try out the simulator to get a better feel for the direct access, Level II world.

4. This exercise will guide you to the most sophisticated programmed ordering platform in the business. This platform can be found at www.trade
   station.com. At this Web site, click on the links that will give you more
   information about TradeStation's strategy testing and "EasyLanguage"
   programming. But be forewarned! The "EasyLanguage" is anything but
   easy—or user friendly. Still, if you can ramp up TradeStation's steep learning curve, the tools available to you using this platform are very powerful
   and useful.

5. Complete your "shopping" for the direct access platform you prefer by also
   going to the Web sites for Tradecast and RealTick. If you are convinced of
   the benefits of using a direct access platform, make the switch to that platform that you find best fits your needs.

PART SIX

MACROWAVE INVESTING IN MOTION

Any investor who ignores the power of macroeconomics over the markets will lose more than they should—and perhaps more than they have.

If It's Raining in Brazil, Buy Starbucks

Chapter 19

PREPARING FOR THE INVESTING WEEK

Genius is one percent inspiration, ninety-nine percent perspiration.

Thomas Edison

If Thomas Edison were alive today trying to protect his 401(k), he might say the same thing about stock market investing, namely, that good stock picking often requires at least some inspired thinking. But mostly it's the "perspiration" in the form of carefully preparing for the market that really pays off. That's why in this chapter I want to talk a little bit about how I prepare for each investing week.

Key Macrowave Points

1. The savvy macrowave investor begins the week with a broad overview of both the short- and long-term trends of the market and scenario-builds accordingly.

2. The savvy macrowave investor reviews the weekly macroeconomic calendar before the start of each investing week, reads *IBD*'s "Big Picture" daily, and systematically scans the Web for the breaking macroeconomic news on a daily basis.

3. The savvy macrowave investor conducts daily stock and sector screens using a variety of Web tools and monitors both CNBC and Bloomberg television.

4. The savvy macrowave investor continually tries to assess and reassess new information about the four dynamic factors and three key cycles as a means of anticipating changes in the market and sector trends.

5. The savvy macrowave investor takes analysis from the media with a large grain of salt and healthy dose of skepticism.

The *Savvy Macrowave Investor* Newsletter

In preparing for the investing week, the vehicle that I use to clarify my thinking—and which I share with the general public on my Web site—is my *Savvy Macrowave Investor* newsletter. What I want to do now is explain the structure of each section of the newsletter and the kind of research and preparation that goes into its writing. This preparation is *the same kind of preparation that I recommend you, yourself, do*. So what follows is an explanation of the five parts of the *Savvy Macrowave Investor* newsletter within the context of the weekly and daily research I do to be ready to write each of the parts. These parts, in the order we shall discuss them, include:

1. The Market Overview and Scorecard
2. The Macroeconomic Calendar
3. Strong and Weak Sectors
4. Media Watch
5. Stock Picks of the Week
6. The Technical Roundup

The Savvy Macrowave Overview and Scorecard

The newsletter always begins with an overview of both the short- and long-term trends of the broad market. For example, the market may be in a prolonged, downward bearish trend. However, over the last several weeks, there may have been a "bear market rally" in which the short-term trend is up. This is a market that is very dangerous to invest in, as it remains uncertain as to whether the market will make a successful transition from a late bear to early bull stage.

Alternatively, we may be solidly in the middle bull phase of an upward-trending market, with both the short- and long-term trends up. Going long into this kind of market will be almost like printing money.

As for how I develop "my take" on the broad market, it begins with my *daily* routine. I use www.dismalscience.com and other sites like www.money.cnn.com, and www.bloomberg.com to keep track of the latest macroeconomic reports on inflation, productivity, consumption and so on. I carefully read the "Big Picture" column of *IBD* and quickly scan the rest of the paper for possible stock picks. I do my daily stock and sector screens using a wide variety of Web tools, including *IBD*, Market Edge, and BigCharts. I monitor both CNBC and Bloomberg Television for news and analysis (taking any of CNBC's stock picks or market

short side of market has biggest profit potential &
probably risk in most times & circumstances

forecasts with more than a grain of salt). And I always read *Barron's* cover-to-cover. And lest you think this all takes a lot of time, it doesn't. My daily routine *does* fit neatly in to the 5 to 10 hours a week I have recommended to you as the minimum amount of time necessary to manage your own portfolio well.

Finally, please note that at the end of the newsletter's first section, I also provide a macrowave scorecard. It rates the various elements of the macrowave market equation on a bullish versus bearish scale. These elements are organized along the lines of the four dynamic factors and include the outlook for corporate earnings, the major elements of the GDP equation (consumption, business investment, and net exports), both fiscal and monetary policy, and various exogenous shocks like war, terrorism, and oil price spikes. By keeping this macrowave scorecard each week, I am able to carefully monitor the important macrowaves that are moving the markets.

The Macroeconomic Calendar

The second part of the *Savvy Macrowave Investor* newsletter reviews the macroeconomic calendar for the coming week, specifically which reports are coming out on what days and what the consensus estimates are projected to be. Importantly, this section also identifies *which of the reports are likely to be the major market movers*.

Perhaps most interestingly, I also speculate on the best "odds on" play of the week on the macro data front. What I am looking for is one or more reports where the effect of a data surprise on the markets will be "asymmetrical." What do I mean by this?

In many cases, the relative macroeconomic risk that the Wall Street consensus is wrong is *not* symmetrical. That is, a positive upside surprise like an improvement in consumer confidence or productivity will *not* provide anywhere near the same amount of "lift" to the market indices as a downside surprise will provide "drop."

This is a profound observation because the existence of such asymmetrical risk turns trading on pending macroeconomic news from what would otherwise merely be a 50-50 gamble into an intelligent speculation in which the odds are now clearly in your favor. The reason: You can enter a position where the potential reward of winning is significantly higher than the risk of losing—and a favorable reward-to-risk ratio is the hallmark of intelligent speculation.

For example, and most aggressively, you can short a rising market if the risk of a negative macrowave surprise is significantly greater than that of a positive one. More conservatively, you can simply hedge your portfolio on the eve of a major macroeconomic report (or set of reports) against any impending macrowave risk.

why hedge if getting out has sa cost? Taxes?

For example, if your portfolio is long and you fear an impending negative surprise, you can short a market index like the Nasdaq 100's QQQ and/or the S&P 500's SPY to hedge that risk.

Strong and Weak Sectors

The third part of the newsletter draws the latest bead on the patterns of sector rotation. By doing so, it identifies emerging strong sectors and weak sectors in which there may be good opportunities to buy or short stocks.

To prepare this section, I use the sector screens from both Market Edge and IBD along with a proprietary sector analysis model developed by David Aloyan. Periodically, I will also go to www.bigcharts.com and download every single firm in a sector and put it through both a technical and fundamental screen using the fundamental analysis tools of www. investors.com (as explained in Chapter 13) and the technical analysis tools of www.marketedge.com (discussed in Chapter 14).

Media Watch

The fourth part of the *Savvy Macrowave Investor* newsletter focuses on the follies, foibles, and often sheer genius of our esteemed media. As I indicated earlier, as part of my research, I regularly monitor the financial press. Besides *Investor's Business Daily* and *Barron's*, I scan the *Wall Street Journal's* editorial page. I do this because the *WSJ's* op-ed articles and editorials provide an early warning system of possible changes in both fiscal and monetary policy.

For an invaluable foreign perspective, I skim the *Financial Times*, and for the news from "Main Street," I regularly read the *Los Angeles Times* (but would likely read the *Boston Globe*, *New York Times*, *Washington Post*, *Chicago Tribune*, *San Francisco Chronicle*, or any one of a number of excellent newspapers, if I lived in any one of those cities). As I mentioned, I also watch CNBC and Bloomberg TV, particularly in the morning before the market opens to see where the S&P and Nasdaq market futures are heading.

Note that I conduct this media survey with a very high degree of skepticism. While I value the analyses of these influential outlets, I also find that there are many times when they get it just dead wrong. It is precisely those kinds of occasions that the newsletter typically tends to focus on. Put simply, *I am trying to warn people not to buy into what often are examples of either irrational exuberance or pessimism and equally often examples of just plain bad analysis.* Here are just a few examples:

CNBC's Kudlow and Cramer pound on the table declaring a new bull market that, in reality, is in the throes of just another bear market rally. *Barron's* runs a story pimping what, on closer inspection, is a Boeing stock ready to swoon. An *IBD* reporter inaccurately concludes that higher oil prices will lead the Fed to raise interest rates—when such an oil price shock will have just the opposite effect. The point: Don't believe everything you read or see, and especially don't buy or sell stocks on such information.

Stock Picks of the Week

The fifth part of the newsletter offers some stock picks for the week. Often, with these picks, I will offer up a "macroplay" such as I described in Chapter 7. For example, in the sample newsletter below, I suggest a possible short sell on the Carnival Cruise Line based on an outbreak of the Norwalk virus that turned some of the company's ships into what the media caustically referred to as "Barf Boats."

Now please note this important point. I offer these stock picks as *mine*. *They shouldn't necessarily be yours*. When it's all said and done, it must be *you* who assumes responsibility for making your own market choices. It is *you* who must learn to sort out the Wall Street wheat from the huckster chaff.

Technical Roundup

The last section of the newsletter is prepared completely by David Aloyan. It features a complete technical analysis roundup of the three major stock market indices: the S&P 500, the Nasdaq, and the Dow. You should find this section very valuable when it comes to gauging the broad market trend as well as any pending reversals or weakening of that trend.

That, then, is the structure of, and logic behind, the *Savvy Macrowave Investor* newsletter. Let's conclude this chapter with a sample of the newsletter, which can be found each week at www.peternavarro.com.

QUESTIONS

1. The *Savvy Macrowave Investor* newsletter always begins with the broad market outlook. Suppose that the newsletter describes the market as being in a prolonged, downward trend. However, over the last several weeks, there may have been a bear market rally. Is this a safe market to invest in?

2. The macrowave scorecard rates the various elements of the macrowave market equation on a bullish versus bearish scale. Name at least four elements of that scorecard.

3. In many cases, the relative macrowave risk that the Wall Street consensus is wrong is *not* symmetrical. For example, a positive upside surprise like an improvement in consumer confidence might not provide anywhere near the same amount of lift to the market as a downside surprise will provide a drop. Why is this an important observation?

4. Why does the *Savvy Macrowave Investor* newsletter include a section on strong and weak sectors?

5. What is the main purpose of the "Media Watch" section of the *Savvy Macrowave Investor* newsletter?

6. Should you run right out and buy or short the latest stock picks of the week in the *Savvy Macrowave Investor* newsletter?

7. The last section of the *Savvy Macrowave Investor* newsletter features a technical analysis of the broad market. How can this help you in your investing?

EXERCISES

1. Visit www.peternavarro.com on a Monday and read the latest version of the newsletter. Then, during that week, closely follow the release of the macroeconomic data at www.dismalscience.com and compare the newsletter's analysis to the actual events. Also, follow the "stock picks" over the next several weeks to see whether we got it right or wrong. (*Note*: As we learned in Chapter 16, if you obey strict money management principles, you only have to be right with your stock picking 60 percent of the time to make a *lot* of money.)

2. Using the left-hand side of the macrowave scorecard that appears in the sample newsletter in this chapter, give your own assessment of current conditions. That is, try to assess whether each of the various elements in the scorecard seem bullish or bearish *now*. After you do so, look at this scorecard and see if it helps you come to some deeper conclusion about where the stock market might be headed in the next few months.

3. Here's an exercise that I love to give my business school students at the University of California as I teach them how to follow the markets. Pick up a copy of *Barron's* on Saturday and read it cover to cover. As you read it, jot down all of the stocks that *Barron's* gives significantly positive *or*

negative coverage to. Then, try to pick the one stock that you think will drop the most on Monday when the stock market opens because of unfavorable *Barron's* coverage. Also, pick the one stock you think will jump the highest on favorable coverage. Lastly, at the close of the market on Monday, check the stock price movements of *all* of the stocks on your list. In a typical week, you should see the "*Barron's* effect," namely, bad coverage drives most stocks down and good coverage drives them up, at least for a day or two.

Chapter 20

THE STIMULATION OF PORTFOLIO SIMULATION

> Only three things in life are certain: Death, taxes, and that every new investor inevitably pays "tuition" to the market.
>
> *Ron Vara*

Novice investors invariably make rookie mistakes that needlessly cost them some of their hard-earned capital. For example, the novice may use a market order before the opening bell and get caught in a gap up opening. Or the novice may set a stop loss too tight and get pushed out of a stock for a loss—after which the stock quickly and maddeningly takes off. Or the novice may forget to set an appropriate stop loss altogether—and lose far more than intended.

One very effective way to avoid paying such "tuition" to the market is to simulate investing in a "mock portfolio." With a mock portfolio, you can use "play money" before you actually put your real money down—and save a lot of cash by doing so.

In this last chapter of our book, I am going to show you how both novices and experienced investors alike can greatly benefit from the use of "portfolio simulation" using a very powerful but very easy-to-use software. The software is called STOCK-TRAK and it is available at my Web site at www.peternavarro.com.

Key Macrowave Points

1. STOCK-TRAK is a versatile portfolio simulation tool that allows you to invest in real time using all the regular tools of modern investing.

2. Novice investors can benefit greatly from portfolio simulation. Invest for at least three to six months before committing real money to the market as you master the art of savvy macrowave investing.

3. Portfolio simulations can help experienced investors break a string of losses by uncovering flaws in their investing systems.

4. All investors who want to overcome "shortaphobia"—an aversion to short selling the market—may find a cure using portfolio simulation.

Key Point #1: Simulate Your Portfolio With STOCK-TRAK

STOCK-TRAK is used by tens of thousands of students and the general investing public each year. It provides the ideal method to practice investment strategies, test theories, . . . learn about the various markets, and compete against your classmates, friends, and colleagues.

Mark Brookshire, CEO

STOCK-TRAK is a portfolio simulation tool that allows you to invest in real time using many of the tools of modern investing. With STOCK-TRAK, you can trade virtually every type of financial instrument traded on the major exchanges—from stocks, options, and futures to mutual funds, bonds, and international stocks. You can also use many of the tools of modern investing—from setting stop losses and buy stops to buying on margin and short selling.

Importantly, the software also charges you "commissions" on every trade. This is so you will learn about how these "transactions costs" can wind up consuming a large share of any profits you might make—particularly if you overtrade.

Now here are just some of the reasons why both novice and experienced investors can benefit from portfolio simulation.

Key Point #2: The Tuition Bill Always Comes Due

"Don't confuse brains with a Bull market."

A Wall Street Wag

Many novice investors who began their investing career in the middle of the last bull market thought they were brilliant because initially they made so much money. Of course, many of these same investors wound up losing as much—or more—than they first made when the bull turned into one of the worst bear markets in history. The reason: The stock market is a very dangerous place to be, and it offers countless traps for the novice investor. That's why virtually every new investor at some time pays "tuition" to the market in the form of losses.

For example, in an effort to diversify his or her portfolio, a novice may buy 10 different stocks—but buy them all from the same sector. Of course, when the sector tanks, all of the stocks will fall in undiversified tandem.

Similarly, the novice may unwittingly buy into a stock that is rallying on rumors of a positive earnings announcement. However, this same lamb to the slaughter may quickly see his or her profits get vaporized when all of the smart money sells on the earnings news.

The list of such traps for the novice goes on and on. To avoid falling into them, *I strongly recommend* that you simulate your investment experience for at least three to six months before you put real money down. During this "training time," you can hone your skills as a savvy macrowave investor. Tune in to the flow of the four dynamic factors, following the movements of the key cycles. Comb the Internet and publications like *Investor's Business Daily* every day for strong stocks in strong sectors to buy and weak stocks in weak sectors to short. You can also apply every single investing tool you've learned about in this book.

So go ahead and make all your early rookie mistakes and perhaps lose a ton of money. But at the end of the day, if you first simulate a portfolio, all you will have will be *paper* losses—and a solid base of experience.

Key Point #3: Stop the Bleeding and Find the Right Bandage

It's not just the "newbie" investor that can benefit from portfolio simulation. This is because *any experienced investor can suffer a string of bad losses.* Such losses can happen for one of two reasons: It is truly bad luck or, more perniciously, there is actually some fatal flaw in your investing system.

In the bad luck category, remember that we savvy macrowave investors are, first and foremost, intelligent speculators, *not* gamblers. What we are trying to do as we analyze the markets and apply our macrowave investing methods is to move the odds in our favor—away from the house's advantage of 51–49 to something more like 60–40 or 70–30 in our favor.

Note, however, that even if the next 10 stocks you want to speculate on all have a very legitimate 60 percent chance of being profitable, every single one of them also has a 40 percent chance of being unprofitable. That means that it is well within the laws of probability to pick 2, or 3, or even 10 losers in a row—even though taken individually, every single one of them was an intelligent speculation.

So how do you tell the difference between such bad luck and perhaps a more fundamentally flawed stock picking system? It can be very difficult to do so.

But let me say this. If you do hit a big string of bad stock picks, *stop* pouring real money down into what may be a rat hole, take several very deep breaths, and move into cash. Then, spend some time analyzing your losses. After you pinpoint what you think might be some of your problems, go ahead and test out your solutions *not* with more real money but rather through simulated investing.

Key Point #4: Conquer Shortaphobia

Short weak stocks in weak sectors in a downward-trending market.

The Second Golden Rule of Macrowave Investing

One of the most curious facts of stock market investing is that over 90 percent of all individual investors shun the short side of the market and only buy stocks. At first glance, this may seem puzzling. After all, there will be many months, and even years at a time, when the stock market is in a prolonged bearish down trend.

In such down trends, you can make vast sums very quickly short selling the market. In fact, you can generally make more money in a much shorter period of time shorting a bear market than you can going long in a bull market. This is because bear market moves tend to happen in a much more compressed period of time.

So why do investors shun the short side? One reason is precisely because the stock market tends to move down a lot faster than it moves up. That's not just a golden opportunity to make money quickly. It's also a lot more risk if the market suddenly reverses.

The other reason, however, is that short selling simply runs against the grain of the typical investor's psyche. For whatever reason, we seem to be more conditioned to both expecting—and indeed *wanting*—the market to go up rather than down. These basic emotions of hope and optimism seem to make us very uncomfortable with the short side.

Now here's the point: If you have the same aversion to short selling that most investors do, there is no better risk-free way to overcome such an aversion than to simulate investing in a "short side–only" portfolio. That's right. Go ahead and set up your mock portfolio with STOCK-TRAK and limit yourself to *only* trading the short side, even while you may be buying stocks with real cash.

You will see very quickly that this "short-side" portfolio exercise will be a great way to conquer your "shortaphobia" at the same time that short selling will toughen you up as an investor and sharpen your stock-picking skills. Moreover, such experience will help you better pinpoint weak stocks and weak sectors even in an upward-trending market.

QUESTIONS

1. What two types of investors can benefit from portfolio simulation?

2. Why is simulating your portfolio for three to six months *before* you put real money down such a good idea for novice investors?

3. Under what two circumstances will experienced investors benefit from portfolio simulation?

EXERCISES

1. Visit www.peternavarro.com and check out the STOCK-TRAK link.

2. Even if you are managing your own *real* portfolio, use STOCK-TRAK to try out some new investing ideas.

3. Trade a short sell–only portfolio on STOCK-TRAK to conquer your shortaphobia. Find weak stocks in weak sectors.

4. Visit www.academic.nasdaq.com/headtrader/. You can fruitfully spend several hours perusing this site and playing the Head Trader Game.

ANSWER KEY

Answers to Questions for Chapter 1

1. If rain comes to break a drought in Brazil, why might the stock price of Starbucks stock go up?

   Brazil is the largest coffee producer in the world. If rain comes to break a drought, coffee beans will be cheaper. That means a coffee retailer like Starbucks will make a few pennies more on each cup coffee they sell. As profits rise, so too should a stock price.

2. List at least five of the major macrowaves that helped bring the Nasdaq Stock Market Index down from over 5000 to well below 2000.

   The major macrowaves included inflationary pressures, a 50-point interest rate hike by the Federal Reserve, the collapse of Microsoft antitrust talks, oil price spikes, presidential election uncertainties, terrorism and war, a bad case of Enronitis, oil and gold prices spike, and tensions in the Middle East.

Answers to Questions for Chapter 2

1. At a minimum, how many hours a week should you devote to actively manage your portfolio?

   If you can't devote at least 5 to 10 hours a week to your portfolio, you may be better off putting your money in a very broad index fund.

2. Should you view the stock market more as a game of roulette or poker? And what is the difference between gambling and speculation?

   You should view the stock market more as a game of poker rather than of roulette. With gambling, the odds are against you. When you speculate intelligently in the stock market, you are using your analytical skills to put the odds in your favor.

3. Besides making money, list two other important investing goals.

   Two other investing goals besides making money should be (1) taking pride in the craft of investing well and (2) enjoying the challenge of a very complex and subtle pursuit.

4. What is the minimum level of capital you need to be an efficient active investor?

   You should start with a minimum trading account of least $25,000 and preferably $50,000.

5. Why is it important only to invest money that you can afford to lose?

   If you are using money in the stock market that you can't possibly afford to lose, you will likely wind up making bad decisions because of added pressure.

Answers to Questions for Chapter 3

1. What are the Three Golden Rules of Macrowave Investing?

   The savvy macrowave investor (1) buys strong stocks in strong sectors in an upward-trending market, (2) stays out of the market and in cash when there is no definable trend, and (3) shorts weak stocks in weak sectors in a downward-trending market.

2. Name the four stages of macrowave investing.

   The four stages are: (1) Process the flow of information from the four dynamic factors. (2) Use a mastery of the four key cycles to determine the broad market and sector trends. (3) Use fundamental and technical analysis to find strong stocks in strong sectors. (4) Use direct access investing with sound money and risk management principles to enter and exit positions.

3. Name the four dynamic factors.

   The four dynamic factors are (1) corporate earnings news, (2) the macroeconomic data, (3) fiscal and monetary policy, and (4) exogenous shocks.

4. Name the three key cycles.

   The three key cycles are (1) the business cycle, (2) the stock market cycle, and (3) the interest rate cycle.

5. Why does a better understanding of the patterns of sector rotation help you become a better investor?

By understanding the patterns of sector rotation, you are better able to identify strong and weak sectors.

6. Upon what does technical analysis purely focus?

Technical analysis focuses purely on the price action of a stock.

7. Name at least one of the traps that the fundamental analyst tends to fall into.

The fundamental analyst will invest in a fundamentally strong company in a bad overall market. Or he or she will invest in a great company in a bad market sector.

8. What are the first three rules of money management?

The first three rules of money management are cut your losses, cut your losses, and cut your losses.

9. Before you actually ever buy a stock, you must also decide both how and when to do what?

You must decide how and when to exit the stock.

Answers to Questions for Chapter 4

1. Over the longer run, what does a company's stock price depend on?

It depends on investor expectations about the company's future stream of earnings.

2. In processing the earnings news, the savvy macrowave investor wants the answers to what three major questions?

The three major questions are: (1) Is the company's earnings likely to meet, beat, or fall short of the consensus estimate? (2) Is the company likely to meet, beat, or fall short of its earnings whisper number for the quarter? (3) Is the company likely to change its earnings guidance?

3. When do companies typically release their earnings news?

They release earnings news after the close of the market or right before the next day's open.

4. If a company releases bad earnings news, what is likely to happen to the stock price when the market opens the next day?

The stock price will likely "gap down."

5. Provide at least two reasons why the stock price of a company may *gap down* after very *good* earnings news.

   (1) The real increase in a stock's price may come before the earnings announcement. Once the news hits, many investors may take their profits and run even as the stock's price plunges. (2) Earnings might be good, but the stock price may still gap down if the company changes its guidance about the profitability of future quarters. (3) Reported earnings may be above the consensus estimate but below the so-called whisper number.

6. Why do consensus estimates tend to be unreliable?

   Strategically, company executives attempt to keep the analysts' estimates below the company's internal targets. If actual earnings beats the consensus, the company's stock price usually rises.

7. Who provides the consensus estimates?

   They are provided by professional stock market analysts.

8. Why does the savvy macrowave investor also check the earnings calendar for other stocks in the sector in which he or she may be investing?

   The savvy macrowave investor checks it for companies that are leaders in a sector or that may be bellwethers for the broader sector.

9. Why is it useful for the savvy macrowave investor to look at the earnings reports of the economy's largest companies?

   It is useful because these companies are bellwethers for the broader *market* and help a savvy macrowave investor gauge the broad market trend.

10. Most broadly, what does a healthy earnings season signal and, conversely, what does a dismal earnings season signal?

   A healthy earnings season signals a bullish market. A dismal earnings season signals a bearish one.

Answers to Questions for Chapter 5

1. The process of speculating on the likely effects that the key macroeconomic reports will have on the stock market is called "macro scenario building." What are the goals of such speculation?

   At a minimum, we don't want to be caught in any big positions on the wrong side of the economic news. The broader goal is to use the macroeconomic news to better gauge the market and sector trends and thereby exploit profitable opportunities that may arise when the actual news is different from the consensus estimates of the Wall Street experts.

2. When we say that all macroeconomic indicators are not created equal, what exactly do we mean?

   We mean that some economic indicators are likely to have a much greater effect on the stock market than others.

3. Why does the stock market hate inflation?

   It hates it because inflation raises the probability that the Federal Reserve will raise interest rates.

4. Is the Federal Reserve more likely to raise interest rates in the presence of demand-pull inflation or cost-push inflation?

   The Federal Reserve is likely to very swiftly raise interest rates in the presence of demand-pull inflation. But the presence of cost-push inflation can actually reduce the probability that the Fed will raise rates because cost-push inflation is contractionary.

5. Why does the stock market hate recessions?

   It hates them because recessions mean lower production and sales and ultimately lower prices for the products firms sell. As earnings fall so, too, must stock prices.

6. Why are both auto sales and housing starts regarded as key leading indicators?

   They are key leading indicators because the auto and housing sectors are typically the first to surge when the economy is recovering from recession.

7. Why does the stock market love increases in productivity growth?

   It loves them because the U.S. economy can grow much faster without fear of inflation.

8. What happens to productivity when the economy begins to slide into recession? Is this likely to worry the Federal Reserve?

   Productivity typically tends to fall as the economy slides into recession because businesses cut back on production at a faster pace than they lay off workers. This kind of short-run fall in productivity is not likely to worry the Federal Reserve.

9. Why does the stock market hate budget deficits?

   It hates them because budget deficits can cause inflation and higher interest rates and discourage private-sector investment.

10. Why does the stock market (mostly) hate trade deficits?

It hates them because trade deficits can weaken the dollar and are inflationary.

11. If the trade deficit increases because the U.S. economy is growing faster than the European and Asian economies, is this bullish or bearish?

In this case, a trade deficit is less worrisome because it has resulted from robust U.S. economic growth. That's bullish, at least in the short run.

Answers to Questions for Chapter 6

1. What is the difference between fiscal and monetary policy when it comes to fighting recession?

Monetary policy expands the money supply and lowers interest rates to stimulate a recessionary economy. Fiscal policy uses increased government spending or decreased taxes to achieve the same goal.

2. Why is it important to understand that interest rate changes are part of a cycle by the Federal Reserve rather than isolated events?

The interest rate cycle has a huge impact on the broader market trend. It is very difficult for the market trend to continue moving up once an increasing interest rate cycle takes hold.

3. What are some of the sectors likely to be hurt by a Fed rate hike?

Interest rate–sensitive sectors such as autos, banking, brokerage, financial services, home finance and construction are all likely to be hurt by an interest rate hike.

4. How might an interest rate hike by the Federal Reserve affect the housing sector and the various sectors that depend on home construction?

An interest rate hike leads to higher mortgage rates, a fall in new-home sales and, eventually, a decline in new-home construction. Slower new-home construction reduces consumer spending on appliances such as washers and dryers, dishwashers, and refrigerators, as well as carpet manufacturers and other home improvement businesses.

5. Is the Federal Reserve more likely to be successful fighting inflation or recession? Why?

Raising interest rates to fight inflation usually is very effective at contracting the economy. However, when the Fed cuts interest rates to try and stimulate the economy back to full employment, there is no guarantee that either consumers or businesses will respond to the interest rate reductions. This is the case of being unable to "push on a string."

6. What are the two main ways to finance a budget deficit created by expansionary fiscal policy? What are the problems associated with each of the two methods?

   The government can either sell bonds or print money to finance the deficit. Selling bonds can crowd out private investment while printing money can cause inflation. Both are bearish for the stock market.

7. Is it better for the government to use a tax cut or increased government spending to stimulate a recessionary economy?

   Increased government spending provides a more certain stimulus. This is because there is no guarantee that if you cut someone's taxes that that person will actually spend the money.

Answers to Questions for Chapter 7

1. Define, and provide several examples of, exogenous shocks.

   An exogenous shock is a term that economists use for events that come from outside the economic system. Such shocks range from oil price spikes, war and terrorism, and natural disasters to more human-made phenomena like accounting scandals and the advent of disruptive technologies.

2. Why are oil price spikes very bearish for the stock market?

   They are bearish because they act as a contractionary tax on the economy.

3. Is war bullish or bearish for the stock market?

   Some wars, like World War II, have been very bullish because they stimulate the economy. However, the government's shift in budgetary worries from "butter" to "guns" can lead to larger budget deficits, higher inflation, higher interest rates, and lower productivity—all of which are decidedly bearish in the longer term.

4. What is the nature of the "terrorist tax"?

   In an age of terrorism, we are going to have to spend more for security. This cost is going to have a long-term weight on the economy and stock market.

5. What is likely to be the single-most important source of large movements in stock prices in the twenty-first century?

    The single-most important source of large movements in stock prices in the twenty-first century is likely to be disruptive technologies.

Answers to Questions for Chapter 8

1. What are the Three Golden Rules of Macrowave Investing?

    The Three Golden Rules are: (1) Buy strong stocks in strong sectors in an upward-trending market. (2) Short weak stocks in weak sectors in a downward-trending market. (3) Stay out of the market and in cash when there is no discernible trend.

2. At any one time, the stock market trend will be in one of three possible states. What are they?

    The three states are an up trend, a down trend, or a sideways trading range where there is no discernible trend.

3. Why is trading against the trend a bad gamble rather than an intelligent speculation?

    During an up trend, 8 out of 10 stocks generally are moving up with the trend. That means you only have about 20 percent chance of being right about a short position. The reverse is true in a downward-trending market—going long is the gamble.

4. What is the hardest thing for the undisciplined investor to do when there is no clear trend?

    The hardest thing to do is sit in cash.

5. Does a market or a sector trend move in a straight line?

    No. Movement is more like "two steps forward and one step back" for an up trend and the reverse for a down trend.

6. Name two advantages of exchange-traded funds over mutual funds.

    First, exchange-traded funds trade exactly like stocks. That means if you want to invest in the broad market or a particular sector, you don't have to rely on a mutual fund. Instead, you can buy an exchange-traded fund, which has much lower fee and expense ratios.

    Second, unlike mutual funds, you can also short-sell exchange-traded funds, and they are not subject to the so-called up-tick rule.

7. Name the exchange-traded funds for the Nasdaq market, the Standard & Poor's 500 Index, and the Dow Jones Industrial Average.

    The exchange-traded funds are QQQ, SPY, and DIA, respectively.

8. Name the exchange-traded funds for the semiconductor and biotechnology sectors.

    The exchange-traded funds are SMH and BBH, respectively.

9. The 3-point-break method is a very useful shorthand tool to identify what? How can this knowledge help you in your trading and investing strategies?

    The 3-point-break method is a very useful tool to identify trends and trend changes. It can help you because it generates buy, sell, and short signals.

Answers to Questions for Chapter 9

1. Stock prices and the broader stock market cycle reflect nothing more than what?

    They reflect changing shareholder expectations of a future stream of earnings.

2. Take out a pencil and pad of paper and draw the business cycle. Do the same for the stock market cycle and show the relationship between the two. Compare your drawings to the figures in the book.

    Go to the figures in Chapter 9 in the book to compare your drawings.

3. Which peaks first, the business cycle or the stock market cycle? Which one of the cycles is a "leading indicator" of the other?

    The stock market cycle peaks before the business cycle and is therefore a leading indicator of the business cycle.

4. What can we say about the duration and amplitude of the business cycle and what might this mean for your investing and trading strategies?

    Both the duration and amplitude of the business cycle can vary significantly. For example, an expansion can last as little as six months or as long as five years or more just as a recession can be mild or severe. Because both the duration and amplitude of the business cycle vary considerably, the cycles are harder to predict, which means more risk for your investing.

5. What does the term "sector rotation" refer to?

    At different points of the stock market cycle, the stock prices of the companies in some sectors will rise, on average, faster than the stock prices of companies in other sectors. As a result, these sectors outperform both the general market and the other sectors.

6. Which sectors do the best in the early bull phase of the stock market cycle?

Transportation, retailing, and semiconductors all do best in the early bull phase.

7. What are some of the so-called defensive sectors that do well in the late bear phase of the stock market cycle?

Food, drugs, and medical care all do well in the late bear phase.

8. In what phase of the stock market cycle does the energy sector typically peak?

It typically peaks in the late bull phase.

9. Which two sectors generally lead the recovery?

Autos and housing usually lead the recovery.

10. At which phase of the stock market cycle is the Federal Reserve likely to begin *raising* interest rates, and at which phase is the Fed likely to begin *lowering* interest rates?

Typically, the Federal Reserve begins raising interest rates in the late expansionary phase of the business cycle as inflationary pressures build. It typically starts to lower interest rates in the middle to late bear phase of the stock market cycle during the recessionary phase of the business cycle.

Answers to Questions for Chapter 10

1. A typical interest rate cycle goes through four clear stages. What are they?

The stages are (1) a series of rate hikes, (2) steady higher rates, (3) a series of interest rate cuts, and, once again, (4) steady but lower rates.

2. When does the first stage of the interest rate cycle typically occur?

It typically occurs in the late expansionary phase of the business cycle.

3. Why does the Federal Reserve hold interest rates steady in the second stage of the interest rate cycle?

The Fed holds rates steady to allow its tight money medicine to slow the economy down and eventually wring inflationary pressures out of the economy.

4. Once the Federal Reserve begins to lower interest rates in the third stage of the interest rate cycle, does the stock market and economy immediately recover?

   Not necessarily. Sometimes it can take a very long time for an "easy money" policy to revive the economy. The problem is you "can't push on a string," meaning that just because interest rates are low, consumers and businesses won't necessarily increase their spending.

5. Why does the stock market not like rising interest rates?

   It doesn't like them because they choke off growth and earnings.

6. Do Fed rate hikes hurt some sectors more than others? If so, which sectors are hurt most?

   Key interest rate–sensitive sectors such as banking, brokerage, and finance as well as autos and housing will all be hurt relatively more than other sectors by interest rate increases.

7. The Federal Reserve started the upward portion of the interest rate cycle with a 25-basis-point hike on June 30, 1999. How long did it take before the stock market crashed, and how long did it take before the economy went into a recession?

   The Nasdaq market reached its peak of over 5000 in March 2000 and then crashed. The recession officially hit one year from the stock market peak in March 2001, graphically illustrating the power of the stock market to predict future economic conditions.

8. What is the par value of a bond? What is the coupon rate?

   The par value of a bond is its face value. The coupon rate indicates the amount of interest you will receive upon purchase of that bond.

9. Suppose you buy a bond and then interest rates rise. Suppose further that you want to sell your bonds after this increase in interest rates. Will you be able to sell your bond at par, at a premium, or at a discount? Why?

   Bond prices move in an inverse relationship to interest rates. If interest rates rise, the price of your bond will fall, and if you sell it, it will be at a discount. If on the other hand, interest rates fall, bond prices will rise, and you will be able to sell your bond at a premium.

10. How do you calculate the current yield of a bond?

    To calculate the yield, simply divide the bond's coupon rate by its current price.

11. The "risk and term structure of interest rates" refers to what relationship?

    The "risk and term structure of interest rates" refers to the relationship between the yields of Treasury and corporate bonds of different durations and risk levels.

12. In general, what can we say about the relationship between the credit risk of corporate bonds and their yields?

    The riskier the corporate bond, the higher the yield.

Answers to Questions for Chapter 11

1. The yield curve is determined by the relationship between what?

    It is determined by the relationship between short-, medium-, and long-term interest rates on Treasury securities.

2. Why does the savvy macrowave investor carefully follow the yield curve?

    It is one of the most important leading indicators of both bearish recessions and bullish expansions. Following the yield curve is therefore useful in anticipating changes in the broad market and individual sector trends.

3. What is the short end of the yield curve determined by and what is the long end determined by?

    The short end is determined by the discretionary decisions of the Federal Reserve regarding short-run interest rates. The long end of the curve is determined by inflationary expectations in the bond market. As inflationary expectations rise, current yields on the long end of the curve rise as well.

4. What are the four key shapes of the yield curve?

    The four key shapes are normal, steep, flat, and inverted.

5. In what stage of the business cycle and stock market cycle are we likely to observe a normal yield curve?

    A normal yield curve is typically observed during the middle expansionary period of the business cycle and the early to middle bull phase of the stock market cycle.

6. When do we typically observe a steep yield curve? What is the macrowave logic behind this observance?

    We typically observe a steep yield curve at the start of an economic expansion just after a recession ends.

7. What are the two major factors that work to steepen the yield curve?

Increased capital demand and the first stirrings of inflationary expectations after recession drive the long end of the yield curve up in anticipation of economic expansion.

8. With an inverted yield curve, short-run interest rates are higher than long-run rates. What two forces cause the yield curve to invert?

At the short end, the Federal Reserve has begun to raise interest rates to fight inflation. At the long end, bondholders might be willing to lock in yields that are lower than current short-term rates if they believe that the Federal Reserve's contractionary medicine will trigger a recession and therefore be deflationary.

9. In almost all cases, the inverted yield curve signals what?

It signals the coming of a recession and new bear market.

10. The stock market reached a peak in March 2000. Within a year, the economy was in recession. How could the yield curve have helped you as an investor profit from the market crash?

The savvy macrowave investor who observed the March 2000 inverted yield curve would have surely cashed out his or her long positions and may well have gone short.

11. In 1992, the yield curve steepened significantly. What did this presage?

It presaged one of the longest economic expansions in U.S. history, as well as one of the most robust bull markets ever recorded.

Answers to Questions for Chapter 12

1. What kind of stocks does the buy low, sell high approach look for?

It looks for underpriced bargains.

2. In what kind of a market does the buy low, sell high approach work best, and in what kind of a market are you likely to sustain heavy losses?

The buy low, sell high approach works well in a trading range market but underperforms in up markets and can lead to heavy losses in a downward-trending market.

3. What kind of stocks does the buy high, sell higher approach look for?

It looks for stocks that have built a strong base and are about to burst through their pivot points to new highs.

4. In what kind of market does the buy high, sell higher approach work best, and in what kind of market does it perform poorly?

This approach performs very well in an upward-trending market. However, when the market is trading in a tight range, it can be risky. In a downward-trending market, it is very dangerous because of the possibility of failed breakouts.

5. How does the high-volume mover approach work?

It looks for stocks that are moving sharply upward and breaking out on above-average volume or moving sharply downward and breaking down.

6. Name two of the major problems that arise when you depend on the ratings of Wall Street analysts.

Many Wall Street analysts are very slow to downgrade a weak stock or upgrade a strong stock. At least some of these analysts are corrupt and tell you to buy a stock when they're telling the private clients to sell.

7. Summarize the approach to stock picking of the legendary Peter Lynch.

Lynch believed that the key to making money in the stock market is sticking with what you know. He simply said: "Look around you. Look for the new companies and products and trends that are likely to lead to a stock price's rise."

8. Name some of the magazines that are useful to read when searching for stocks.

The following magazines are useful to read when searching for stocks: *Red Herring*, *Technology Review*, *Forbes*, *Fortune*, *Kiplinger's*, *Money*, *Smart Money*, and *Worth*.

9. Why is it wise to ignore the hot stock tips of your friends, acquaintances, or even stockbrokers?

If the hot stock tip comes from inside information, it would be illegal for you to trade on that information. Many times, a hot stock tip originates with the scam artist who wants to pump up the stock and then dump it on the market. Finally, by the time the information gets to you, it is often too old to use.

Answers to Questions for Chapter 13

1. Every stock you consider should go through what two types of screens?

It should go through both a technical screen and a fundamental screen.

2. According to the efficient market theory, stock prices always reflect what? What does this imply for the possibility of finding any stock bargains?

   Stock prices always reflect all available information, and it is impossible to ever find any bargains.

3. According to the random walk theory, stock prices move for what kinds of reasons? What does this assumption imply for trying to pick stocks?

   Stock prices move for totally unpredictable reasons, and it is useless to try to pick winning stocks.

4. If you believe in the efficient market and random walk theories, what should your investment approach be?

   You should either invest in a broad market index fund or, alternatively, create a widely diversified portfolio and hang on for the random ride.

5. Fundamental analysts reject the efficient market theory. What is their alternative belief about stock prices?

   Their belief is that every stock has an "intrinsic" or "fair" value, but stock prices do not always reflect fair value in the short run. These price discrepancies provide profitable opportunities to buy undervalued stocks or short overvalued stocks.

6. A stock market analyst is looking for companies that make products that are easy to understand, have a history of running a high rate of return, are not burdened by excessive debt levels, and have a trust of the management. What famous stock market guru is this stock market analyst likely trying to emulate?

   The analyst is trying to emulate the Oracle of Omaha, Warren Buffett.

7. Name several quantitative and qualitative measures that fundamental analysts look for when evaluating a stock.

   Quantitative measures include profitability, growth in the revenue base, and the degree of leverage and cash flow. Qualitative measures range from whether the company is well managed or prone to labor strikes to the company's rate of technological change and innovation.

8. To use the method of the savvy macrowave investor, is it important that you know how to conduct your own fundamental analysis, or is it sufficient that you simply know how to conduct a fundamental screen?

   Fundamental analysis is very time consuming and tedious. All you need do using the savvy macrowave investor method is to learn how to use simple fundamental screens, many of which are available on the Internet.

9. What are the two traps that the fundamental analyst typically falls into? How can these traps be avoided?

The first trap is investing in a fundamentally strong company in a bad overall market. The second is to invest in a great company in a bad market sector. To avoid these traps, you can also use a technical analysis screen.

10. Technical and fundamental analysts often fight like cats and dogs. So which camp is right?

Both camps are! Any stock you buy should be both technically and fundamentally strong, and any stock you might want to short should be both technically and fundamentally weak.

Answers to Questions for Chapter 14

1. The savvy macrowave investor uses technical analysis on a daily basis to do what?

The investor uses technical analysis to identify the trend, momentum, and sentiment of the broad market as well as the market's individual sectors and stocks.

2. Name some of the most common and useful terms of technical analysis.

Some of these terms include the "gap up" and "gap down," support and resistance, breakouts and breakdowns, overbought and oversold conditions, pullbacks, and relative strength.

3. Technical analysis has its roots in underlying investor psychology and human behavior. Why is this important?

This basis is important because technical analysis can provide a very powerful graphical and mathematical reflection of the ever-changing moods of the market.

4. What is the crucial first step in analyzing the trend of the broad market, an individual sector, or a specific stock? By taking this first step what are we able to accomplish?

The crucial first step is to create a price chart. A price chart quite literally paints a picture of the trend.

5. If you look at a price chart and see a series of ascending peaks and troughs characterized by prices that are making higher highs and higher lows, what kind of trend are you observing?

This trend is clearly an uptrend.

6. When you see a double top chart pattern, is this bullish or bearish? What is the underlying behavioral explanation for this pattern?

   A double top chart pattern is very bearish. Behaviorally, once a stock has taken a crack at breaking through resistance twice and failed, buyers are likely to give up and the stock price will typically fall.

7. Once the technical analyst has used the price chart to identify the trend and reviewed the basic chart pattern, the analyst typically does what next? Why?

   The technical analyst begins to look more closely at the volume of shares traded as well as various volume indicators. The analyst is looking for some confirmation of the prevailing trend or some signal of an impending reversal of the trend.

8. If the On Balance Volume indicator indicates that a stock is under "distribution," is that bullish or bearish?

   That is bearish.

9. Moving averages are used to clarify and amplify the direction of a trend. How can they do that?

   They help smooth out the noise that arises from price and volume fluctuations.

10. When the technical analyst sees a shorter-period moving average begin to cross above a longer-period moving average, what does that say about the price trend and is this a bullish buy signal or a bearish sell signal?

    This type of crossover indicates the price trend is on its way up. It is definitely a bullish buy signal.

11. The RSI oscillator and the Moving Average Convergence Divergence indicator are what kind of indicators? How can they be used?

    These are so-called momentum indicators. They can be used along with moving average analysis to confirm the current trend, warn of an impending stall, or signal a trend reversal.

12. If the majority of investors are bullish, most likely it is time for you to become what? Why is this so?

    If a majority of investors are bullish, it is time for you to become bearish. If too many people are already bulls, there simply won't be enough cash still sitting on the sidelines to continue to propel the market up.

13. I do not expect any of you reading this book to become technical analysts. I do however expect you to be able to do what after reading this chapter?

    You should be able to conduct your own technical analysis screens.

14. Technical analysis is often used to uncover both overbought and oversold conditions. In which kind of market are these signals likely to be more valuable, a sideways market or an upward-trending market?

Overbought and oversold conditions are more useful in a sideways market. In an upward-trending market, technical analysis will often flash false signals of an overbought condition and thereby discourage entry into the market or prompt an early exit from an otherwise very profitable stock.

Answers to Questions for Chapter 15

1. What are two of the most important keys to successful long-term investing?

Two of the most important keys are managing your risk and protecting your investment capital.

2. Risk represents the chance you will lose what? Because such risk exists, there is also a possibility of what happening?

Risk represents the chance you will lose money investing in stocks. With the possibility of loss there also comes the possibility of reward.

3. Name the three *dimensions* of risk. Explain how the savvy macrowave investor reduces each kind of risk.

The three dimensions of risk are (1) market risk, (2) sector risk, and (3) company risk. The savvy macrowave investor reduces market risk by investing with the trend, minimizes sector risk by buying into strong sectors and shorting weak sectors, and reduces company risk by basket trading.

4. Name at least four *sources* of risk.

Sources of risk include credit risk, country risk, exchange-rate risk, interest rate risk, liquidity risk, political risk, and regulatory risk.

5. When it comes to the risk-to-reward ratio, the savvy macrowave investor follows what rule?

The savvy macrowave investor never enters into an investment unless the reward-to-risk ratio is favorable.

6. What does the Sharpe ratio reveal?

The Sharpe ratio reveals the difference between the lucky gambler who may win by assuming excessive risk and the successful speculator who minimizes risk for a given level of reward.

7. What does the beta tell us?

The beta tells us how risky a stock is relative to the broad market.

8. Contrast the approach to sector diversification of the traditional investor versus the savvy macrowave investor.

The traditional investor believes that a well-diversified portfolio includes stocks from many different sectors at *all* times. In contrast, the savvy macrowave investor focuses on just a few sectors at *any one time*.

9. List at least five risk management rules.

The following are risk management rules: (1) Basket trade. (2) Trade only liquid stocks. (3) Diversify narrowly by outperforming sectors. (4) Don't put all your eggs in one basket. (5) Never bet the farm. (6) When in doubt, go flat. (7) Pyramid your entries and exits. (8) Do your research.

Answers to Questions for Chapter 16

1. How do you calculate your Win%?

To calculate Win%, you simply tally up your winning trades and divide these winning trades by your total trades.

2. What is the definition of your risk capital? What about your maximum drawdown, and how is it calculated?

Your maximum drawdown is the most money you are willing to lose in a worst-case scenario in which you lose 10 times in a row on all of your open positions. You calculate your maximum drawdown by multiplying 10 times your risk capital.

3. What does your actual level of risk capital depend on?

It depends on your own level of risk aversion.

4. If you are a moderately aggressive investor, what percentage of your portfolio should you use as your risk capital? How about if you are a very aggressive investor?

In the moderately aggressive case, your risk capital would be 3 percent of your initial portfolio. In the very aggressive case, it would be 4 percent.

5. The savvy macrowave investor always establishes at least two possible exit points for a trade *before* entering any new position. What are these two exit points, what does each define, and what is their relationship to the reward-to-risk ratio?

This first exit point is your *stop loss*. If the stock hits that price, you're out of it. This exit point defines the dollar value of your position risk. The second exit point is used to *lock in your profits* should the trade work out the way you planned. It defines your position reward. To calculate the reward-to-ratio, you divide your position reward by your position risk.

6. What is a good rule of thumb to use for your reward-to-risk ratio? How is this ratio used?

   A good rule of thumb is to use a 3-to-1 ratio. Any stock that offers you the promise of at least a 3-to-1 ratio is one that you should "green light" while any trade with less than a 3-to-1 ratio is a no-go.

7. To determine your position sizes, what two steps must you take?

   You first divide your risk capital by the number of your positions. This gives you your position limit. You next divide this position limit by your position risk to arrive at the number of shares to hold for that position.

8. Generally speaking, when does the savvy macrowave investor begin to add position risk? How does this strategy differ from the typical investor?

   Typical investors increase their risk when they are losing money. Rather than cut their losses, they try to average down their losses by buying more shares. Savvy macrowave investors only increase their risk when they have earned some profits and are playing with the house's money.

9. What is a good rule of thumb for adding your first unit of risk after you have increased the size of your portfolio through profit-making? What does adding this unit of risk do to the size of your risk capital and stop losses?

   A good rule of thumb is that once you increase the value of your portfolio by 15 percent, you can increase your risk capital by one unit of risk. Since this unit of risk is equal to your initial risk capital, this effectively doubles your risk capital and stop losses.

Answers to Questions for Chapter 17

1. The debate over using market versus limit orders centers around what?

   It centers around the risk of capturing *the spread* between the ask price and the bid price versus *the price movement*.

2. When should you use a limit order and when should you use a market order?

You should use a limit order if the market is trading sideways and/or if the stock is in an overbought condition. You should use a market order if the market is strongly up and/or if your technical analysis indicates momentum.

3. What are the three major rules of setting intelligent stop losses?

   The three major rules to set intelligent stops are (1) avoid round numbers, (2) avoid key technical analysis decision nodes like support and resistance, and (3) set loose stops outside the range of a stock price's normal volatility.

4. What are the two main reasons why you use a "trailing stop"?

   A trailing stop is used (1) to ensure that you "never turn a winner into a loser" and (2) to lock in profits.

5. When is a good time to use a buy stop? What should you be careful of?

   You can use buy stops to play breakouts. But be careful not to run "naked" without a stop loss after your buy stop is triggered, particularly in a volatile market.

6. Why do some investors try to average down a loss? Under what conditions should you do this? Why is averaging down a loss generally a very a bad idea?

   Investors will average down a loss to lower their breakeven point. You should *never* try to average down a loss. Doing so is a bad idea because most trades that move in the wrong direction *will continue to do so.*

7. What is the traditional definition of portfolio "churning"? Why do some online investors today effectively churn their own portfolios?

   Traditionally, portfolio churning has referred to the case where charlatan stockbrokers trade a client's portfolio simply to generate commissions. Today, many online investors do this to themselves out of boredom, greed, inexperience, or an addiction to trading! They do this by overtrading.

8. Name at least three valuable insider tips of effective trade management.

   The following are valuable insider tips: (1) Don't try to pick tops and bottoms. (2) Buy dips in an up-trending market, sell bounces in a down-trending market. (3) Don't meet margin calls; why throw good money after bad? (4) Look at all time frames before making a decision; use intraday charts to time entry and exit points. (5) Don't chase fast markets (gaps up and gaps down); wait for them to come back to you. (6) If a position doesn't look as good as the day you put it on, close it out.

9. Name at least five of David Aloyan's Top Ten Investor Psychology Tips.

The tips are: (1) Trade or invest because you love it; don't do it as a form of entertainment. (2) Never invest on impulse, emotion, or hope; have a plan. (3) Never invest more than you can afford to lose. (4) Never trade to pay your bills. (5) Make your trading decisions away from the outside noise and ignore conventional wisdom. (6) Don't be impressed by hot money. (7) Always believe you will win, and reward yourself for doing so. (8) Analyze your losses to ensure that you are following your rules and methodology. (9) Always take breaks from the market to reflect. (10) Put your personal life first; it will reflect positively in your trading.

Answers to Questions for Chapter 18

1. What are the three ways to execute a trade? Which is the best and cheapest?

The old-fashioned, slowest, and most expensive way to place an order is to phone your broker. The only slightly less old-fashioned and only slightly less expensive way is to use a Level I online broker. The best and ultimately cheapest way is to use a direct access, Level II trading platform.

2. What are the three important pieces of information about a stock price that are provided by a Level I view of the market?

A Level I view of the market provides you with the current bid, current ask, and the last price.

3. What additional pieces of information are provided by a Level II view of the market? What do you gain with this Level II information and why is this important?

With a Level II trading platform, you see all of the bids, all of the asks, and a running ticker of market-clearing prices as well as the market participants and their share sizes. With this additional information, you gain market transparency. Such transparency can help you greatly improve the timing of your trade executions.

4. If you see GSCO, MLCO, and NITE on a Level II screen, who are they?

They are Goldman Sachs, Merrill Lynch, and Knight Securities.

5. What is slippage? What are the four major sources of slippage?

Slippage occurs when you send a market order that gets filled at a price worse than was available in the market at the time you sent your order. The four major sources of slippage range from (1) slow execution due to mismanagement or lack of resources to more unscrupulous broker practices like (2) payment for order flow, (3) front running, and (4) internalization.

6. Why might you be willing to pay slightly higher commission costs for direct access trading?

   You would be willing to pay higher costs because the savings to be gained from increased market transparency and speed of trade execution more than outweigh any higher commission costs.

7. Besides eliminating slippage and providing market transparency, what is the other major advantage of direct access, Level II platforms?

   They allow you to engage in much more sophisticated programmed ordering.

Answers to Questions for Chapter 19

1. The *Savvy Macrowave Investor* newsletter always begins with the broad market outlook. Suppose that the newsletter describes the market as being in a prolonged, downward trend. However, over the last several weeks, there may have been a bear market rally. Is this a safe market to invest in?

   This is a very dangerous market to invest in because it remains uncertain as to whether the market will make a successful transition from a late bear to early bull state.

2. The macrowave scorecard rates the various elements of the macrowave market equation on a bullish versus bearish scale. Name at least four elements of that scorecard.

   Elements of the macrowave scorecard include the outlook for corporate earnings, consumption, business investment, net exports, both fiscal and monetary policy, and exogenous shocks like war, terrorism, and oil price spikes.

3. In many cases, the relative macrowave risk that the Wall Street consensus is wrong is *not* symmetrical. For example, a positive upside surprise like an improvement in consumer confidence might not provide anywhere near the same amount of lift to the market as a downside surprise will provide a drop. Why is this an important observation?

   This is an important observation because the existence of such asymmetrical risk allows you to turn what might otherwise be a 50-50 gamble into an intelligent speculation in which the odds are clearly in your favor.

4. Why does the *Savvy Macrowave Investor* newsletter include a section on strong and weak sectors?

The newsletter is trying to identify emerging strong and weak sectors in which there may be good opportunities to buy or short stocks.

5. What is the main purpose of the "Media Watch" section of the *Savvy Macrowave Investor* newsletter?

The newsletter is trying to warn people not to buy into what are often examples of either irrational exuberance or pessimism and equally often examples of just plain bad analysis. Don't believe everything you read or see on the television!

6. Should you run right out and buy or short the latest stock picks of the week in the *Savvy Macrowave Investor* newsletter?

Absolutely not. It must be *you* who assumes responsibility for making your own market choices. So don't get sucked into the "guru" game of slavishly adhering to the stock picks of some newsletter Web site, even if it's mine.

7. The last section of the *Savvy Macrowave Investor* newsletter features a technical analysis of the broad market. How can this help you in your investing?

You should find this section very valuable when it comes to gauging the broad market trend as well as any impending reversal or weakening of that trend.

Answers to Questions for Chapter 20

1. What two types of investors can benefit from portfolio simulation?

Both novice investors and experienced investors can benefit from it.

2. Why is simulating your portfolio for three to six months *before* you put real money down such a good idea for novice investors?

The novice investor invariably pays "tuition" to the market in the form of so-called rookie mistakes. By simulating your portfolio decisions for three to six months before you actually put your real money down, all you will incur will be paper losses as you gain a solid base of experience.

3. Under what two circumstances will experienced investors benefit from portfolio simulation?

Sometimes experienced investors suffer a string of losses. If you have had such a string, one approach can be to stop using real money to invest, spend some time analyzing your losses, and then go ahead and test your solutions through simulated investing.

A second reason to engage in portfolio simulation rises when an experienced investor is reluctant to short sell and instead only buys stocks. Portfolio simulation can be a very useful tool in conquering "shortaphobia."

AFTERWORD

I will work just as hard every investing week to protect the dollars that I have already earned as I do work hard every day to make my next dollars.

The Savvy Macrowave Investor Pledge

If this book had been written during the 1990s, few investors would have seen any need for it. During those "Roaring 90s," it was almost impossible to lose money in the stock market, and even the most naïve of investors made out like bandits.

That was then. This is now. And today, most individual investors not only know how important it is to more carefully manage their portfolios. They also have the losses and scars from the Great Bear Market of 2000–2003 to prove it.

Still and all, the problem most investors still face is that the traditional investor's buy-and-hold roadmap has turned into a macroeconomic dead end—one quite literally littered with washed-up stocks and broken dreams. Indeed, in today's increasingly volatile world of inflation, recession, war, terrorism, budget deficits, and other macroeconomic shocks, the stock market has become a highly volatile, and very dangerous, reflection of these uncertain times.

In such a rapidly gyrating market, it has become increasingly clear that the methods of traditional investing, which, to this day, are *still* put forth by the preachers and proselytizers of Wall Street, simply won't do. That's why in this book I've offered you a much more powerful and effective approach that is much more in tune with our modern macrowave times.

Table A-1 summarizes this method and some of the major points of this book by way of contrasting the savvy macrowave investing approach with that of the traditional investor.

I hope the message of this table, and the broader message of this book, motivate you to use the savvy macrowave investor method to do what I urged you to do in the book's first two chapters: Take *control* of your own portfolio and take the *time* to manage it well. This book has armed you with all the tools and concepts you will need to do so. The rest is up to you.

Table A-1   The Traditional Investor versus the Savvy Macrowave Investor

The Traditional Investor	*The Savvy Macrowave Investor*
Almost universally favors the "long" or buy side of the market. Increases portfolio value in bull markets but sustains heavy losses in bear markets.	"Rides the train in the direction it is going." Goes long in an upward-trending market, short-sells in a downward-trending market, stays in cash when there is no clear trend. Increases portfolio value in both bull and bear markets.
Favors a bottom-up approach that begins, and often ends, with looking for "great companies." Largely ignores the broader sector and market trends.	Applies a top-down approach that starts with an assessment of the broad market and individual sector trends and concludes with identifying both strong stocks to buy and weak stocks to short.
Relies primarily on fundamental analysis tools like the P/E ratio to screen stocks.	Augments traditional fundamental analysis with modern technical analysis screens.
Diversifies across many sectors of the market, taking the weak with the strong. Earns a merely average market return at best.	Focuses on a few strong sectors in an upward-trending market or a few weak sectors in a downward-trending market. Significantly outperforms the market.
Buys and holds stocks, even if they begin to show heavy losses.	Cuts losses ruthlessly, but lets profits run.
Engages in highly risky practices such as averaging down losses and generally ignores the principles of sound money, risk, and trade management.	Diligently applies sound money management, risk management, and trade management principles on every single trade.
Relies on a stockbroker or a Level I online broker to receive slow and expensive trade executions.	Uses a direct access, Level II trading platform for fast and efficient trade execution.

The Traditional Investor	*The Savvy Macrowave Investor*
Is clueless as to how the broader macroeconomic environment determines the market and sector trends. Is oblivious to the role of macrowaves like inflation, unemployment, Fed rate hikes, oil prices, war, and terrorism on the markets.	Has a very clear idea of how the major macrowaves move the markets and individual sectors. Constantly monitors the flow of information from the many macrowaves embodied in the four dynamic factors.

In this regard, it has always amazed me how many people are downright lazy when it comes to managing their own portfolios. The irony is that while so many people work so very hard to earn their *next* dollar, they are seemingly totally unwilling to work equally hard to protect the dollars they have already earned.

I don't know if you fit at all into this category. I do know that if you have read this book carefully and diligently completed the questions and exercises after each chapter, you are not only well prepared to do battle with Wall Street's "meannest men in pinstripes," you are also equally committed to being a success.

Now that you have listened to me, I want to listen to you. I'd like to know not just what you thought of this book. Over the years, I also want to hear from you about the many different ways that this book may have helped you.

So visit my Web site at www.peternavarro.com and drop me an e-mail. At this Web site, you can also read the weekly *Savvy Macrowave Investor* newsletter.

So do stay in touch. I would love to hear from you.

Peter Navarro
Irvine, California

INDEX